Stringing Pearls

A Collection of Gems from Nursing Leaders

Leslie Furlow, Editor

PESI®
HealthCare

PESI HealthCare
PO Box 900
Eau Claire, WI 54702-0900

Printed in the United States of America

ISBN: 0-9790218-6-3

PESI HealthCare strives to obtain knowledgeable authors and faculty for its publications and seminars. The clinical recommendations contained herein are the result of extensive author research and review. Obviously, any recommendations for patient care must be held up against individual circumstances at hand. To the best of our knowledge any recommendations included by the author or faculty reflect currently accepted practice. However, these recommendations cannot be considered universal and complete. The authors and publisher repudiate any responsibility for unfavorable effects that result from information, recommendations, undetected omissions or errors. Professionals using this publication should research other original sources of authority as well.

For information on this and other PESI Healthcare educational products, please call 800-843-7763 or visit our website at www.pesihealthcare.com

Cover photograph provided by Bob Bagwell

Introduction

Stringing Pearls

by Leslie Furlow, PhD, RN, MSN, FNP

Why another leadership book? Well, because there are so many stories to tell. I have been intrigued by this concept for more than ten years. Because pearls are always appropriate, I believed that a string of pearls would be the best way to tell the stories. And this book has pearls of every description, from classic, to cultured, to baroque. It is divided into sections that begin with the beginning. To find pearls, you have to find oysters, and they are in the water, so you have to get wet! Next you have to select the right ones, string them and, if they are worth it, you restring them.

As a consultant, administrator, teacher and clinician, I have met some of the most spectacular nurses in the world. Many of them have quietly gone about their work, doing great jobs, mentoring new leaders and insuring healthcare quality. Some of them have received recognition. Some have been published, elected to offices, or presented to audiences, while others have only been recognized in their corner of the world. I have included both in this anthology of gems.

Some of their stories are funny, some are thought provoking and some are just flat out controversial, but all of them are true and real. Just like the people who wrote them. The idea was to create a book that would inspire, challenge and teach. I believe that has been achieved.

I hope you enjoy reading Stringing Pearls as much as I enjoyed collecting them.

ACKNOWLEDGEMENT

I can't thank my colleagues enough for their willingness to help me realize the dream of producing a work that would teach and encourage today's and tomorrow's nurse leaders. I also owe of debt of gratitude to Yvonne Kuter, of K2 Office Magic, my editor, who spent many hours making everything so readable. And thanks to Valerie Kittelson for her many hours on the page editing and book formation.

I appreciate my publisher Brad Poquette, PESI HealthCare, for his support and encouragement for the last several years as I presented leadership seminars. And I can't imagine how this work could have come to fruition without the AchieveMentors, Inc consultants and associates who have taught me so much about being a leader of leaders. Special thanks to Vanessa Montgomery, my Administrative Assistant and Office Manager, who kept me and all the contributors on track. Without her diligence, "Stringing Pearls" would still be only an idea. Special thanks also to Dr. Sharon Judkins, my partner in Hardiness-Mentors, LLC, who has continued to be an inspiration and complement to me.

Finally, I thank my grandmother, Lennie Mercer, who filled so many roles in my life and taught me the meaning of caring. Her legacy lives on in me and my daughter, Terrell, who also followed us into nursing as a profession and a calling.

TABLE OF CONTENTS

DIVING INTO
DEEP WATER

CHAPTER 1

You've Got to Get Wet - First Steps

by Joy Don Baker, RN, PhD, CNE, CNOR, CNAA, BC

First steps relate to the professional nursing career through a three-leg approach in which education, employment, and service in nursing organizations are the bases. The first steps into a new role within the profession of nursing present with a sense of fear yet passion and a determined desire to succeed. Nursing is about passion for a patient-oriented practice, pursuit of learning, and the power to make a difference in peoples' lives - one person at a time.

The practice of perioperative nursing offered me just that opportunity. When our class went into the operating room during my undergraduate education, most of the students exhibited more fear than any other emotion. We had a tremendous desire to be as close to the instructor as physically possible, expecting that she could protect us from this unknown experience.

It was during this short time of two weeks of half days that I scrubbed in on my first patient's case; she was undergoing a breast biopsy. The person scrubbed in to assist the surgeon allowed me to hand the instruments to the surgeon. The simple processes of meeting the patient, working with her in the operating room, and learning an important new skill were the connections that set the stage for a life-long career in perioperative practice. The procedure itself was short; however, after it was over, I nearly fainted (literally) from relief and at the same time felt the excitement of success and happiness for the patient when we learned that the biopsy result was benign.

That roller coaster of emotions, tied up with the opportunity to demonstrate quality execution of a beginning skill set, is what overcoming fear of a risk for the greater reward is all about. We accept that type of risk with each new job we undertake in our professional career path. Without the determination to overcome fear, change cannot occur. The determination required to sustain one through the novice phase (Benner, 1984) is at the same time the challenge that can spur one forward. Making mistakes is scary and has become an over-whelming problem within health care today (Bates, 2007). We can no longer be tolerant of the error rates, yet we cannot continue to crucify the nurse and other health providers through litigation.

One morning as a young student, I was to deliver medications to a group of patients. The normal procedure was for all 9:00 a.m. medications to be pre-pared at the same time and then distributed in a rounding process going from room to room. The medications were set up on a single tray in small cups. I went into a room occupied by two patients and gave the person in the first bed the other patient's medication. When I went to the second patient, I realized my error with horror and immediately went to the charge nurse and the instructor to determine what next course of action I needed to take.

The patient was informed of the mistake, the physician was called, the documentation was completed, and all of the right steps accomplished to address the issue. From my perspective at the time, I was convinced my practice and career in nursing were over. Fortunately, the medication was a mild sedative and the charge nurse, instructor, and physician were all seasoned leaders. No harm came to the patient, yet the learning that took place for me was tremendous and I still think of that lesson when I give a patient a medication today. Health care has made remarkable improvements in the medication delivery system since my first frightening mistake as a student. Yet, coming face to face with the reality that I could cause someone harm created a respectful fear, balancing and enhanc-ing my desire to help others.

It has been said it takes a village to raise a child. I believe it takes a village of mentors to raise a nurse. Throughout my career, I have enjoyed the wonderful benefits that emerge from being mentored. Mentorship is about offer-ing someone else critical and essential feedback, opportunities, and sometimes challenges that can help advance the mentee or novice along a path toward the desired successes.

Have you ever completed a task or job and taken it to a supervisor and all you really wanted was for the work to be blessed and told how wonderful it was? That is what happened to me. At one point in my career, I had just fin-ished rewriting the entire set of Job Descriptions for the department for which I was responsible. This had taken me a great deal of time and hard work; I believed I had captured every detail that needed to be addressed. I presented the final document in a binder, complete with page protectors, for my supervisor's review, and I wanted her approval very much. A week went by and she called me to the office. I had hopes of her saying what a terrific job I had done. When

I arrived, I noticed the documents had the sheet protectors removed and there were red marks on the top page. My bravado was waning.

However, her insight and method of delivering a difficult message set a wonderfully rich stage for how to provide critical and valuable feedback that may be difficult to hear and, as I learned later, may be difficult to give. She went through the first job description page by page, showing me how to improve the document by strengthening the outcomes and focusing on the major underlying components. I managed to get through the meeting with clear eyes and a true understanding of the improvements she was suggesting. All her corrections made sense; I just kept asking myself why I hadn't seen those needed changes.

After the meeting, I rushed back to my office. There, I could close the door and let the tears flow, as a result of the disconnect between the response I had wanted, and the improvements she had suggested in a wonderful and sensitive manner. Her critique was extremely important to the outcome of the project and it had a lasting impact on my future approach to feedback regarding my own work. I have learned to seek that type of feedback, welcoming it for the richness it offers and the improvement it lends to the overall results. Her manner of mentoring suggested future hope and optimism (Grossman, 2007) that I could accomplish the desired outcome.

In my career path, I have enjoyed the richness of being mentored on several other occasions. One such instance occurred early in my advancement in the national AORN organization and continues to be an influence to this day. I first met Carol when she was running for the Board of Directors and I was on the stage seated next to her (when I was seeking election for the Nominating Committee). It was my first time to speak to a group of that size that also held the outcome of the election in their hands. The three-minute talk each candidate gave was critical to success in the election. The anxiety on the stage was palpable and yet the speakers somehow overcame that when presenting their own speeches.

The Nominating Committee candidates presented first and in alphabetical order by last name. As my name is early in the alphabet, I was the first to speak. There was an advantage to going first. I actually got to listen to the remainder of the speeches, instead of half listening while being frightened about my own upcoming presentation. That day, as I watched and talked with Carol, I learned that it is okay to feel anxiety and, at the same time, convert anxiety into motivation for success. She exemplified the national nursing leadership I so respected and had watched from a distance in the past. Now, I was seated next to her on stage, what an adventure. While she waited, her hands shook, she squirmed in her seat, she made notes on her speech - she was normal! Then she delivered a phenomenal speech that won her the election; her voice never wavered and her commitment and passion showed through. I learned it is okay to be real and to be afraid, and to overcome that fear and assume your place of honor.

From that moment on, I sought out Carol's advice, critique and support, and she has continued to give freely with care and compassion to see me succeed. You see, critical analysis can seem harsh and difficult; however, when given with true caring and compassion, the recipient can hear it and take action for improvement. There are times when the mentee may disagree with the mentor. When disagreement is clearly understood as being okay, the mentee begins to develop in a more in-depth manner. The final decision and action always rests with the person being mentored, not the mentor. The mentee must ask for the help; the mentor shares experience and ideas to encourage success or to console the mentee during times of disappointment. The focus is always on the mentee. The hope and realism the mentor offers may be the turning point in a person's career, helping to shift the focus away from fear to a Can Do attitude.

Family and friends are the final connection creating the frame to stabilize and balance this nursing career three-leg approach to first steps of education, employment, and service in professional nursing organizations. Many people may not have had family to support them in their lives and yet they have gone on to create beautiful outcomes for themselves. No one creates a life centered on quality values without some kind of human support system and a faith in something far more powerful than self.

Friends and family may also be mentors in one's life. They are often the individuals who provide unconditional love when life seems to be crumbling around us. They are the ones who pat us on the back saying, "There, there - things will be fine," and they really mean it, even if they have no clue about how to help. They offer support because they believe in us, simply because we exist. A parent with a young child protects her from running into the street. As the child ages, the parent begins to step back from the role of protector and decision maker, allowing the young person to make her own decisions and even mistakes. The pain (and sometimes guilt) in the heart of the parent watching as those mistakes are made can be overwhelming, yet it must be allowed for the child to grow and learn. This kind of growth in a relationship parallels that between a mentor and mentee.

I have been fortunate to have wonderful family and friendships to enrich my entire career in nursing. My parents have attended every academic graduation, have been there during my struggles toward desired achievements, and have embraced me when nothing else could be offered except comfort while I cried. That kind of passion for life and desire to make a difference set the cultural stage for the type of person I want to be, fostering the enthusiasm I want to bring to the nursing profession, utilizing the three legs of education, employment, and service in professional nursing organizations.

8

References

Benner, P. (1984). From Novice to Expert: Excellence and Power in Clinical Nursing Practice. Menlo Park, CA: Addison-Wesley.

Bates, D.W. (2007). Preventing Medication Errors: A summary. American Journal of Health System Pharmacy 64 (9) S3-S9.

Grossman, S.C. (2007). The Mentor Perspective on How Nest to Encourage Others. In Mentoring in Nursing: A Dynamic Collaborative Process. New York, NY. Springer Publishing Co, LLC.

Joy Don Baker, RN, PhD, CNE, CNOR, CNAA, BC

Joy Don Baker has been a practicing perioperative nurse for over 30 years, serving in roles from staff nurse to assistant vice president levels in hospitals across the United States. She has taught in the undergraduate program and currently teaches in the graduate nursing administration program at University of Texas Arlington. Dr. Baker operates her own consulting service providing administrative, assessment, planning, and research consulting.

Dr. Baker has served national AORN as vice president and as a member of the board of directors. Currently, Dr. Baker is serving on the AORN Journal Editorial Board and as chair-elect for the Texas Council of Operating Room Nurses. She is also an accomplished author and presenter on topics such as Critical Thinking and PNDS in Academic Education. Dr. Baker was invited to be the keynote speaker for the Texas Association of PeriAnesthesia Nurses (TAPAN) in 2003; in 2002; she was the keynote speaker for the Japanese Operating Nursing Academy Annual Congress in Chiba, Japan.

Dr. Baker holds certifications in perioperative nursing, informatics nursing, and advanced nursing administration. She also recently achieved the certification of nursing education and is the first faculty member at the University of Arlington School of Nursing to achieve this recognition.

CHAPTER 2

Braving the Deep-Entrepreneurship

by Kim Richards, RN

I'm often amazed when I talk with nurses about becoming an entrepreneur. They will say, "It must be so great to be out of the rat race; you're so lucky." Luck has nothing to do with it. And, as for being out of the rat race – no way. My job moves at warp speed! Don't get me wrong; I'm forever grateful to be able to do what I truly love to do, but my life is not the simple, carefree path that many believe. It is multi-tasking mania! As I meet nurses at conferences and they see my in my new suit, manicured nails, and freshly cut and colored hair, the illusion of a glamorous life may cross their minds. I have an office in my home so, in reality, my daily 'uniform' typically consists of ultra casual 'workout wear' with a pair of scuffies! Not always a pretty picture! With my four dogs by my feet, "life is good," but certainly nothing resembling glamorous. But it is my life on my own terms, my own schedule (most of the time!) and building my own legacy.

When a nurse asks me about opportunities outside of the traditional hospital setting, I am reminded of my own unique career path. Unlike most of my colleagues who functioned as nurse managers and directors, I was a staff nurse when I left the clinical arena. While I enjoyed my role as a young staff nurse, I was compelled to broaden my horizons and venture into unknown territory. I don't really know the reason, I just felt like I could contribute in a different way. I thrive on challenge, connection and change and yet, I had much to learn about focusing my talents, tempering my enthusiasm and listening to my inner voice. Perhaps the intensity and sometimes very personal witnessing of life-ending tragedy made me truly understand that my own life is not to be taken lightly. My life purpose is be used as a vessel through which a higher power can flow.

To be of service to others is an honor, and when lives are changed through my words, actions or focused energy, it is very rewarding.

Entrepreneur Magazine has consistently named "Executive Recruiting" as one of the hottest industries. The need for high level, talented leaders never ceases - especially in the nursing management market. Almost 20 years ago, I took a deep breath, decided to "let go of the ledge" of corporate employment and started my own executive recruitment firm, specializing in nursing management. Someday, I may "exhale." Even after all this time, the little "panic" that can creep up when you own your own business can rear it's ugly head when I least expect it.

I have had the honor of meeting exceptionally bright, emotionally intelligent, very ambitious nurses who, while they enjoy their traditional nursing roles, feel a sort of "calling" to contribute to patient care in a different manner. They speak of their inability to "figure it all out" and "know for sure what they want to do." My response is always this: Listen to your inner voice, follow your passion. Write down specifics about how you want your life to be, what you want your daily activities to be. When do you feel the most joy and pride and when do you feel completely like "you"? Surround yourself with people who encourage your personal and professional growth and talk with leaders you admire. If your current "circle" doesn't include positive people and mentors, think fast about developing a new one! It is of key importance to believe in your ability to achieve your goals, regardless of stumbles in the past or "perceived" failures; however, it is also very comforting to have a "soft place" to land as you are slaying some difficult dragons. Jiminy Cricket (a likely hero!) once sang, "If your heart is in your dream, no request is too extreme." That quote was painted across the wall of my office for years. YOU have to be your best supporter and if you don't believe in yourself, no one else ever will.

Having interviewed hundreds of nurses over my career, and hearing common threads of sentiment regarding lack of work/life balance, I started thinking about how I could best contribute to RETENTION of good, experienced nurses. With the current environment of our aging workforce, innovative measures are urgently needed to focus on retaining talent, not simply recruitment. A "revolving door" will never solve the underlying situation. As I meet experienced nurses, it's clear that most nurses do not set aside time needed for personal physical and mental health. Typically, we nurses are so occupied with being good caretakers that much too often, we are so tired, so stressed, so emotionally exhausted that we just want to go home after work, often to our "other" jobs. This dynamic or "treadmill" that we sometimes create leaves little room for focusing on our personal nurturing and re-energizing.

In response to that need, I developed a mind/body program dedicated to taking care of nurses. Having been a fitness instructor and a nurse for over 25 years, I understood how combining stress reduction and physical strength is vital for continued overall health, allowing us to feed and renew our spirit. **NurseFit** was a labor of love for me to create, encouraging and motivating nurses to easily and conveniently attend hospital based, hospital-funded classes designed specifically for the physical and mental demands of their jobs. The results have been transforming and have fostered teambuilding and camaraderie; the participants report a feeling of empowerment and improved outlook. The business structure also sends a strong message to nurses that their hospitals value them and are willing to invest to keep them healthy and happy. I have had the time of my life working on this project!

Along my journey to happiness and successful entrepreneurship, it was up to me to determine the path; each such journey is very personal and unique. There is no single path to success and no road maps; however, "wrong turns" are usually followed by opportunities to make "U" turns. I have been the most successful when I approach a project with an open mind and heart. Regardless of the industry, any successful entrepreneur must be resilient to adversity, learn from failure and keep moving forward.

This is how my personal journey started

After a few years in Labor and Delivery, ER and ICU, I began working as an office nurse for a very busy family practitioner, which seemed, at the time, like a mistake ... remember "U" turn! Part of my responsibilities during that time involved interaction with pharmaceutical sales representatives. When opportunity knocked, in the form of a vacant position, I was recruited by SmithKline and French (now Glaxo SmithKline) as a pharmaceutical sales representative and was motivated to be successful in a competitive market. Even though I had never been in sales, I was a nurse and the education and skills I had used everyday were applicable to this new position. Upon reflection, I can clearly see how nurses use sales skills everyday, through negotiation, empathy, compromise, focused listening and producing positive results. Such 'Emotional Intelligence' is mandatory for a successful career. Learning when to "push or pull back" is a skill used by nurses everyday. I flourished during this time and was promoted to a hospital representative and trainer. My boss was a wonderful mentor and, after significant personal success, I was fortunate enough to become a mentor myself.

As the years went on, I enjoyed financial success, but was feeling ready for a new challenge and experiencing a genuine longing to live life on my own terms. At that time, unsure of my next step, I contacted an executive recruiter who specialized in healthcare. As I visited in her office, I observed her on the phone interacting with clients and candidates. I said to myself, "I can do that!" It was a 'light bulb' moment! I knew then that this was my next opportunity. Realizing that I needed to hone my skills for this particular role, I took a position with a national recruitment company for a year. I learned as much about executive recruitment as I could, then I left to start my own firm.

The fear of failure was, at times, overwhelming. Fear of rejection, fear of criticism; fear of not being smart enough, or of not being educated enough. This is where I learned that belief in oneself does not mean the absence of self-doubt. I realized I had to be willing to be uncomfortable while facing my fears. It was during this time that I realized that my "real work" needed to be done from the inside out. Self-reflection and assessment can be brutal, but despite many obstacles, setbacks and disappointments, I learned how deep my reservoir of resilience could be.

Keeping my goal of building my own strong, high-quality network in mind, I consistently made the tough calls and put myself at the center of events. I developed relationships with influential clients by earning their trust and filling their needs. I am often asked how on-line 'career centers' or 'job boards' affect my business. The answer is, "Not much." Any successful recruiter will tell you that this business is all about relationship building. It's about staying in touch with great candidates who have dreams of moving to "ABC" town. It's about knowing what really makes people get excited and motivated about their lives and their careers.

Sometimes that motivation comes from family needs, often from a pure desire for opportunity and career advancement. Sometimes I can offer a person the team of leaders with whom she has dreamed of working. And sometimes, it is just good timing. Healthcare is constantly changing and there is often a complete change at the top of an organization, which makes smart leaders realize it's time to start planning their exit strategies. The days of working in a hospital in the same role, for an entire career are virtually obsolete. But, regardless of the reasons and motivating factors, the relationships nurtured and maintained are paramount to success. When in doubt, there are always people to whom I can turn for help, if needed. But by doing the right things consistently, by being open to possibilities and, most importantly, by believing in myself, business has flourished.

After some significant personal crises, I made the decision to move to Colorado from Arizona, not knowing what lay ahead. The world was wide open and I was scared to death.

I was hired by AORN, the Association of PeriOperative Nurses, to evaluate and re-launch their interim management and consultation services. It was agreed that, given the overwhelming need for experienced perioperative leaders, this was an opportunity to grow this particular niche. Through target marketing and sales efforts, the business grew significantly over the next three years. As the General Manager of AORN Management Solutions, I had the opportunity to interact and network with national perioperative leaders, with whom I developed strong and lasting professional relationships.

I made the decision to leave AORN Management Solutions and re-start my own executive search firm. I've enjoyed the opportunity to network with other experienced, ethical recruiters, which allows me to offer my clients full-service nursing management recruitment and consultation, even outside of my particular niche. Focusing on the urgency of connecting experienced perioperative leaders with outstanding opportunities, I was fortunate to experience an abundance of business synergy, which created the "tipping point" in my own business. By surrounding myself with committed, open-minded and creative "out of the box" thinkers, the business has flourished. We all share a common goal of creating a pool of talented, experienced nurse leaders and consultants. More importantly, we love creating our own legacy, as well as enjoying a Work/Life balance. I am very fortunate to have other recruiter colleagues whom I can call upon to vent, bounce ideas off and get some honest truths. These are people with whom I have worked for most of my career and trust implicitly. We have all been in the business long enough to have seen proof of the adage, "What goes around, comes around." I've seen some real 'paybacks' - you don't mess with universal law!

Here are some real-life truths I have learned about being an entrepreneur

Owning your own business is incredibly stressful. Working from home often feels as if you rarely leave the office, at least mentally. Especially in this wireless world, I have been half way around the world on a work-related conference call, without leaving my home office. Flexibility, managing multiple "irons in the fire" at once and multitasking are all mandatory. Work/Life balance can become skewed quickly and when your time, money, passion and creativity are invested in your own business, it can border on obsession. There is no shutting the door, turning off the lights and using PTO. The workload is intense and there is always something more you can be doing - the pipeline needs consistent priming.

Owning your own business is never-ending. Meeting your own deadlines without anyone "to do your pushups" is tough. There's nothing like working without a safety net to light the fire of the "GSD Rule" (Get Stuff Done)! Talking is easy, but taking action and following through determines success. It's like being a duck. You may appear calm and unruffled on the surface, but you need to be paddling like hell below the surface of the water. Every morning, you may feel the fear and have the doubts, but you go for it anyway.

On a daily basis, you wear many hats, knowing that, at the end of the day, whatever happened that day was because of you. The "self talk" you provide yourself is vital to your productivity and success. Whatever it is that gets your hackles up, you have to get it off your chest and off your shoulder. In other words, "Just get over it already." Your mind is your most powerful weapon in the entrepreneurial arsenal. It is more powerful than education, experience, your title, or who your parents are. If you don't think you can do something ... you are wasting your time.

The truth is that you never know what is around the corner and you must remain open to possibility. There have been a lot of times when there was great opportunity and I wondered if it was way too much, but I did it anyway. It required guts, strong intention and the absolute belief that I could achieve anything to which I put my mind. The situation may have been uncomfortable and intimidating, but it always pushed me to the next level - often in earnings, usually in skills, always in self-esteem. The most successful people take the situations that make them anxious and turn those challenges into lifestyle choices. I have found that the more times I practice this truth, the more satisfied and engaged I feel.

Owning your own business can be extremely frustrating. The "hurry up and wait' attitude of others can drive you nuts! Most people do not share the same sense of urgency that you have and don't understand the work involved in putting a "match" together. You can expect a never-ending string of unreturned voicemail messages, being passed off to an unsuspecting, unknowledgeable underling and the occasional just out-and-out rude comment. Those things are just part of the business and you can't take them personally. The key is to be persistent and organized in your follow-up. Especially early in your business when every minute counts, panic can set in quickly and problems that occur seem to have a domino effect on your day. Sometimes, just navigating a hospital phone system can seem like an endless chore and I often wonder if the process is intended to force callers into giving up. Often, you could probably get in your car and drive to the hospital faster!

The business of "doing business" can be very frustrating; that's just reality. So your only choice is to change the way you let it affect you. There will always be negative, rude, sarcastic people to deal with in any job. Executive Recruiting has plenty! This is a stellar example of how your "self talk" can 'make or break' you on a daily basis. Rejection is never fun, in any form. I will admit to having been the brunt of a particularly nasty comment or slight and it is difficult not to take such attacks personally. They hurt one's feelings. Especially when you know the comments are unjustified. When difficult situations arise,

I will take a hard look at my accountability for the situation; if there is a wrong to right, I do it. However, even with all of the best intentions, "stuff" happens … sometimes even when you are unaware you are participating in a problem, or making someone uncomfortable. I have found that, in those situations, all you can do is apologize sincerely, accept responsibility, and ask what you can do to right the wrong. There are occasional situations where no matter what you do, it will not be judged as right. But you **have** to move on. Respond, learn and move on … quickly. Don't dwell on it.

I find it mandatory to incorporate daily activities, and lots of humor, into my life that help me deal with the frustration of business and the resultant impatience that is always just below the surface of most entrepreneurs. Here are a few that work for me:

My day starts with a little meditation - actually not with candles, Zen music and a "warrior pose," but just quiet stillness the moment I awaken. I try to feel my breath moving in and out, feel my heart beating and quiet my thoughts. I am a "list maker" so, if I don't concentrate on keeping myself focused, I will have a very long mental list of things to do before I even get out of bed! I start every morning by expressing gratitude for my abundant life. I have a wonderful husband who supports me unconditionally, and who graciously and unselfishly assumes more than his fair share of responsibility. The acceptance that I feel has allowed me to grow both personally and professionally, and I would be remiss if I did not acknowledge my husband's contribution to my successful businesses … it is truly a team effort.

I have been teaching fitness classes for many years and still continue to be as consistent as possible with those activities, even with a hectic travel schedule. There are numerous times, as I am juggling a phone, sending an e-mail while getting dressed for class, trying to get a cup of coffee and find my car keys, that I swear I am going to stop teaching because it is just too much - too much physical effort, too much planning, too much time, and way too much emotional effort to motivate myself (much less others). Then I really get into the downward spiral of excuses! I'm too old, too stressed, too bloated, too frustrated, and too tired and the list goes on and on. But then I walk into my class, turn on the music, someone smiles at me and I am transformed. Wow! This is the best job ever! I get paid to sweat and yell and scream and they love it! After an hour, I am "pumped up" enough to face any obstacle. It is pure mental and physical stress relief and motivation to "keep on keeping on." I find that I am more grounded and anticipate great outcomes for my day after class. In addition, practicing Yoga creates a much needed mind/body connection and allows me to naturally flow into centering my breath and my thoughts, and strengthening my body.

I find great stress relief in being outdoors in my beautiful state of Colorado. My husband and I love to bike and hike with our four dogs as often as possible. I love the freedom of downhill skiing alone on a cold, sunny day, usually listening to Andrea Bochelli on my IPod. Pure heaven! I listen to music almost all day and I choose the type based on my activity. Music has the capability to relax and de-stress me almost instantly, so I use it as needed.

I also love to travel. I feel my mind opening to new possibilities and ways of doing things as I interact with different cultures. Invariably, when I return home, I am incredibly more thankful for living in the USA. But talking with people of other cultures and observing their customs is fascinating for me. Traveling allows me to think outside of my everyday world and dream. While traveling, I often reaffirm my life/business purpose and have time to develop new avenues of exploration. I also have time to reconnect with my husband, which can often be difficult in our fast-paced world.

In addition, I have been blessed with the world's best friends and an amazing mother. It is with them that I can disconnect and laugh forever. My girlfriends are like sisters to me and I find it mandatory to make time to have fun outside of my career, knowing that my relationships with them are paramount to my state of wellbeing and life balance. I appreciate the honesty they bring to my life and the unconditional support they provide to me. "I never saw a hearse with a u-haul behind it." I read that Denzel Washington said in an interview. I love that!

The most successful people I have met or heard speak all concur: "Money does not buy happiness, but happiness has a lot to do with your earnings." That's great motivation to get happy. Do whatever makes YOU happy and do it often. Your attitude is infectious and people will continue to do business with people they like.

So, with this kind of stress, workload and pressure involved in becoming an entrepreneur, why would any nurse subject herself to it?

The rewards are abundant, both emotionally and financially, and deeply personal. There is no better feeling than knowing you were the catalyst in connecting top, talented nursing leaders with the opportunities for which they have been waiting their whole lives. Your clients are thrilled, your candidates are ecstatic and life is good. You are the hero. It's exciting to bring people together when you know you have done your best to provide excellent service. The results are gratifying when both clients and candidates tell you that you have made a difference in their lives. After launching NurseFit, the transformations that occurred in the participants were magical. Some of the nurses had never taken time to care for themselves and faced a plethora of mental/physical problems that were sure to debilitate them. To see the results of a mind/body connection in their faces was very personally rewarding to me. They have become stronger and happier people who are able to continue to give their best care.

I've read and heard others say that once you work for yourself, it's common to feel you could never work in a conventional environment again. I share that sentiment and I believe it's due to the flexibility, the ability to call your own shots and work more efficiently and not always according to the clock. I have had incredible opportunities to travel the world while continuing the progression of my business. The freedom can be exhilarating.

Many entrepreneurs like myself are driven by the need to build something great, to create a better, more valuable business service, to create something from nothing. It becomes your 'baby' and your legacy. My businesses may not be around forever, but I take pride in knowing that the lives I have touched during my career will continue to be enriched, and that I contribute to excellence in patient care by identifying outstanding nursing management talent and assisting in retention. It is rewarding to help hospitals become more efficient and vital to their communities by providing them with talented nursing leaders who contribute to the healthcare within their administrations. As baby boomers, including myself, grow older, the service I provide today could quite possibly end up saving my life in the future. I have a vested interest in making sure hospitals have access to and take special care of great nursing leaders.

If this all makes it sound as though I have had an ideal life, let me assure you that it has been anything but an easy journey. There was a time I experienced a very personal and debilitating crisis that hit me like a ton of bricks. Up to that point, I thought I had all the resources to "just shake it off" and "gut it out." I was wrong. I waited too long to reach out and get professional help while sliding down the slippery slope of depression, and almost lost it all. Well-meaning friends and family tried their best to help, but I was in agony and didn't know how to climb out of what seemed like a steep black hole. I could not work, I could not sleep, and I could not smile. I was numb. While this had nothing to do with being an entrepreneur, it had everything to do with the "inner work" that I mentioned earlier. As expressed in one of my favorite books, Secrets of Six Figure Women, by Barbara Stanny, "An empty vessel has little to offer. Obligatory or guilt-driven self-denial is always undermining, leading to anger, resentment and pain. Without taking care of ourselves, we engage in self-sabotage."

With the aid of a wonderful counselor, short-term medication, and renewal of my dormant spiritual faith, I was able to slowly rebuild my life and my courage. "One day at a time" did not always work for me. There were times when I literally had to just take it "one minute or one hour at a time." After much personal discovery, meditation and prayer, I was able to pull myself out of that black hole and get on with life. What I had learned about myself during those painful and difficult times fueled my resolve to start a new life. I was committed to building an authentic, purposeful life and didn't really know how to start. This defining, pivotal point in my life has proven to be the best gift I could ever have given myself. I finally learned that I must love, accept and respect myself more than anyone. I learned that I am the most important person in my life and, by doing things that make me happy, my soul is genuinely free. The abundance of love, energy and possibility is endless and infectious when you allow yourself to actively participate in your own life. My level of happiness is my responsibility. How I choose to live my life is directly related to my spiritual beliefs. I have the opportunity every day, by my words and actions, to demonstrate the grace of goodness, generosity and purposeful living. Sometimes this can be difficult in business, but there is always a higher road to take.

I am now aware of "triggers" that can diminish my "sense of self" and will not hesitate to stop myself dead in my tracks, preventing any situation or any person from ever defining my direction or intent. I don't allow others to set my standards. Yes, I work intensely, but I make the time I need to fill up my soul and look around at the amazing life with which I have been blessed. Giving time, energy, and financial aid to others has also enriched my life tremendously and has allowed me to connect with people on a more intimate level. Volunteering has a boomerang effect on my psyche and I find the more I give, the more the rewards are multiplied. I had an opportunity to be part of a medical mission in Africa that rekindled my passion for expanding my life purpose. I was allowed to grow in a different direction and live in the moment. The broader sense of empowerment and influence created by that ability to greatly improve the lives of others has inspired me to take my ideas to the next level and stay focused.

Self-awareness and objective reflection, while sometimes brutal, are mandatory to being a successful entrepreneur. That is where "angels along the way" have played a key role in my success, both professionally and personally. I have been blessed with wonderful mentors in my life who somehow saw beyond my impatience, "knee jerk reactions" and stubbornness, and took time to offer me help, advice and another chance to do it better. They told me the truth when I didn't want to hear it, and I owe a deep debt of gratitude to all of those "angels." I appreciate their wisdom and kindness, and honor them by always striving to implement the lessons they taught me, and always looking for ways to "pass it on." Some may not seem like "angels" because they said hurtful things like, "You are way out of your league! You are nuts!" (I still have that e-mail! She was right!) To those cherubs, I say, "Thank you so very much for being the bitter, mean, angry person that you are," and then I simply allow my success to speak for itself. The emotional "fuel added to the fire" that happens when someone tells me I can't do something only serves me well. "Angels" and the valuable lessons they teach can come in many forms.

Like most nurse leaders, my life and career have been blessed with many twists and turns, successes and failures, painful losses and great joys. My belief in myself and my clear goals have acted like a firm, but gentle hand against my back, urging me to keep going. I remember that my intentions become my reality. For me, the best way to predict my future is to create it from an open heart and gratitude, and always be aware that great possibilities are endless.

Kim Richards, RN
Kim Richards and Associates, Inc., President
NurseFit, LLC, Founder/Owner

Kim Richards attended Watts Hospital School of Nursing in Durham, NC before graduating from Colombia Basin College in Pasco, Washington. Kim was a staff nurse in various clinical areas before being hired by Smith Kline and French Pharmaceutical Company, where she worked as a Seattle area Hospital Sales Representative and Regional Sales Trainer. After almost eight years with SKF (now Glaxo Smith Kline), Kim moved to Scottsdale, Arizona where, after working a year for a national recruitment firm, she started her own firm, Executive Connections, Inc. Kim remained the President of the successful firm for twelve years before selling the business and relocating to Littleton, Colorado. She was hired by AORN, (the Association of Perioperative Nurses) to evaluate and re-launch their interim management and consultation department. As the General Manager of AORN Management Solutions, Kim led the business to significant growth through targeted marketing, development of strategic partnerships and relationship building. After three years, Kim left AORN to restart her own executive search firm, Kim Richards and Associates, Inc., which specializes in national recruitment of top perioperative talent. The company has been successful in providing interim, permanent and consultative services for hospitals around the country.

She also is the Founder and Owner of NurseFit, LLC, a company that is dedicated to retention of nurses through convenient, hospital-based, hospital-funded yoga classes. NurseFit was created to help prevent the most common work related injuries and teaches awareness of mind/body connection. Kim has been a certified fitness instructor for over 25 years and has been successful in demonstrating to hospital administration the relationship between nurse retention and regular participation in classes designed to increase flexibility, strength and reduce stress.

Kim is a featured presenter for national conferences, including those of The American Staffing Association, The National Association of Personnel Services, and The Association of California Nurse Leaders (ACNL). She is an active member of the Association of Nurse Executives (AONE), where she serves on the publications committee. Kim is also a member of the American Society of Healthcare Human Resources Administration (ASHHRA) and The National Association of Women Business Owners (NAWBO).

Kim was honored to be on the cover of Nurse Leader as the "Leader to Watch" in April 2007. She lives in Littleton, Colorado with her husband, Bill, and their four dogs. Kim enjoys a very active lifestyle of hiking, biking and skiing in the Rocky Mountains. She enjoys traveling, volunteering, and decorating for special occasions, and is the owner of "Designs by Kimberly," an Interior Decorating business.

CHAPTER 3

It's Very Deep - We Were on the Evening News

by Joan Burritt, DNSc, RN

Introduction

Picture yourself naked on a rock at the shoreline with the tide going out and a gaggle of paparazzi standing on the dunes nearby. When a significant patient care error occurs and there is media involvement, the organization must brace itself for intense scrutiny, probing questions, and a sense of utter vulnerability. Every aspect of the organization is exposed, examined, and evaluated – from policies and procedures to leadership oversight and competence. Moreover, there is limited opportunity to control or influence what information is communicated to the public. Without a doubt, a serious patient care error with media attention is the ultimate test of an organization's values, leadership and commitment to transparency.

For most healthcare leaders, discovery of a care delivery error – even a minor one – evokes a visceral response of deep regret, concern and embarrassment. Instinctively, there may be a desire to contain and control, to minimize, or to address the issue internally quietly and quickly. Full disclosure, while the right thing to do, is not an easy road to take.

So, why be transparent? Clearly, there are ethical and legal imperatives to inform patients and families of an error in the care delivery process. These imperatives also apply to the reporting criteria for regulatory agencies, such as the Joint Commission, Department of Public Health, and Centers for Medicare and Medicaid Services. Beyond the ethical and legal imperatives, organizations also have moral and professional obligations to take the transparency high road to a broader scale in the interest of patient safety. Candid, forthright and widespread sharing of information about a care delivery error may prevent a similar event from occurring in other facilities. There is much wisdom and numerous potential benefits to many patients that can be gained from learning through other people's mistakes. Regulatory agencies have taken on a critical and invaluable leadership role in communicating the lessons learned from organizations by their dissemination of sentinel events and other alerts.

Most, if not all, healthcare organizations embrace a culture of transparency in relation to sharing information about a care delivery error with patients, families, physicians, staff, regulatory agencies, the governing body, and other care facilities. It's the right thing to do. While acknowledging a mistake is distressing and difficult, leadership has the opportunity to direct and control the investigation, communications and actions taken. It is an organized, measured, methodical process. However, when there is media attention, this process can turn into a white knuckle, harrowing river raft ride through turbulent rapids.

Media Attention

Media attention around a serious patient care error intensifies the event to a crisis level suddenly and swiftly. In addition, the focus of control is shifted to some degree from the organization to the press. Without question, the defining element in this kind of situation is leadership. The leader – and the entire leadership team – will make the difference between successful navigation of the experience or calamity and chaos for the organization.

There are three equally important roles of leadership during a serious care error event with media attention. The first is to manage the crisis. Secondly, leadership must set the organizational tone for communications – both internally to patients, families, staff and physicians, as well as externally to the media and public. The third role of leadership is to continue oversight for operations and patient care delivery. Although the patient care error and media involvement will require focused attention, leadership must reserve enough energy and time for their "prime directive" – their responsibility and accountability for the care of patients in the hospital.

Of these three leadership roles, managing the crisis is usually the most challenging. Typically, the organization has no internal references or experience with a significant patient care error and media exposure from which to draw guidance. It's not unlike feeling one's way along a dark, unfamiliar hallway. The many decision points encountered during the crisis require a "collective think" to determine actions and next steps. It truly necessitates a full team effort.

Managing the crisis is a difficult balancing act of simultaneously investigating and correcting the patient care error, communicating with patients, families and authorities, and responding to the media. Media attention may force acceleration of the investigatory and communication process, depending on the point at which the press becomes involved. When the media enters the picture, the organization must be prepared to relinquish an element of control over events, time frames, the message conveyed, and priorities. Understanding key principles of managing a crisis and the media will help an organization maintain a maximum level of control in this kind of situation.

Johnson & Johnson, following the Tylenol tampering events in 1982 and 1986, has shared their lessons learned from that experience in publications and countless presentations. They have identified ten principles of crisis management to follow when a significant error has occurred and there is media attention:

1. The scale of a crisis depends on how it is handled, not what triggered it from the start – people will wait to see how the company acts, then assign blame.
2. The biggest costs associated with a crisis are to the corporate reputation and the marketplace – legal and communications costs are least significant.
3. Good instructive decision-making and clear communications are vital – detailed plans and manuals are secondary.
4. Adopt "worse case scenario" planning, keeping ahead of the media, regulators and public – don't rely on wishful thinking.
5. Emotional stories from eyewitnesses will be believed ahead of statements from company spokespeople.
6. Defensiveness – or silence – is usually interpreted as admission of guilt.
7. You cannot control the situation – events will escalate quickly and unexpectedly, often driven by rumors.
8. You must make decisions without adequate information and in the public spotlight.
9. Others will take advantage of your problem to suit their own needs.
10. Media will exaggerate the scale of the problem.

In addition to the ten principles of crisis management, Johnson & Johnson has provided invaluable insight regarding the media. When dealing with the press, organizations must bear in mind that reporters are seeking a good story, one with news (i.e., the uncommon). Reporters see themselves as the public's surrogate and, in a situation involving an error, they are searching for cause or blame. To that end, when an organization is faced with media attention around a patient care error, it must accept that the focus will be on the error itself, the harm or potential harm to patients, and the culpability of individuals, especially leadership. Efforts to communicate actions taken by the organization to care for the patients involved, correct the problem, and ensure the event will never reoccur will not receive the same level of attention.

One of the most critical decision points for the leadership team is determining what will be communicated to the media by whom. While the truth is clearly the best and only option, the message must be carefully crafted. Critical elements of the message should include the incident, patient safety risks, actions taken to mediate the risks, and steps taken to prevent the incident from happening again. Selecting the appropriate spokesperson is a strategic decision, requiring much deliberation. The message itself, as well as the audience, are key drivers in determining the right person(s). Equally important is the confidence and comfort level of the individual when confronting the media. Speaking to the press is not for the faint of heart. There is no second chance to get it right. The careful crafting of the message can be completely derailed if the messenger is unable to deliver the content precisely as intended or if the person cannot answer the difficult questions posed.

Johnson & Johnson has outlined tips for an organization to use in preparing and conducting interviews with the media. In preparing for the interview, there are four essentials:

1. Know what you want to say before your interview.
2. When preparing, ask yourself the hardest questions and listen to your answers from the public point of view.
3. Think about the headlines you want to see when deciding your key messages.
4. Practice out loud, not in your head.

Conducting the interview is an art and a science. While it is absolutely critical to prepare and rehearse for the meeting with the press, it must be understood that the organization cannot anticipate all the questions that may be asked. To that end, the spokesperson must be able to think on his/her feet. Johnson & Johnson offer the following advice for media interviews:

1. Project yourself as open and credible.
2. Focus on delivering key messages, not "conversation."
3. Support key messages with examples and evidence.
4. Don't wait for the right questions – take control.
5. Align with the public interest/concerns whenever possible.
6. Don't bluff, lie or get angry.

7. Avoid negative, defensive language or emotional responses.
8. Turn negatives into positives.
9. Project appropriate body language.
10. Don't speculate – if you don't know, offer to find out.
11. Don't speak for the competition or other organizations.
12. Don't be tempted to fill the silences – long pauses are often a trick.
13. End on a positive key message.
14. Don't accept the interview if you are not prepared.

To illustrate how organizational values, leadership and commitment to transparency come together to successfully navigate a crisis event that attracted media attention, a case study will be used. The example involves a premiere, highly respected facility with a regional and national reputation for excellence and a designated Magnet facility. In this hospital, a significant patient care delivery error occurred, the seriousness and magnitude of which were unprecedented in the proud history of the organization. How the leadership responded to both the event itself and the ensuing media attention is a testimony to their commitment to "doing the right thing," effective management of a crisis, and their culture of transparency. The example and lessons learned from their experience may help other organizations when faced with a similar situation.

One Hospital's Experience

The Event

At an acute care facility in California, a Registered Nurse made a unilateral decision regarding the terminal cleaning of gastroscopes which was not in accordance with the hospital policy. The gastroscopes were used in gastric bypass surgical procedures, a high volume, high visibility service line for the organization. When the issue was discovered, the hospital learned the divergence from policy had been occurring over an extended period of time. In addition to scrutiny from regulatory agencies, the incident attracted local and national media attention.

Priority #1: Patient Safety

When a care delivery error occurs – no matter how big or small – the first priority must be patient safety. Upon discovery of the gastroscope incident, immediate steps were taken to ensure hospital policy was followed in the equipment cleaning for future procedures. Simultaneously, the hospital engaged experts in the field to conduct an extensive analysis of the risks to patients who had undergone procedures using the gastroscopes that had not been terminally cleaned. While the cleaning method employed by the Registered Nurse did not comply with best practice outlined in the hospital policy, the experts determined it posed nominal or no risk to the patients involved.

Although the expert findings generated a sense of relief among the leadership team, they also created a critical decision point. Given the nominal or absence of risk to patients, what were the appropriate next steps in light of the evidence? Driven by the ethical values of the organization and the commitment to transparency, the leadership team unanimously decided to contact all patients who had had surgical procedures involving gastroscopes during the period where policy was not followed. The total number of patients was 297.

Priority #2: Communication

Communication Strategy Considerations

At the very least, care delivery errors should be shared with the patients, families, physicians and staff involved in the incident. Communication beyond these constituencies is guided by many factors. To some extent, the seriousness and magnitude of the error itself is a determining factor. The greater the error, the more extensive the communication process, as regulatory reporting criteria, risk management considerations, and patient safety obligations to other organizations influence the scope of information sharing.

The $64,000 question for an organization is whether or not to proactively contact and alert the media to a significant patient care error. This is a tough decision to make. Much depends on the organization's ongoing relationship with the media and the perceived quality of the reporting in terms of bias and communicating the 'full story.' While proactive reporting may provide an organization with the opportunity to exert greater influence on the content and timing of the message conveyed to the public, the degree of influence is usually more perception than reality. If the organization elects not to share a significant error incident with the media, it should nevertheless prepare itself for potential press involvement. Serious care delivery errors are newsworthy events. Reports to some regulatory agencies, such as the Department of Public Health, are a matter of public record. Reporters 'trolling' for a good story can access the documentation and pursue the matter. Family members or even staff members may feel obligated to inform the media to promote patient safety or to achieve a sense of justice served for the error occurring in the first place. To that end, it is important for the organization to consider the media in their communication strategy.

Critical Elements of Communication: Who, What and How

While patient safety is clearly the #1 priority in a serious patient care error situation, the communication strategy is of utmost importance. In short, successful navigation of the event is contingent upon communication. There are three crucial aspects of communication: who, what and how. Although these aspects may seem simple, they are extremely complex and require much thought. Who is told is the easiest of the three. The length of the list will be dictated by the magnitude of the error, those required to know, and those who need to know.

Determining What is told to who, and by whom, is the most difficult part of the communication strategy. In a serious patient care error, there are usually multiple individuals or bodies who must be informed. Although the message to each must be consistent, the content should consider the audience and be adjusted accordingly. For example, patients and families may not need the level of detail required by the governing board of the organization. Similarly, the audience will 'drive' the selection of the spokesperson or messenger. With the multiple constituencies who must be informed, it is unlikely that 'one size will fit all' and that a number of individuals will be needed in the communication process. When identifying individuals, the caveat is choose the right person – which may or may not be linked to one's formal position or the table of organization. Given the criticality of the communication process, it is better to select the person(s) who can effectively and accurately deliver the message, rather than to stand on ceremony or protocol.

How the information is communicated is guided by strategy, mandated processes and organizational culture, norms and values. The how in communication has much to do with the audience. For example, an established process will dictate how regulatory agencies are informed of an error, whereas how that information is shared with staff members will depend on the organization's systems and standard approaches. What is most important in determining how the event will be communicated is selecting the method, medium and messenger that will ensure the accuracy and intent of the information shared.

The Gastroscope Incident: Initial Communication Strategy

In the gastroscope incident, the communication strategy required a "collective think" by an expanded leadership team. This included the Chief Executive, Chief Nurse Executive, Chief of Staff, Chief of Staff Elect, Infection Control Officer, Risk Management, and the Administrative Directors of the clinical areas. Other key stakeholders and resources were added to the team for their input and guidance. They included the physicians involved in the procedures, legal counsel and marketing leadership. As noted in the table to follow, the initial communication strategy focused on the patients, families, and key constituencies who needed to be informed of the error, such as the Department of Public Health, health system leadership, and governing body. Contacting the media was not considered at that time. The communication priority and commitment was to the patients and families, with regulatory agencies and internal leadership groups as a secondary, but equally important, priority.

Initial Communication Strategy

Who	What	How
patients / families	scripted message describing: the incident • level of risk • availability of follow-up testing (funded by the hospital) • ongoing communication / support • hot-line number for other questions	telephone contact by a hand-selected group of hospital staff who were specially trained for the project
regulatory agencies	scripted message describing: • the incident • number of patients involved • level of risk • immediate steps taken to follow hospital policy • incident investigation status • steps taken to inform patients and ensure follow-up testing	telephone contact by the risk manager
health system leadership	same message shared with regulatory agencies	telephone contact by the Chief Executive
governing body	same message shared with regulatory agencies	telephone contact by health system President / CEO

Who	What	How
managers	same message shared with regulatory agencies	reviewed through leadership council structure by Chief Executive and Chief Nurse Executive
staff	same message shared with regulatory agencies	reviewed at staff meetings by the manager
medical staff	same message shared with regulatory agencies	reviewed at Medical Executive Committee by the Chief of Staff and Supervisory / Section meetings by hospital leaders
other hospitals within the health system	same message shared with regulatory agencies	reviewed at the established forum structure by the Chief Executive

The Gastroscope Incident: Arrival of the Media

Shortly after the organization self-reported the gastroscope incident to the Department of Public Health, the hospital was contacted by the local media for information regarding the error. It is not clear whether the media learned of the incident through monitoring the Department of Public Health website or by another means – nor was it a critical factor to know. What mattered most was the effect of the media involvement on managing the event, especially the communication process.

The arrival of the media had a tremendous impact on the course of the event and leadership in three ways. First, it greatly accelerated the communication process with patients and families. The media believed they could and should play a key role in informing patients and families of the incident in the press or on the evening news. However, the organization felt deeply obligated to inform patients and families personally through the telephone call process, which was underway but not yet completed. The media refused to wait until all individuals had been contacted to run the story. Additional staff were quickly trained and deployed to the telephone team and the pace of the calls intensified in order to reach as many patients and families as possible before the evening news and morning paper.

A second effect of the media involvement was the impact on leadership. Responding to the press consumed an enormous amount of time and energy. Yet, given the seriousness of the error and patient safety concerns, the organization could not stop or delay its investigation or efforts to resolve the situation. To that end, managing the media was an additional stressor and burden on an already overloaded agenda. Virtually every member of the leadership team was called upon to help with the crisis, either through a direct role in managing the situation or to cover responsibilities for those who were involved.

Thirdly, the media attention brought a new dynamic into play: addressing the concerns of hospitalized patients and families, and supporting the morale of the staff. Understandably, patients and families had questions about their own safety, given the breaking news. Hospital staff, many with over 20 years of service and with deep organizational pride, where devastated by the negative media coverage. Emergency meetings were held with the managers to discuss the incident and media attention. In addition, 'talking points' were distributed to guide discussions at staff meetings, and with patients and families. Finally, leadership pursued every opportunity to personally meet with physicians, staff, patients and families to engage in dialogue.

Responding to the media required a customized communication strategy specific to the press and television stations. Carefully crafted scripts were developed by the expanded leadership team, which utilized the 14 tips for media interviews outlined by Johnson & Johnson. Key messages were identified which focused on the facts, such as the nominal risk to patients, the steps taken to personally contact patients and provide follow up care, and the actions implemented to correct the error. In addition, much thought was given to selecting the most appropriate individuals for the interviews. An important note is that the spokespeople differed, depending upon the medium. Moreover, the individuals were not always the most senior members of the leadership team or the designated spokesperson for the organization. As an example, for the television interviews, the comfort level of the individuals chosen to speak in front of a camera and live audience was as important as their credibility, knowledge of the incident, and communication skills.

The media attention continued for approximately one week – although it felt like a lifetime – with local newspaper, radio, and television coverage. During this period, the regional and national newspapers also picked up the story. Once the media involvement evolved to the regional and national level, the organization had no control over the information communicated. It was not contacted for comment, nor was it made aware of the planned coverage. The organization learned about the coverage after the story had aired, through a variety of sources, including friends, colleagues, and staff members attending conferences, who called to say, "You were on the evening news." It was an extremely difficult period for the organization - where one simply had to wait for the storm to pass.

Priority #3: Root Cause Analysis

When a care delivery error occurs, ensuring patient safety involves a two-step process consisting of: 1) immediate correction of the error and 2) conducting a root cause analysis. Without an in-depth examination, identification, and regulation of risk factors that contributed to the error event, there is potential for reoccurrence. All too often, the immediate correction of the error serves as proxy for the root cause analysis process, leaving the organization and ongoing patient safety at risk.

In the gastroscope incident, the risk manager conducted the extensive root cause analysis. Participants included physicians, clinical leaders, staff members from the Operating Room and Sterile Processing Department, and the Infection Control Officer. Although the divergence from the gastroscope cleaning policy had been a unilateral decision by a Registered Nurse, the team sought to identify factors which allowed this to happen in the first place and continue unchecked and undiscovered over a prolonged period of time.

A number of risk points were identified, some of which were painful for the organization to acknowledge. Among the more difficult was recognizing that the culture in the Operating Room and Sterile Processing Department did not promote professional accountability for adherence to policies or for reporting deviations from protocols. As a result of the findings, the scope of the investigation was expanded beyond the gastroscope event itself to examine all sterilization processes, policies, and leadership oversight. In addition, management and staff accountability for practice in all other areas of the Operating Room were examined and evaluated.

Following the root cause analysis, a comprehensive redesign of the Sterile Processing Department was initiated to eliminate identified risk points in the cleaning and sterilization processes. In addition, decentralized sterilization processes, for example, in the GI procedure suite, were placed under the oversight and direction of the Sterile Processing Department to ensure consistency of the standards and practices. Finally, a comprehensive program was designed and implemented in both the Sterile Processing Department and Operating Room to transform the culture and promote professional accountability for practice.

Priority #4: Addressing Performance Management Issues

One of the most difficult decision points in a patient care error event is the human resources aspect. Care delivery errors usually involve a mistake by one or more individuals. While every organization strives to promote a culture of "no blame" around patient care errors, leadership also has the ethical obligation to ensure the delivery of safe, patient care by all staff members. Determining whether disciplinary action should be taken with the individuals involved in the error situation is a complex, and often painful, process but a critical part of the error investigation and resolution. Among the key factors to be considered are:

1. Seriousness of the error.
2. Was the action intentional, deliberate, and/or the consequences understood?
3. Prior performance of the individual(s).
4. Mitigating factors which contributed to the action taken.
5. Insight, remorse, and ownership for actions demonstrated by the individual(s) and commitment to improvement.
6. Level of confidence that the practice, clinical judgment, or other issues which led to the error can be corrected by education or training.
7. Risk to the organization in potential litigation actions if the individual(s) involved in the error remain employed.
8. Internal reference points for disciplinary actions taken in similar situations.

As part of the organization's investigation and address of the gastroscope incident, extensive interviews were conducted with the staff members involved. In addition to the Registered Nurse who made the decision to diverge from the terminal cleaning policy, there were individuals who followed her instruction even though they knew that it was not in accordance with protocol. For confidentiality reasons, the disposition of the individuals associated with the patient care error will not be discussed. The important point is that the organization believed it had an ethical and professional responsibility to take action, based on the egregious nature of the error and the findings from the interviews.

Priority #5: Lessons Learned

An important part of any significant event in an organization is reflection on the experience and lessons learned. This process helps to identify areas of improvement that can be applied to future situations. Additionally, analysis of the event has a way of memorializing it, which allows the organization to move on. In order to move on, one has to let go. Reflection, combined with identifying lessons learned, facilitates that process.

In their retrospective reflection on the gastroscope incident, the leadership team was extremely proud of their response and approach to an extremely difficult and devastating event. At each step of the way, the safety and well being of patients and families remained at the forefront, even when the media became involved and created tremendous distraction. Another source of pride was the extent of the investigation, which went well beyond the incident itself to evaluate all aspects of cleaning and sterilization processes for every procedure. The teamwork at every level of the organization, which enabled the facility to respond to the many complex, emergent demands during the crisis, continues to be a hallmark of the hospital. Other perspectives and lessons learned from the leadership team are as follows:

A huge lesson learned for me was the importance of proactively contacting the Magnet Credentialing Center to inform them of an error event when the media becomes involved. In the midst of the swirling activity, I did not think to alert them. As a result, the Credentialing Center contacted me when they learned of the event. They couldn't have been more supportive or understanding. Their sole concern was to know more about the event so they could help field questions or concerns in case they were contacted by the media or another organization. Although I sincerely hope I will never experience another serious patient care error event with media attention, if I do, the Magnet Credentialing Center will be a priority call for me.

Vice President/Chief Nurse Executive

I'll always remember one of our board members coaching me and saying, "The media will kill you but talk, talk, talk with your patients and you'll be fine." He was absolutely right. Having an organized process in place with someone speaking directly to patients was critical. We had the same person speak with virtually all patients and she maintained ongoing contact with a hot line, always returning phone calls within hours. We also provided follow up calls with physicians as needed.

An interesting and unexpected byproduct of being in the media is that this turned out to be a very "freeing" experience. Once in the media, the events and corrective actions could be talked about more openly with staff and the public. We were able to use the event as a platform to further the hospital's agenda for patient safety and quality improvement and used the event as an opportunity to educate staff about the need to follow policies and have a questioning attitude. The public exposure made us organizationally humble and helped leadership make the case for change in processes.

Several other actions were key in communicating with our patients. We stayed focused on this as a clinical issue rather than the administrative functions. In this way, the patients could focus on getting their tests completed and communicating results. We also stayed very connected and aligned with the affected physicians, making sure that our communications with patients were consistent. Importantly, this also helped avoid any blaming of each other in the process.

Another important step was coordinating all actions with the appropriate regulatory agencies and accepting their guidance. Besides the fact that their opinion trumps yours anyway, they had good advice.

Chief Executive

I would have to say that transparency was the key to the success in our handling the gastroscope issue. I think that a lot of the controversy was blunted by our facing the issues head on and not giving the impression of hiding anything. I also think that having an effective, honest (appearing), direct, open spokesperson dealing with the press was also helpful. Many of my neighbors commented that they were swayed by my delivery of the information.

Effective (personal) communication with patients on multiple occasions was also very helpful.

Chief of Staff

The things that we did well were:

1. *Acknowledge that there was an issue and not try to bury it. The news services weren't able to scandalize the issue beyond being a problem that we identified and are addressing. There weren't any subplots. One of the spokespersons for the hospital did a magnificent job discussing the nurse who was involved in objective and straightforward terms. That the original clip used her discussion was powerful in my opinion.*
2. *Disassociate between what happened and what needs to happen going forward. That there was a problem with the gastroscope is effectively water under the bridge, and the immediate concern is what do we provide the patients to deal with this problem. From my experience, we were able to get the patients to not dwell on what happened and instead concern themselves with what needs to be done to address their exposure.*
3. *Scripps developed a flattened hierarchy very quickly so that domain "experts" could make decisions and things were implemented quickly. I was able to make suggestions about testing and get a response back for approval very quickly.*
4. *Everyone involved contributed in whatever way necessary and there was a minimum of turf issues.*

Chief of Staff Elect

1. *A small strategic team needs to be identified early; it should include Risk Management, Legal, Marketing, Patient Contact Coordinator (whomever is assigned), Key Pathologist, Lab contact - Manager/Director (someone with enough clout to be able to get results tracked down) & Private Physician involved (plus a main contact at his/her practice).*

2. *All patient calls should be routed through your patient coordinator - it allows the patient continuity, one phone number that is answered regardless of time of day or day of week – it's all about information at that point. Utilization of a blackberry so that it can be answered immediately turned out to be crucial.*

3. *A brief education on the labs (for example what is a PCR, why are you testing for multiple types of Hep, etc.) in order to allow the patient coordinator, marketing, legal etc. to be able to speak specifically with regard to whys & wherefores.*

4. *A database that allows you, at any given time, to know patient status. This involves daily updated e-mails on patient calls, results & comments. Always with a cc. to legal. Good documentation saved us numerous times.*

5. *When a "challenging" patient is identified and it requires a physician phone call, the patient coordinator should be in the room as a scribe in order to deflect the "what was said vs. what was heard syndrome" that is common in a stressful communiqués.*

6. *The team should anticipate at least a 6-month timeline depending on patient volume. We were still getting calls almost a year later.*

Director, Community Benefits
Coordinator, Patient/Family Contact Team

1. *I was impressed by how much the patients appreciated our personal phone calls - it seemed to take away the anger factor at the incident and instead focus them on what they could do now, such as get tested. It helped us identify those who were extra anxious and put them in touch with our pathologist, epidemiologist and/or risk manager depending on their concerns. I think this greatly reduced the potential for negative fallout or their concerns being played out in the media. It also helped me appreciate the barriers some patients had to getting tested. For instance those up in Alaska without a lab nearby. Again, the personal calls helped us identify these issues up front and ensure other arrangements would be made. We also identified other payment options. Bottom line, I learned just telling them to get tested was not enough and there was great value in helping identify concerns as well as barriers that would have made letters through the mail ineffective.*

2. *I was surprised by the profile of the folks who were most effective in making the initial phone calls to patients. I would have thought it would be RNs intimately knowledgeable and involved with the surgical experience. But, in fact, the best folks were those not at all involved, but who had excellent communication and relational skills. We scripted the message, which helped with consistency and helped those who weren't involved understand what we were trying to do. Most were RNs, one was a clinical director, but not an RN. Besides patient care folks, we also used marketing professionals. It may have been their lack of intimate involvement that allowed them to focus on the people and the issues at hand, rather than being held back by any sense of guilt.*

3. *I learned that marketing was an invaluable resource, not just for the camera and newspaper pieces, but for supporting us through the incident, thinking through many of the ramifications, giving valuable insight into how the public and patients may respond, helping craft letters and scripts, on and on. They have battle experience; while any given nurse, MD, manager may only deal with something like this on a rare if ever occasion, they are trained to handle such ordeals and really came through, keeping level heads in dangerous waters, and able to muster what control we did get over the media.*

Administrative Director, Clinical Services

1. *Be prepared - make sure leadership (physician, clinical staff, administration) is comfortable in front of the camera and that they know what to say. Interestingly enough, the day we got the call regarding the gastroscope incident, the marketing directors were meeting with a media consultant for our own media training as well as developing schedules for each site's media training sessions. We had just identified the key people from the hospital we needed to get into a training session, and voila, we have a "media worthy" event. So we were able to work with the same consultant for intense media training for our COS, CE, pathologist and nurse administrator. We not only identified the key representatives for media but the key talking points and hypothetical questions (including the "what ifs?") early on in the process, which helped us tremendously when it did hit the media.*

2. *What you do today affects what happens tomorrow - cliché, but true!! Due to the media relationships that have been developed over the years by the PR manager and corporate PR director, we received a heads up call from one of the TV stations which allowed us enough time to pull together a press conference to address the issue relaying our key messages about*

patient safety, the impact of the issue on our patients, our process for communications with patients, what happens going forward, etc.

3. *Which leads to, don't leave anyone out! We also learned that we need to include EVERYONE in the press conference. And, because the press conference was at 8 p.m., past the print deadline, we did not alert the local newspaper health reporter, and she was not very happy with us. Although we were ready with messages and had our media representatives in place, she made it difficult with additional probing and accusations and additional coverage.*

4. *Full disclosure - tell all... they find out anyway! As this was mostly a site issue, we wanted to manage it as such, so we didn't talk about the 5 patients at a system hospital. When the media found out about them, it led to more questions and made it look like we had something to hide, or that we were protecting someone, i.e., the doctor and kept us in the media longer than we wanted.*

Director, Marketing & Communications

What we did well:
- *Have good relations already established with the media.*
- *Maintain good internal communications during the crisis.*
- *Provide script for PBX operators.*
- *Media training for spokespeople.*
- *Established talking points and hypothetical Q&As.*

Manager, Public Relations

I would add that any organization facing a serious patient safety issue that will be publicly reported needs to consider the following:

1. *When you start to notify patients, you have to assume that the information will leak to the media and have a plan for telling everyone. Don't wait to reach all affected patients before you provide information to the public.*

2. *It's never too early to brief your senior public relations/communications staff on the issue so that they start preparing a communications plan.*

3. *Do everything you can to get in front the story - it's always better to be the driver. While we were able to throw a quick news conference together, we could've been more organized and prepared if we had planned it more than an hour beforehand. And the lateness of the hour prevented us from getting it to the newspaper -- which agitated them and set a worse tone for the story. It also gave the story another day because we held our news confer-*

ence Monday night, it was on TV Monday night and Tuesday morning and then ran in the paper on Wednesday morning.

4. *In hindsight, I wish we would have told the whole story up front (rip off the band-aid with one tug!). By not releasing the information on another system hospital up front, we allowed the story to have a second wave and made ourselves look like we were trying to hide something.*

Corporate Director, Public Relations

Summary

Managing a significant patient care error event when there is media involvement is time consuming for the leadership team, as well as physically and emotionally exhausting. However, it can be a transforming experience for an organization. If done well, the organization will emerge stronger with an even deeper commitment to living its values and beliefs around quality patient care and transparency in that process.

References

Swearingen, David. Presentation on Reputation/Crisis Management. Scripps Health. 8 November 2007

Joan Burritt, DNSc, RN
Clinical Professor

Joan Burritt has over 24 years of administrative practice in complex healthcare organizations. She has held senior and executive level nursing leadership roles at Yale-New Haven Hospital, the Hospital of the University of Pennsylvania, and Scripps Memorial Hospital La Jolla, the flagship of the Scripps Health system. Dr. Burritt is also deeply committed to nursing education, serving as a lecturer and preceptor to students. Her previous and current faculty appointments include Yale University, University of Pennsylvania, University of San Diego, University of California Los Angeles, and San Diego State University. Dr. Burritt recently assumed a consulting role with Lakier & Sullivan

After graduating from the Grace School of Nursing at Yale-New Haven Hospital with a diploma in nursing, Dr. Burritt earned her BSN at Boston University. She received her MSN and doctoral degrees from the University of Pennsylvania. Prior to returning to Yale-New Haven Hospital in 1983 to begin her administrative practice, Dr. Burritt worked as a staff nurse in obstetrics, oncology, and general medicine.

Dr. Burritt has been recognized as an "Emerging Leader to Watch" by the American Organization of Nurse Executives and as one of the "50 People to Watch in San Diego" by San Diego Magazine. She has contributed to two textbooks and authored a number of articles. Her most recent, "Achieving Quality and Fiscal Outcomes in Patient Care: The Clinical Mentor Program," which appeared in the December 2007 issue of the Journal of Nursing Administration, reflects her interest and concern regarding the increasing gap between the clinical abilities of staff and the needs of acutely-ill patients in a complex care environment. Dr. Burritt has presented at local, regional, and national conferences and served as a keynote speaker at many commencement ceremonies and other special events. She has received numerous honors and awards for her leadership and contributions to nursing and the community.

CHAPTER 4

There Are Rules out Here – Joint Commission

by Marsha Barnden, RN, BSN, MSN

The Conspiracy

Any nurse executive knows the scenario. It is two minutes after seven in the morning and, on any other second Tuesday of the month, you would have already arrived at the hospital for a seven-thirty Family Practice Committee meeting. But today is the day that you jump in your car, juggling a travel mug of decaf and a bent Styrofoam bowl of cereal and yogurt, when you realize you grabbed a plastic knife instead of spoon. You dash back into the house and return with the appropriate eating utensil, only to find that your seventeen year-old has left you with a fuel tank on fumes. You skillfully stuff your legs into a pair of panty hose (between stoplights, of course) and make your way to the nearest gas station when your cell phone rings. "They are here. YOU said you didn't think they would come for two more months, but Joint Commission is in Administration and they look really serious. There are four of them and the physician is the team leader. He is already asking for so many things and I am freaking out! I am going to put them off until you get here - please hurry!"

You rush out of the station with only half a tank of gas before you remember that you also have your six year-old daughter, who must be dropped off at school. You drive twice the speed limit to the school and, as you slow down to a rolling speed, you instruct her to open the door and jump. As she tumbles out, she yells, "I forgot mommy, I need my frog costume, because we have to practice our play today"! You tell yourself to breathe and go to a happy place as you see a text message reminding you of your 3:30 hair appointment. Alas … so much for any previous commitments, as your calendar has now become obsolete. It is going to be a very long week and you resolve that you will just have to live with your gray roots a little longer.

The "Enemy"

Who is the "Joint Commission" anyway and from where did they come? It is unlikely that one would encounter a patient care executive anywhere who was unfamiliar with this renowned organization. However, many of those familiar with the organization may not fully understand its origin. In 1951, the Joint Commission on Accreditation of Hospitals originated as a not-for-profit organization whose primary purpose was to provide voluntary accreditation. This was the genesis of a process that would transform the way healthcare is provided across the nation. The name was changed to the Joint Commission on Accreditation of Healthcare Organizations (JCAHO) in 1987, to better reflect an expanded scope of activities. Another pivotal change came in 1993, when the standards manual was reorganized around vital patient care and organization functions to shift the focus from standards that measured an organization's capability to perform to those that assess an organization's actual performance. Thus, a performance-based accreditation process was born.

The JCAHO announced its 'Shared Visions - New Pathways" initiative in 2002. This new and innovative direction was designed to progressively focus the survey process on patient care systems that are key to the safety and quality of patient care. Included in this design was the patient tracer methodology, a groundbreaking approach intended to bring the survey team to the bedside, where an in-depth assessment of systems and processes could occur. In 2003, the National Patient Safety Goals and associated requirements were established and aimed at improving the safety of patient care. This same year, JCAHO announced plans to transition all scheduled triennial surveys to an unannounced survey by 2006. The Shared Visions - New Pathways survey concept, including the patient tracer methodology, was successfully launched on January 1, 2004 and the JCAHO began conducting on-site accreditation surveys on an unannounced basis in 2006.

Much about the JCAHO has changed over the years. Today, the organization is called The Joint Commission. The accreditation manual consists of eleven chapters and hundreds of standards ranging from medication management to management of the environment of care. The standards cross all functions within a healthcare institution, including those that are patient-focused as well as those standards that specifically address organization-wide functions. This is quite an evolution from the single page "Minimum Standard for Hospitals" list created by the American College of Surgeons (ACS) in 1917. The Joint Commission continues the legacy of the ACS in that the accreditation process focuses on the end result: improved patient outcomes. The Joint Commission accredits and certifies more than 15,000 health care organizations and programs in the United States. Joint Commission accreditation and certification is recognized nationwide as a symbol of quality that reflects a healthcare organization's commitment to meeting or exceeding specific performance standards.

Although The Joint Commission has evolved through the years to become a very sophisticated and professional organization, one aspect remains intact. The Joint Commission has been, and will always be, committed to its mission: "To continuously improve the safety and quality of care provided to the public through the provision of health care accreditation and related services that support performance improvement in health care organizations." Despite a pragmatic and attainable mission statement, it is unfortunate that The Joint Commission is often regarded by many in the healthcare industry as intimidating at best. Some feel that the standards required for accreditation by The Joint Commission are unreasonable and far too difficult to fulfill. Others simply don't want "outsiders" perceived as having great power to do harm coming into their organization. It is within those organizations that The Joint Commission is considered the enemy. But is that a fair accusation?

I believe that The Joint Commission is a friend rather than foe and that the survey process is not a war between the good guys and the bad. I say this as a regular run-of-the-mill hospital worker and not as a Joint Commission surveyor. Although I do function as a part-time surveyor, I base my belief more on my day-to-day job, rather than my exposure to the inside. However, you will see that the inside exposure does provide a glimpse of The Joint Commission that can only be seen from that vantage point. That view also shapes my feelings toward the organization. If you decide that The Joint Commission is your friend, even with some reservation, there are some common obstacles that can be overcome so as to ensure that your survey experience is a good one.

The "Attack"

On-site hospital surveys for any reason (state licensing, accreditation, OSHA review, etc.) have been notoriously stressful and somewhat overwhelming for almost everyone involved. Joint Commission surveys are no exception, particularly with the recent addition of the stealth arrival at 0730 hours. The surprise element has been a highly charged occurrence across the nation, as many surveyors have been greeted with a look of sheer horror and the following response: "Uh … let me get someone else." It would seem that the survey team has been lying in wait in some obscure hotel on the outskirts of town and dining surreptitiously in a dark steakhouse that none of the locals frequent. And then, as if materialized from thin air, here they are on your doorstep. No matter how much effort may or may not have been exerted prior to the visit, it seems there is always some degree of panic among the forces. The panic is really an innate response, a feeling that you are stark naked before the world and everyone is looking at all your stuff. There you are, completely exposed and vulnerable. Not just bare to the "intruders" but to your very own staff. Who cares what the surveyors think, but what will your staff think about you and the leadership team if you don't put on a good "show"? The thought of it all makes you want to run for cover. After all, if you wanted to be entirely exposed, you would have sought to be a centerfold. There are innumerable ways in which you can stay home and embarrass yourself, so why would anyone want to endure such a degree of potential public and personal humiliation? Who wants to be the community poster child for the "you definitely don't want to go there" hospital? The exposure concept can be by far the biggest obstacle to hurdle. Dirty laundry smells even worse when it is not your own.

Marching Orders

The standards contained within The Joint Commission accreditation manual are the standards by which hospitals and their affiliated services have been surveyed since the inception of The Joint Commission. The standards were developed with much consideration given to the realities of hospital operations. There have been many changes made to the standards over the years as a result of input from the healthcare organizations and several standards and chapters have been rewritten to provide necessary clarification and make the requirements easier to meet. Once standards compliance is achieved, organizations are encouraged to raise the bar, to strive for as close to perfection as can be reasonably expected, given the available resources. Having been a part-time Joint Commission surveyor for nearly three years, I have seen, firsthand, the inner workings of the organization. Despite any misconceptions that may abound concerning The Joint Commission, I am convinced that they have much to offer the ever-changing healthcare arena in this country. I can say emphatically and without reservation that The Joint Commission lives by their mission statement and the mission statement is the driving force behind the required standards. It must be emphasized that the standards contained in The Joint Commission accreditation manual are not extraordinary. The standards are doable, if an organization makes a commitment to prioritize the standards and associated requirements. This commitment must come from top leadership. There is no other way.

The Allies

The Joint Commission carefully screens and hires professionals who, like the organization, believe that every healthcare institution must strive to be the very best possible, always placing safety and quality first. I have had an opportunity to work with very high caliber physicians, nurses, and administrators who share a desire to see organizations do well. Along with many of my surveyor colleagues, I actually delight in the opportunity to provide hospitals with an enormous chance to showcase the wonderful things they do day to day to improve patient outcomes. Believe it or not, surveyors are on your side - it is not a "you" versus "them" situation. Surveyors are your allies and the best interests of the organization are foremost in the surveyors' minds. Even when suggestions need to be made (observations of "findings"), a surveyor is always thinking of the very best for the organization and, ultimately, safe and quality patient care.

You may still be asking yourself why anyone would want to endure such vulnerability. I can tell you that you do want to undergo the scrutiny. Really, you do. Not only should an organization want the stamp of approval that validates that they are meeting minimum standards for patient care, but organizations should not want to miss the opportunity for some very talented individuals to shine a different light on systems and processes. Different eyes see different things and, when hospital staff see the same things day in and day out, they may easily miss the prospect of improving even the slightest step in a process that could change the entire system and make a difference that might save a life.

Most surveyors who do not work full-time for The Joint Commission work in a hospital, just as you do. They are often senior leaders, just as many of you are nurse leaders. They live your life in a different place. Your struggles have been theirs at one time or another. They have walked in your shoes and understand the challenges of healthcare in an environment where money has never been tighter, resources thinner, and patients sicker. Surveyors do understand your roles and they aim to do whatever they can to help you perform your job better to produce quality patient outcomes. Surveyors will often go the extra mile to work with your teams in determining the best course of action in any given area. Most are eager to impart best practices they have seen at other organizations and appreciate hospitals that allow them to share the sound practices they may have observed during your survey with other organizations.

The bigger question should be related to how an organization can endure such an incursion. You can have a successful Joint Commission accreditation site visit and it is possible to survive a survey unscathed and with ego intact. To my knowledge, survey teams have not taken any hostages or left any dead bodies. Some essential survey survival tips follow, in the hopes that you can facilitate a smooth and successful survey process.

Battle Strategy

There are countless explanations as to why organizations struggle through Joint Commission accreditation surveys, but one premise bubbles to the top of the list. Hospitals are challenged with the survey process for the same reasons they so often suffer less than stellar survey outcomes: the organization is not performing optimally or consistently in limited or multiple areas. Often, if an organization is performing consistently, the consistency is headed in the wrong direction. This is a very a bold statement, but one that can certainly be substantiated. We have all encountered such phenomena to some degree at various intervals throughout our careers. It seems that, with precise predictability, hospitals experience periods of heightened excitability as they gear up for Joint Commission, but the exuberance soon wanes. Why can't the excitement be sustained? It is much like the initial, but short-lived, exhilaration one might feel for the soup of the day, only to have it changed the next day. Some would view Joint Commission compliance like the soup of the day – "gung ho" on Tuesday, but over it on Friday.

The Joint Commission standards simply require that organizations maintain a minimum level of patient safety and continually investigate ways to improve performance. Will it ever be possible that folks will understand that hospitals owe patients safe, quality care and that we have an obligation to always look for better ways to do what we do every day? We all know that the answer is that, while not every member of the organization's care team will "get it," there are far more who will! It is those individuals on whom you must focus your energies. The others will eventually fall off, because they will not be able to survive in an environment that is moving forward toward a mutual goal - that of meeting or exceeding regulatory requirements. Those who struggle against the positive changes will become outsiders who will begin to feel very uncomfortable in their efforts to thwart progress. Just a word to the wise – don't worry about those staff members who are going in a direction other than where the organization is going as a whole. Surveyors sniff out those folks immediately and recognize that they are outsiders. The surveyors will focus on the 'platoon members' who are committed to the organization and are following the marching orders because they care about their mission and the rest of their troop.

Survival Tips

We're not ready! How many times have you heard that? Even knowing the general time frame during which the Joint Commission may visit, I find that most organizations procrastinate their efforts to ensure standards compliance. When will you be ready? Will you ever be ready? The reality is that an organization cannot "get ready" for a Joint Commission survey. Organizations must be ready at all times, every day. This requires tremendous work on the part of the entire team, but it is the only way to survive. It is painful to watch organizations that have ramped up for a survey. This usually becomes apparent to the surveyors early during the first day. Don't get caught in this trap! Rather than "be ready for Joint Commission," why not always be ready for the next patient. If staff members are always prepared for the next patient, the chances are great that they will be well prepared for a site visit by Joint Commission. The Joint Commission does not require perfection, but they do survey to the standards as outlined in the accreditation manual. Organizations have been given the manual in order to prepare for an open-book test. To have a successful survey, it is crucial that hospitals demonstrate to the survey team that they are aware of all of the requirements and have exercised due diligence in their efforts to comply with the standards.

If you invite someone to dinner, your invitee would expect that you have made preparations for a meal. Hopefully, you have purchased food and gone to the effort of cooking something very nice. If you are really energetic and proud of your culinary talents, you make something spectacular and even provide entertainment, in the way of a movie or special music. A Joint Commission survey is much the same. You know they are coming to visit, but are not sure when they will arrive. So you buy all the groceries and make the food ahead of time; just keep it simmering until they get there!

Be proud of your organization and accomplishments - show the surveyors what you've got! Let the surveyors know that you and your team are excited to identify any opportunity where patient care might be improved. Under no circumstances should you withhold anything from the Joint Commission team that they are authorized to access. Your attitude should always be that you have nothing to hide and you very much appreciate the opportunity to have a review from a different set of eyes, eyes that truly understand the underpinning of a healthcare organization. During the most successful surveys in which I have participated, both as a surveyor and surveyed, the organization was very open with the survey team. This attitude very quickly sets a collegial tone for the entire length of the survey.

We've Been Hit!

It is the first day of survey and you have finally made it to the hospital. You may find your team a bit on the frazzled side, but happy to see you! It is important to maintain a positive and calm demeanor. Staff members very quickly pick up on anxiety vibes from senior leaders. Being matter of fact in your conversations will most definitely keep your team from buckling under the stress. The old adage, "never let them see you sweat," is appropriate for this situation. There is no reason for staff to succumb to paralysis at the mere sight of a survey team! The surveyors do not bite and you should always find them pleasant and friendly from arrival forward.

Do be certain to ensure that staff or volunteers who work the Front Desk know exactly what to do and who to call, should a survey team arrive. The Front Desk attendees should all understand who to call and where to take the surveyors, so that they are not left seated in the Lobby. It is not always possible to have a designated room that is kept unoccupied for such a purpose. Have a back up plan, so that hospital personnel know where to direct the team. Having the logistics planned ahead of time will serve you well and make the survey activities flow smoothly.

Your Papers, Please

The sure evidence of ramping up for a survey is an organization that presents massive quantities of documents (by way of the proverbial binders), to include an infinite number of policies, most of which demonstrate very recent approval dates. Be reminded that organizations are not required to produce every policy the organization owns. Only the documents listed in the material received before the survey are necessary. Surveyors will certainly ask for additional policies throughout the survey, but only as the need arises. One word of advice is to ensure that there is not a 'single owner' of the policies intended for use during a Joint Commission survey. The required policies should be copied and made readily available anytime a survey team should arrive. Ideally, the policies should be maintained in a location that is accessible to several hospital staff members. Additionally, all other hospital policies should also be readily available to multiple hospital employees, so that they can be obtained easily, if they are requested. It is most frustrating to surveyors to ask for policies that never seem to materialize.

Give Me Your Numbers!

As good as patient care can be, there most always exists an opportunity to further refine and perfect a process. These refinements go a long way to enhance the care provided and boost staff morale, as well as patient satisfaction. Surveyors will want to see that organizations are always looking for improved patient care processes, so "good" useful data is absolutely a must! Organizations should present data that has been aggregated and analyzed. The key thing to remember about data is that, unless an organization uses the data to positively affect patient outcomes, the data is not meaningful or useful. The single most common observation I have made regarding data is that many organizations are "data rich and information poor." Because the organization may have fallen victim to the old quality assurance model, they have tracked and trended data over a long period of time, without ever really analyzing the data and making decisions based on that data. The organization is then left with an enormous amount of raw data, accumulated over eons, that simply get reported to various committees on an ongoing basis. Even when a Performance Improvement committee has been commissioned to oversee all performance improvement activities, there is often lack of evidence that the committee has discussed the data in terms of possible process changes necessary to improve patient outcomes. You have heard real estate agents chant, "location, location, location!" Well, as far as data is concerned, the mantra should be, "outcomes, outcomes, outcomes!"

Patient Tracers: The Interrogation

The patient tracer methodology is an obvious departure from the previous framework utilized by the Joint Commission surveyors. Formerly, much of the survey time was spent reviewing policies with very little interaction with staff and patients. Well, hasn't that changed now! Anyone who has undergone a survey since the implementation of the Shared Visions - New Pathways initiative will tell you that the process is quite different indeed. The majority of hospital employees I encounter (both front-line staff and senior executives) have indicated that they very much prefer the new way and appreciate that the survey process has been brought to the bedside.

Surveyors will most definitely want to talk with the persons providing care for a given patient. Surveyors are keenly aware that managers will almost always have the answers they are looking for, so they are not interested in talking with those at the management level. Whoever the direct caregiver may be, whether a nurse, respiratory therapist, dietician, or EKG Technician, the surveyor will want to spend considerable time reviewing the patient's course and focusing on the specific care provided by individuals from all disciplines involved. I have found, even in my own hospitals, that staff do not need to be coached if processes have been put in place and all the appropriate individuals have been well educated about those processes. I tell those with whom I work to simply share what they are doing for the patient and be prepared to answer questions just as if they were giving a report to a co-worker. There is much focus on interdisciplinary care and how that care is coordinated. Therefore, communication is emphasized at all transitions of care. Staff should already be proficient in whatever communication methodology has been implemented to ensure safe handoffs. Much like the patient's plan of care, providers should be able to paint a picture for the surveyor to illustrate why the patient is receiving services, how they are responding, what care has been modified if the response is not as intended, and what the ultimate goals are for each patient.

It is most interesting to note that I rarely, if ever, see the use of the nursing process as it was taught to those of us who are now getting on in age. Newer nurses very often struggle with the concept of assess, diagnose, plan, implement, evaluate. Because of this, many newer nurses have difficulty with problem-solving and critical thinking skills. I suggest that perhaps preprinted care plans may have contributed to this, as many examples lack the content necessary to effectively "paint the picture." Additionally, preprinted care plans are frequently not made patient-specific and individualized and, as such, they appear to be generic in most cases. Whatever care plan may be used throughout your organization, the take away message is to ensure that the reader can get an idea of exactly what is currently going on with a given patient.

There is another key tip for patient tracer activities. Staff members often get extremely nervous when there is an audience. This is most especially true if the staff member's manager or another senior leadership person is in attendance during the tracer. It is most helpful if escorts are limited, so as to facilitate a less threatening atmosphere when care providers are interviewed. It is not uncommon for a surveyor to ask some audience members to excuse themselves, if it appears that the interviewee is exceptionally anxious. Better to prevent that from occurring by limiting the number of people involved at the outset.

The single most important thing for staff members to remember is that the surveyor is on their side and they do very much want to see the employee do well. Surveyors want staff to have the answers and will give them every possible opportunity to provide whatever is necessary in the way of explanation or evidence. Surveyors do not want to trip up staff members or trick them in any way. The intent of the surveyors' visit to a patient care area is just to learn more about patient care processes and systems. The focus is not on the staff member, so staff should be encouraged to relax and tell their story!

Foxholes - Run for Cover!

It may happen that a difficult situation arises whereby a surveyor is not able to find the appropriate answer to a question and the staff member becomes frustrated or otherwise freezes up. If this occurs, it is acceptable to have another staff member, perhaps a colleague, offer assistance in providing whatever is needed to clarify the question. Staff members should be instructed that they can always tell a surveyor that they do not understand a question and to please state it another way. If the staff member understands the question, but does not know the answer, that is perfectly okay, as well. Admitting that they don't know is far better than attempting to bluff their way out. That never seems to work well for anyone. It is also acceptable if the staff member states that she doesn't know the answer, but she knows who to ask or where to look.

Again, the surveyors want to see the hospital be successful, so they will be as helpful and supportive as possible. Organizations simply need to give surveyors something to work with! Staff should not need to run and hide when they see a surveyor approaching their unit. It is a wonderful learning experience when a small group of team members from any unit sit together with a surveyor and review a patient's course of care. Surveyors love to teach! Not only does the primary care provider get support from his co-workers, but the others who participate always learn so much about communication, collaboration and team-work! I never cease to marvel when I see eager staff members who are just hanging around because they are interested in what is going on during a patient tracer. It tells me that they care about the work they are doing, and that is always so refreshing!

Calling in the Reinforcements

A vital part of the survey agenda involves system tracers that include groups of individuals who are key stakeholders in whatever organizational or patient care function is to be discussed. These groups may include members of the organization's medical staff, as well as senior leaders. It is critically impor-tant to ensure that the right people are present for these discussions. If the phar-macist is responsible for Pharmacy and Therapeutics Committee activities, then that individual should be available when medication management is discussed.

On a similar note, it often becomes painfully clear to surveyors that only one or two individuals really know what is going on with a particular issue being discussed. This is commonly an indicator that the organization is not effective in the area of communication and collaboration. Additionally, ineffective com-munication is a red flag that performance improvement and other activities are occurring independent of the committee structures that have been put in place to direct those activities. It should be evident during any group session that all the appropriate players are actively participating in the efforts required to accomplish the task at hand. During group sessions, it is imperative that each person in attendance offers something to the conversation concerning his/her role in the process. The more that individuals speak up, the more it is evident that the organization has mechanisms in place to ensure collaboration and coordination of efforts. Nothing is worse than a room full of people with no one talking. The eye contact and other body language speak volumes about the organization! If staff members are nervous about any scheduled activity, they should practice a round table by discussing with each other what part each of them plays in the activities currently underway. Each participant should share his/her contributions and explain how those contributions fit into the bigger picture.

Give Me Your Papers, Again, Please: Minutes

I have but one word to the wise about committee meeting minutes. The most common observation I make with regard to minutes (and this includes my own hospitals) is that the minutes do not consistently and accurately reflect when outstanding items have achieved some resolution. I so often review minutes where long-standing issues keep cropping up, but the loop is never closed. Then I am unable to determine the outcome without further investigation.

Additionally, I frequently identify an issue in meeting minutes that is of some significance; however, I may not be able to find any mention of that issue in subsequent minutes. It is almost as if it never existed. Closing the loop is not always easy to do, but it is a 'must' in the area of performance improvement! Those given charge for taking minutes should be educated about the amount and type of detail that should be reflected in the minutes, including documentation of those responsible for a particular item and any specified timeframes for completion. Any time an item is outstanding, it should be brought forward on each meeting agenda until resolution has been accomplished and documented. Evidence of problem resolution is a key component to good performance improvement work and is necessary for establishing a monitoring process to ensure that whatever gain is made is sustained for a defined period of time.

Special Forces Assignment: National Patient Safety Goals

I would be incredibly remiss not to address the Joint Commission's National Patient Safety Goals (NPSG's), as they are, without a doubt, a major focus during a Joint Commission survey. Given the inordinate number of medical errors, the NPSG's are much needed and long overdue. It is expected that the goals will not be going away anytime soon and, in fact, will most probably continue indefinitely. We will likely see many of the goals retained year after year and new ones added based on commonly occurring errors within the health care environment. When one thinks about the types of things that are done to patients when they enter a health care setting, it is not far reaching to agree that hospitals are very dangerous places. The opportunities to cause patient harm are abundant and, in many cases, those who are in a position to cause harm are ignorantly unaware of the risks. It cannot be over-emphasized that organizations need to provide considerable resources dedicated to making certain that the NPSG's are fully implemented throughout the organization and that monitoring efforts support significant compliance with all of the goals. Where noncompliance is identified, immediate action should be taken to improve performance with regard to the requirements, as stated within the goal.

Wave the White Flag

Ready to give up those preconceived notions about the demon Joint Commission? I hope that organizations will understand that undergoing a Joint Commission survey is not a war between them and us. Although there may be slight battle fatigue and perhaps a bit of combat stress, there should be no battle scars beyond a limited number of findings that may require some specific action. If an organization receives a requirement for improvement, it is just an opportunity to make a process better, perhaps make a patient safer. Should your organization receive such a finding, ponder this: do you think your organization would take the time and effort to make the necessary changes if it were not required of you? Chances are an organization may not choose to do so. Not because they don't want to make the change or improve in a given area and not because they don't care about their patients. The simple truth is that they may not change anything because the problem will most likely fall right off their radar screen. Without the pressure that accountability creates, it is far too easy to let things fall through the ever widening cracks, the big black holes. Oh, the problems won't go away forever. They'll just stay in the holes and grow until they get so big that they squish right back out of the holes and hit you in the face.

Perhaps you will make peace with the enemy and come to understand that the Joint Commission survey process does not have to be traumatic. Work with what you have been given and rest assured that will be enough. Keep in mind, it's all about doing the right thing and doing it consistently. Once you reach the right thing, stay there and don't back down. Clench it like a dog with a bone and, eventually, others who "get it" will follow you on the road to excellence. They will either come along, or be left behind. Ahhhh … surrender is such a relief!

Remember: everything is always okay in the end. If it's not okay, it's not the end!

References

The Joint Commission. (2008). *Facts about The Joint Commission*. Retrieved June 13, 2008, from: http://www.jointcommission.org/AboutUs/Fact_Sheets/joint_commission_facts.htm

Marsha Barnden, RN, BSN, MSN

Marsha Barnden has been a Registered Nurse since graduating from Bakersfield College in 1980 with an Associate Degree in Nursing. Marsha later obtained a Bachelor of Science in Nursing in 1994 and Master of Science in Nursing in 1997, both from California State University, Bakersfield, where she was Nursing Class Valedictorian and Dean's List Student.

Marsha chartered and was President of the first Nursing Explorer's Post in Kern County. She has served on the San Joaquin Valley College Board of Directors and been President and Treasurer of the Xi Epsilon Chapter of Sigma Theta Tau Nursing Honor Society, Treasurer of the Los Angeles Chapter of the American Association of Legal Nurse Consultants, Treasurer of the local chapter of AWHONN, President of Kern Nurse Administrator Council and member of the Kern RN Society. She is certified by the Association of Women's Health/Obstetrics/Neonatal Nursing in Inpatient Obstetrics.

Marsha works full time for Adventist Health as Director of Standards and Clinical Processes, where she is responsible for patient care policy development, implementation, and compliance. She is also employed by The Joint Commission as a part time hospital surveyor and surveys hospitals nationwide. Marsha maintains her clinical skills working per diem as a Labor and Delivery/Maternal-Child Nurse. She currently resides in Bakersfield, California where she lives with her husband Keith.

CHAPTER 5

The Power of Apology in Nursing Leadership

by Donna Hart Reck, MSN, RN, NE-BC
and David Gage, PhD

There's a Buddhist saying that even your worst enemy can be your Buddha. Similarly, a CNO's worst management nightmare can be her Buddha. This chapter describes one CNO's nightmare and the lessons she took away from it.

As Dragnet's opening narration cautioned, "Ladies and gentlemen: the story you are about to hear is true." We, too, have changed the names, along with some of the other details, "to protect the innocent." Our case study unfolds inside the walls of an academic medical center.

An Ed in Crisis

This academic medical center had been experiencing rapid growth and increasing patient visits for several years following a failed merger with a large, for-profit health system. After the unwinding of the failed merger, it was an exciting time to be working in the center, and specifically in the Emergency Department. The ED environment was complex, growing rapidly and constantly changing, with new challenges around every corner. To be sure, there were problems: staffing issues, communication glitches, and equipment or supply shortages, to name a few. The department had reached its maximum capacity, which would require eventual physical expansion, but typical for EDs, patients kept pouring through the doors anyway. Balancing the department's needs against individual physician, staff and patients' expectations was a daily challenge. Employing people in interim roles in nursing and physician leadership positions had become a necessity. Interim nurse and physician leadership lasted for an extended period of time. Particularly for nursing, we seemed unable to hire and keep a manager who could settle in and tackle the challenges. Finally, an extensive and costly national search ultimately yielded a permanent nurse manager.

The new manager, Lisa, seemed more than eager to tackle the myriad challenges awaiting her and jumped in with both feet. Her energy and enthusiasm seemed the perfect prescription. She was young and inexperienced and, staff said, brash and loud at times. She had a military background and embraced the gung-ho work ethic of the U.S. Marines. It was a stark contrast to the laissez-faire approach of the male nurse manager who had preceded her. After shadowing the interim nurse manager for only a few days, she felt ready to take over.

Lisa's first initiative was targeting what she correctly believed to be a major source of trouble: communication. To demonstrate rapid progress on this issue, she decided to restructure the assignment board, the department's central control and communication channel. She made the changes before she left one evening – without telling anyone. When she marched in the next morning, she was taken aback to discover that her changes had been reversed. Speechless at first, she became determined to uncover who was responsible for undermining her first attempt to prove her value and authority. The act of undoing her initiative became hugely significant and, given her military background, she seemed inclined to view it just one way: insubordination.

There's nothing like a bad kick-off. She was green, she was eager, and she wanted to be successful. The nurses she was trying to manage had decades more experience than she did. She was following a style that was the opposite of her own. No matter what she did, it seemed to be wrong. It was a downright hostile situation. The harder she tried, the worse things got. It was a classic case of staff-management conflict. A storm was brewing with no shelter in sight.

Regrettably, no one had the patience or willingness to tolerate the shortcomings of a new nurse manager, given the daily challenges of increasing patient volumes and physical space limitations. The experienced nurses petitioned for help. They shared their concerns with the unit director and eventually with Human Resources. Even though she was nearing the end of her probationary period, given the issues and concerns expressed, Lisa was placed on a performance improvement plan so her behavior would be monitored on a weekly basis. She carefully pushed back and characterized her treatment by the staff as nasty, abusive and slanderous. Her director agreed with her. Morale declined and employee turnover and call-offs increased. When I (Donna) questioned the director about the increasing turnover and call-offs, she assured me it was okay because the staff members who were leaving were the "trouble makers" and needed to go.

The director also assured me that she was working closely with Lisa to help her acclimate to the environment and, together, they were making progress on resolving issues with the staff. Later, I discovered that the conflict was actually continuing to escalate. Lisa began disciplining staff more forcefully for what she deemed inappropriate behavior. She tried to bring people in line by doling out consequences, such as denying time off, vacation leave and requests to attend educational programs. She forced one nurse – a single mother with a long-standing arrangement allowing her to work primarily day shifts – to work nights because Lisa perceived that nurse as "agitating." The staff responded strongly, feeling that the action was arbitrary and capricious. They complained to the director about this and what they perceived as other inappropriate behaviors and comments by the manager. Lisa reacted to these complaints and other attempts to go around her by tightening the screws. She issued a memo that epitomized how bad the power struggle had become and how desperate she was. The memo directed all of her staff to cease and desist all discussions regarding unit management – both inside and outside the workplace. That included communicating about the ED by telephone with one another in their own homes.

The ED had reached a nadir. One physician later described the distrust as "palpable" and said the nurses genuinely feared retaliation for questioning the manager's decisions. A feeling of paranoia crept into the unit. Security cameras were installed in response to staff raising legitimate security concerns, but many nurses believed they were put up to catch them breaking the manager's rule prohibiting them from congregating in groups and talking about her.

With new nurses, Lisa might have gotten away with such strong-arm tactics, but the unit had a large number of experienced staff, who knew she was treading on thin ice. They had questioned her clinical competence to begin with, and now they had no confidence in her managerial abilities either. The combination of experienced staff and a green manager is a combustible mix, and explode it did! The manager felt increasingly threatened and began doling out harsher discipline without warnings or clarifying her expectations. Initially, the staff tried to resolve the situation on their own, taking their story to the clinical head nurses and the director, and by getting physicians involved. Unfortunately, nothing seemed to change and they grew ever more hurt, confused and angry.

Some of the staff decided to take matters into their own hands by going outside of the medical center because they believed no one was listening to their pleas and nothing was going to change. Unbeknownst to anyone, they made several anonymous reports to the Department of Health, the Patient Safety Board and the State Board of Nursing, most of which took direct aim at the manager.

In hindsight, it's easy to see that Lisa was inadequately prepared for the task she faced. She was dropped into a medical center's team-oriented emergency department fresh from a command-and-control world. To make matters worse, the failed merger created a sense of urgency and confusion that required experienced team leadership to move the unit forward. In addition, the medical center was in the middle of a three-year journey to achieve Magnet recognition and was instituting new initiatives and a shared governance model for nurses.

Lisa needed close guidance and supervision from the unit director and, as soon as the problems arose, her director did successfully lobby for resources and assistance. An outside consultant was provided to help facilitate the situation, resolve the issues and provide coaching to the manager and director. Possibly, though, the extra supervision and resources were too little or too late, because the turbulence continued to escalate. The manager cancelled the scheduled shifts of three per diem nurses whom she perceived as threatening and undermining her authority, and then banned them from working in the department. She decided it was necessary to fire one senior nurse, Sarah, whom she saw as a ringleader bent on usurping her power and destroying morale. Following the termination, two clinical head nurses, each with decades of experience, resigned, further crippling the management team and isolating the manager.

A meeting of Sarah, Lisa, the director and a union rep was supposed to occur regarding Sarah's dismissal, but it had been cancelled multiple times without good communication or prior notice between the parties. Sarah was distraught and the staff was confused about why the meetings kept getting cancelled. They grew increasingly upset and concerned for her. One fateful morning, after yet another mix-up about the meeting, a spontaneous meeting of Sarah and nine of her colleagues occurred on the unit floor. They didn't understand why the meeting appeared to be cancelled again. They decided to go as a group into Lisa's office, where Lisa and the director were meeting.

Lisa and director were caught completely off guard when Sarah and nine staff members suddenly entered, demanding an explanation. Lisa later said she felt cornered, intimidated and threatened, and that the staff were abusive. The spontaneous meeting took on enormous significance. To the staff, it felt like an expression of concern and support for their peer. To the manager and director, it felt like an insurrection was underway and heads needed to roll. While attending an AONE conference I (Donna) received a barrage of confusing emergency phone messages that made the incident sound like the second storming of the Bastille!

From the perspective of the manager and the director, prompt disciplinary action was necessary to send a clear, strong message. Immediate measures were taken against Sarah and the nine staff, in consultation with the Chief Human Resource Officer in my absence. The staff involved received disciplinary letters and Sarah was terminated. In response, the union immediately filed a class action grievance on behalf of the disciplined nurses.

The grievance process catapulted the entire matter squarely into my lap when I returned. As part of the process, a meeting took place with the nurses, who came to be known as "the disciplined nurses," the manager, director, union leaders, HR and me. Each side had time to present its version of the story to me. As I listened to the staff members' stories, I remember saying to myself, "Oh my gosh, how did this happen, and how did it progress this far without me knowing?" I had to figure out what I was going to do – and quick!

Clearly, this was a case of "dueling realities." The nurses were on one side. The manager, director and HR were on the other. Each side had its own perspective and belief about what had transpired and, for all intents and purposes, their stories were mutually exclusive. Unsure of the veracity of either side's story, I believed we had to reduce the disciplinary consequences stemming from the spontaneous meeting in Lisa's office. Together, we agreed that Sarah would be suspended instead of terminated and that she could work on a different unit after she attended anger management classes. The nine other individuals involved would receive disciplinary letters in their files.

Listening to the nurses during this process, I realized that the tension, anger and resentment were so great that much more had to be done. The unit was in a crisis and on the brink of a major meltdown. Without some swift, decisive intervention we could lose more staff. I knew I needed to remove the manager and consider my options regarding the director but it was necessary to do more than that, especially given the fact that we were returning, again, to interim management. I needed to provide leadership, structure and a path for resolving the deep, underlying issues and I knew I would now have to play a major role. I had to design a plan to rebuild and repair the relationships. But where to start? It was clear the staff was distrustful and felt abandoned and betrayed. As I considered my options, I began to realize everything that was at stake.

The Stakes

One way or another, the crisis would be resolved, but the quality and timing of the resolution would have lasting consequences at many levels. Most importantly, it would affect individual nurses and other staff. Several nurses had already left the medical center because of what had happened and others had transferred to different units within the hospital. Some remaining employees continued to interview for other jobs.

The resolution would undoubtedly affect the culture of the department, as well as the medical center as a whole. Anecdotes of the situation spread throughout the medical center and it was implicitly understood that the resolution of this crisis would set precedents for how other problems would be handled in the future.

Without a doubt, the resolution would reflect on the character and integrity of the leaders at the medical center, including me. Finally, it would have a direct effect on the bottom line of the institution. Recruiting and training every nurse who decided to leave for a more conflict-free setting would wind up costing the institution tens of thousands of dollars, not to mention a precious intangible: their experience. A great deal is lost every time a nurse with twenty years of experience leaves and is replaced with a graduate nurse. Most of those who left, or were considering leaving, were the most experienced in the department. Of course, they were also the most sought after by competing institutions.

As bad and painful as the situation was, though, I knew it could get worse.

I knew we needed someone who could help us resolve the mess in the ED and help us get the ED on its feet. That someone was going to have to come from outside the medical center, given the distrust that the nurses and the union felt toward management and HR. I knew it had to be someone considered neutral by all parties, with enough experience to handle the situation. I also knew we would be incapable of uniting staff in a change effort if we failed to adequately address the pain caused by the manager situation. Finding the right person to mediate the situation would be critical.

I was sure our Vice-Dean for Administrative Affairs, Dr. Kevin Grigsby, who is an ethnographer and expert in conflict resolution, would know the right person. Coincidentally, he had recently published an excellent article on organizational pain, entitled "Managing pain in academic medical centers." In his article, he wrote, "Emotional pain, often in the form of anger, sadness, fear, and confusion (and often heading to overt conflict between individuals and groups), is generated in the course of everyday workplace activity. Left unchecked, an undesirable byproduct known as *organizational toxicity* will emerge and manifest in a loss of self worth, feelings of hopelessness, and a loss of energy and drive on the part of individuals in the organization." Without question, we had an abundance of organizational toxicity!

Dr. Grigsby had experience with a mediation firm and recommended them to me. He said the firm had a unique multidisciplinary approach that would be extremely desirable, given the complex mix of psychological dynamics and management, organizational and labor issues. He was confident they would be able to help us resolve the conflicts and set us on a course toward rebuilding the department. I wanted them to start immediately! Little did I imagine that the medical center's need for competitive bidding would take six weeks. Unfortunately, the six-week delay reinforced the doubts some people had about my commitment to resolving what had occurred. I had little patience but they had even less. The only good thing about it taking so long was that it gave me time to firm-up support from executive leadership (the acting COO and the CFO) and get the union's buy-in and support.

With the delay, however, some of the nurses went outside for help. With the union's help, they filed a class-action grievance. Two individuals hired their own personal attorneys. A small group of nurses contacted the Department of Health for the Commonwealth, alleging unsafe care of patients by the manager. Others filed claims with the Department and with the State Board of Nursing, alleging unsafe practices and incompetent management by the manager, the director and me. That certainly stung. This was going to be a big job!

D.G.: A very big job, indeed. And complex. It was the kind of conflict situation no one would ever walk into alone. I asked three highly skilled mediators at our firm to work with me on the initial interviews and strategy. To say, "emotions were running high," would have been an understatement. There were no bullets flying, but plenty of grievances and threats of lawsuits were in the air. There were many moving parts that seemed unrelated; though we knew they had to be connected, we didn't know exactly how. The risk of getting caught in the crossfire from either side shooting at us seemed high.

We knew our entire team had to pass muster with Donna and the acting COO in order to be hired. After clearing that hurdle, we understood we would also have to go through a review and approval process by the disciplined nurses and their union advocates. That was necessary, even though they wouldn't be paying part of our bill, because it was important for them to be on relatively equal footing with Donna with respect to working with us. We carefully answered a page of written questions from them about our experience with hospitals and unions, and they were relieved to hear that we had considerable experience mediating and consulting in healthcare settings, including working successfully with unions.

From what Donna had described, and our initial phone calls with a couple nurses and a union rep, we understood that the job ahead of us had multiple levels, consisting of:

1. The individual nurses who felt they had been mistreated,
2. The other nurses in the ED who were involved but had not been inappropriately disciplined or mistreated,
3. The other constituents (e.g., techs and physicians) in the department and their strained relationships,
4. The relationships between staff and management, and between staff and administration and,
5. Various problematic relations between the ED and other departments.

We would address all of these issues in our interviews, not just the problems surrounding the crisis. (Later, we would refine our understanding and add to this list, but the initial list was more than sufficient for a starting point.)

The Mediators' Interviews

We had gotten assurance from Donna that she understood we would be impartial, and that we were not there to bolster anyone's stance, including hers. We would coach her and others to put their perspectives and ideas forward in the most effective manner possible, but that wouldn't mean we were taking sides. Ultimately, as mediators, we were not there to decide who was right and who was wrong, as arbitrators would do; we were there to assist all of them in reaching a better resolution than they might have achieved on their own. Donna assured us that she could live with whatever we discovered and would do her best to follow our recommendations for how to proceed. Her openness was welcomed and refreshing, and a bit unusual. Typically, clients begin (and some end) with more reservations than she exhibited. Guardedness usually slows down progress, but it usually goes with the territory.

By the time the three other mediators from BMC and I had arrived to begin the interviews, we had worked up, with Donna's assistance, a list of 20-30 nurses, doctors, technicians, union reps, and administrators to interview. It was crucial to earn the trust and confidence of everyone, but most critically, that of the disciplined nurses. We needed to see a healthy cross section of the department to get a complete perspective, and also to convey to people that we were being fair and unbiased from the very start. It is sometimes nearly impossible to recover from even a small misstep during this initial stage, so we had to establish ourselves as neutral and independent, in both perception and reality. Also, in order to create a feeling of safety for everyone to talk openly, we established ground rules and addressed confidentiality. (We explained to people that, if they told us something that they did not want attributed to them, we would honor that request.)

We had no idea how significant that feeling of safety was going to be. It slowly became clear in the initial interviews that the nurses' repeated experience of the manager's retribution had conditioned them to fear speaking openly. They even feared retaliation for talking to us! I couldn't remember seeing adults so afraid to speak their minds. Of course, some could express themselves, especially their anger and disdain for what had transpired. Also, the supporters and colleagues of the disciplined nurses spoke articulately about the history of the problem and its aftermath.

Three days of listening to the stories, perspectives, insights, and suppositions of a cross section of the department led us to conclude that the level of trust had never been lower in the history of the department. The relationships among nurses, between nurses and physicians, and between nurses and HR were in tatters. Interestingly, despite everything, few harbored ill will toward the CNO. But they were confused about her. They seemed to believe, on the one hand, that her director hadn't told her the truth about what had been happening, but, on the other hand, they couldn't understand why she didn't find out sooner. My colleagues and I could understand their confusion. There was certainly a problem there that needed to be addressed – later, after we had stopped the bleeding.

In dozens of individual and small-group interviews with the staff nurses, techs, physicians, administrators, secretaries and others, we heard the same detailed stories of what happened with the nurse manager. The stories were virtually identical. Importantly, many of the people talking to us were long-time, valued members of the medical center, who came from every perspective within the department. We also interviewed the HR staff and the director. Their stories were different from the staff's stories.

As mediators, we weren't there to determine who was right and who was wrong; but it is nearly impossible not to form impressions. While there was no single truth, it was important to parse out the most accurate version of what transpired.

After the initial round of interviews, we could see a clear, unbridgeable gap – some described it as being as wide as the Grand Canyon – between the reality embodied in the nurses' stories and the reality that had been held by the unit director and HR, based on the manager's story. Suddenly, we too, could see the "dueling realities." Each side's reality negated key aspects of the other's story.

The Letters of Discipine and The Role of HR

The nurses' stories were full of anger over many things. One source of their anger was the disciplinary process.

For months before we arrived, HR had been negotiating with the union and the disciplined nurses over the language of the letters that would become permanent fixtures in their files. During the six-week consultant-approval process, Donna had kept us apprised of the progress on this front. She reported during one conference call that the grievance process related to these letters was coming to a conclusion, meaning that they were nearing agreement over the wording in the letters. She expressed relief over this "positive development."

While it sounded good to her, it concerned us for two reasons. First, it sounded like HR was prematurely tying down one piece of a large and complex puzzle. Mediators understand that it can be a risky strategy to tie down certain pieces of a complex puzzle, because those elements could be closely connected to other pieces. Working in a linear fashion and getting some of the "easier" pieces out of the way can compound the difficulties of resolving the more difficult issues later on.

Second, this development concerned us because we had no way of knowing before we got there how the disciplined nurses felt about what they were agreeing to. Clearly, Donna felt like it was progress, so we voiced only mild reservation. In truth, we feared they were making the situation worse, but we didn't want to sound like we didn't want them making progress without our help, or as though we didn't trust them to handle things.

It turned out that HR and the nurses were still negotiating over the language when we arrived. But what we heard in the interviews from the disciplined nurses about this struck us as somewhat bizarre. Despite the fact that the language of the disciplinary letters reflected the manager's account of what transpired, which was not their reality, they seemed to accept that something was going to go into their files that they didn't believe. We found it peculiar that they were negotiating the wording of clauses in the letters when they didn't even believe the gist of the revised clauses was true.

We could see how that may have been confusing to HR, since it was to us as well. The nurses' negotiations over wording felt to HR like they at least had the essence of the story correct. To claim that Lisa's accusations were false, yet still negotiate and concede the wording, made the nurses appear to be talking out of both sides of their mouths. That, coupled with the anger of the nurses, seemed like confirmation that Lisa's complaint against them (i.e., they were "troublemakers") was true. Furthermore, the nurses felt they had no choice but to negotiate the details because they felt powerless to stop the letters from becoming part of their permanent records.

We discovered that, when the nurses first felt abused by Lisa, they reported it to HR. Unfortunately, they felt that not only was that action ineffective, but also that HR was taking the side of management. This experience only made them more resentful and reinforced the we-versus-them mentality that started with the manager.

Sadly, it was a classic case of how disputes form as circumstances progress from "naming" to "blaming" to "claiming" (Felstiner et al., 1981). First, the individuals involved said to themselves that they had been injured by their manager's heavy-handed actions. The behavior they may have thought of as rude, inept or stupid in the beginning, they now *named* an injury. Second, they attributed the injury to Lisa; thereby *blaming* the party they perceived to be responsible. Next, they voiced a grievance and *claimed* entitlement to a remedy from the offender. Finally, the claim was transformed into a *dispute* when HR essentially rejected their claim for amends and began negotiating over language.

When the situation escalated to a dispute and enlisted a supporting cast of characters, people were forced to save face. The involvement of others confirmed that what had happened was truly egregious. Not being heard added insult to injury. Some nurses then reached out to even more people to get help being heard. As a conflict passed from one stage to the next, people's behavior became more adversarial. People began counting more instances of the other's behavior as offensive. Matters of "principle" developed. More and more outsiders were drawn into the dispute and, as repair seemed more and more implausible, people came to desire vindication and retribution. At each stage, people developed an increased sense of entitlement, more tangible remedies became attractive, and supporters pushed for victory rather than reconciliation.

My colleagues and I believed the internal grievances, complaints to state boards, lawsuits, and threats were as much, or more, about being heard and treated with respect, as they were about seeking compensation and retribution. By the time people bring in neutral outside mediators, however, the offended parties are often more focused on establishing rights against each other rather than in reconciliation (Levi, 1997, p. 1197).

Compared to the mediators, HR was at a distinct disadvantage from the start. It was the manager and director who first had their ear and HR is technically part of management, and certainly viewed that way by staff. The tangled, twisted dance between the manager and the nurses was so complex (perhaps twice as complex as we've presented here) that anyone who was even remotely part of the system was likely to be viewed as biased and untrustworthy.

As mediators, it was tempting to take a pass on the letters of discipline. There were certainly lots of other fish to fry and the nurses weren't demanding we act on them. Besides, we weren't sure what could be done about them at this stage. We told Donna, in summary fashion, that everyone we interviewed, except HR and the director, contradicted the story painted by the letters of discipline. It certainly appeared that what had happened in the ED was not what the letters implied. Without hesitating, she said she would do whatever was necessary to correct the inaccuracies, but she wondered, "If the underlying premises of the letters are spurious, where do we go from here?"

The Intial Plan

The nurses were angry about the nurse manager and the letters, but they were also angry about not being heard, believed, or trusted and the many downstream consequences of having been disciplined (e.g., poor evaluations and smaller pay increases). Following the initial round of interviews, we formulated three short-term goals to address the situation that had consumed the ED, and two longer-term goals to help ensure that the circumstances would not repeat themselves in the ED or anywhere in the medical center:

1. Continue developing trusting relationships with all of the parties,
2. Understand as clearly as possible what actually happened and create a shared reality about it,
3. Develop a strategy for repairing the ruptured relationships and rebuilding trusting, effective, working relationships,
4. Assist the CNO in establishing an effective leadership structure within the ED, and
5. Redesign the leadership and communication structure in the Department of Nursing to ensure that the CNO would always be informed of potentially serious problems in the department.

To begin, we suggested a series of nine one-on-one mediations between the disciplined nurses and Donna. We recommended that she hear for herself what they had to say. I (David) would conduct all of the mediations to provide continuity. We heard in the initial interviews that it was enormously reassuring to the nurses that the CNO cared enough about them to hire outside professional mediators "all the way from Washington." The size and obvious cost of the effort gave them hope that she was actually on their side and that something could change for the better. They knew that she hadn't given up on them. In return, it seemed they hadn't given up on her.

If Lisa's story was inaccurate – if her behavior was self-serving or self-protective, or vindictive – then a lot of work would have to be done to correct the wrongs that had been meted out to the disciplined nurses. The wrongs had been memorialized in the letters of discipline and the letters themselves would become the beginning focal point for the mediations.

Seven of the nine disciplined nurses had met with us for interviews and now agreed to meet with Donna. Two had refused to meet with any of the mediators and they were likewise unwilling to meet with her. Some of the nurses told me they would only agree to meet with the CNO if they could have a union rep with them. From my perspective, that wasn't ideal, but I agreed. Some wanted to meet with the CNO in a group, but I turned down that request. I had already explained to all of the parties that, as the mediator, I would be in charge of the process and, as participants, they would be in control of the outcome. Regarding individual versus group meetings, my belief was that group meetings would diminish the probability that the participants would let down their guards enough to really hear one another and be genuine. If there was to be any hope of real, deep understanding, genuine apology for wrongdoings, and forgiveness and reconciliation, it would be in one-on-one meetings. I also believed the nurses would be willing to meet one at a time if I assured them nothing untoward would happen. So, I explained that we needed to go with individual meetings, but I would meet with them privately before the meetings to coach them, and would be present during the meetings to help them say what they wanted to say. I reiterated my pledge, based on Donna's assurances, that there would be no repercussions for anything they would say. Ultimately, all seven of them agreed to the one-on-one meetings.

On the eve of the meetings, anxiety was running high. The fallout from the battle between the manager and the disciplined nurses was extensive and continuing. In addition to the issue of the letters, Lisa and the director had resigned, one nurse had been terminated and rehired, a dozen nurses had voluntarily transferred out, other nurses had received bad evaluations (and correspondingly smaller increases in pay) and there was constant talk of more people leaving the unit. Everyone knew that the future was uncertain. It was not the best environment for a meeting with your CNO!

I (David) couldn't help sharing that nervous feeling, but I was confident that this was the correct next step. The nurses had important things to say and, given the circumstances, there wasn't a better or more appropriate person to hear those comments than the CNO. I felt sure from my discussions with Donna that she would be open and sympathetic to their concerns and know how to respond. She wanted to know why they were angry with her, but I wouldn't tell her. She had to hear it first from them.

A couple things had to occur in order for the meetings to be successful. First, the nurses had to be genuinely heard by the person ultimately responsible for the department – the CNO. They had originally bypassed the CNO and gone directly to the CEO of the medical center. That had not been an effective strategy, because they had failed to talk directly to the CNO. They had assumed she already knew what was happening. Second, we had to clear up any wrongdoing, including the letters and other inappropriate disciplinary consequences, both intended and unintended.

The Mediation and Apology

D.R.: The BMC mediator team and David opened my eyes to the fact that the situation needed to be addressed on two levels: the substantive (the managerial-financial-legal issues as described in the complaint) and the interpersonal (the relationships that had been damaged). David suggested that the disciplined nurses needed to express their pain and anger directly to me and have the opportunity to explain how their experiences affected them. We agreed that he would make sure we addressed both the substantive and interpersonal issues during each mediation session.

David laid out the basic format of the meetings and said it was important for me to begin the conversation, thank the nurse for coming, and clarify the purpose of the meeting: namely, it was about understanding the past and moving forward. I needed each nurse to feel free to speak her mind without fear of retribution, so that we could clear the air and so I could truly understand her perspective of what had happened.

Prior to the first meeting, I felt anxious about what the nurses would say to me. Would they yell and scream at me, demanding to know what I was thinking? Would they demand that I explain how I could have allowed this to happen? What would they want from me? How would I react to their stories and what would I say to them? Without a doubt, I wanted to feel and show compassion, but beyond that, I wasn't sure how to react. David had coached me to listen carefully to their stories and their feelings toward me. He told me that I would hear things that would not be pretty, but he wouldn't elaborate. I knew he was also coaching them individually to be honest and not hold back, which didn't help my anxiety level.

The meetings were an overwhelming and humbling experience. The nurses came in one by one and poured out their stories, some in a mad rush, others haltingly. They were nervous and understandably fearful. Speaking up is what had gotten them into trouble in the first place, so why would this be any different? Fortunately, they had come to trust David and appeared to rely on his support during the meetings. At times, though, he seemed to be supporting them more than me, and even helping them challenge me! I had to remind myself that he was neutral and unbiased, even though it might feel like he was favoring them at times. He was their guarantee that if they had trouble verbalizing their perspectives and interests, he would step in and make sure I heard exactly what they needed to say.

As I sat and listened to each nurse describe what it had been like to work in that environment, I wanted to cry. Story after story, I felt their pain, hurt and anger. I had always wanted staff to be treated with dignity and respect, never as they had actually been treated. It was obvious, beyond any doubt, that they had been treated unfairly. I apologized for the way they had been treated, for not finding out about it sooner, and for not taking steps to stop it faster.

During each meeting, David encouraged the nurse to tell me how she felt about me personally. One woman related, in vivid detail, how she felt disdain from me during an encounter in a staff meeting at the height of the problem. We went over what had happened on that day in painful detail, and what I was actually feeling. There was no question; she wasn't making up what she had to say. Clearly, she didn't relish revealing her feelings; she was struggling and needed David's encouragement to get it out. I was dumbfounded, because I had not felt anything like disdain toward her. I told her I understood her anger toward me and that I clearly remembered the moment to which she was referring. I was able to tell her my thoughts and feelings – not disdain at all, but something very different. I apologized for my obviously poor nonverbal communication and she graciously accepted my apology.

I understood that I had to listen carefully to their stories for any apology on my part to be real and accepted. Thus, for two days, that was pretty much all I did. They were the most excruciating conversations I've ever sat through in my professional career. All I could do was listen, acknowledge the truth of what they had experienced, accept responsibility for not knowing what was going on, tell them how bad I felt, and that I was truly sorry. No one told me I should apologize. No one had to; after hearing the stories, it was the right thing to do. Moreover, it was the only thing I could do.

Those mediation sessions helped me to see how I had gotten into this predicament. Long before the problems in the ED, I was trying to allow my directors and managers to have real authority over their areas of responsibility. I wanted to empower leaders to do their jobs and not feel as though they were being micromanaged. What I began to realize was that I should have been explicit about needing to be thoroughly informed of any and all problems that arose. I was relying on others to do the right thing, which was okay, but I needed to have systems in place to stay better informed. That was a major lesson for me. I made a mental note about what steps to take next.

I personally apologized to each nurse for what had happened. I took ownership for not knowing what was happening and failing to act soon enough. Some of the nurses reacted tearfully and so did I. I promised that I would take steps to ensure that history would not repeat itself. I told them that it was of the utmost importance that they feel comfortable in the future to come directly to me if they were not sure whether or not I knew what was happening.

As painful as the meetings were, there was a breakthrough in each one. I knew each nurse to one degree or other and, with each one, there was some connection re-established. Certainly, it was the hardest and most important with Sarah. David helped her to talk about the humiliation she felt with her co-workers and even with her own family. She told me she felt she had to keep her firing a secret from her family. "They only knew me as a dedicated nurse who loved nursing. How could I tell them I was fired?"

That tore me up inside. I constantly struggle in my CNO role to help nurses feel proud that they are practicing what I believe is the greatest profession on earth. And here was a nurse who felt so utterly humiliated that she was carrying around this secret from her own family. Despite my efforts to make the medical center the best medical center in which to work, this predicament had happened. All I could do was apologize and tell her I would do everything in my power to help her to feel good about herself as a nurse again.

The meetings were an amazing mix of feelings and substance. On the substance side, we discussed and wrote down numerous specific commitments on my part to right the wrongs as much as possible. The discipline letters had to come out of their files completely. The merit pay adjustments had to be corrected retroactively. Implementing these steps would take time, but I assured them of my commitment to see them through.

D.G.: In some sense, a mediation is a dance that must be choreographed beforehand. People have to be prepared, and the separate "caucus" sessions before the start of mediation are a good way to coach people. In the caucus sessions before the mediation, I helped the nurses understand that they needed to clear the air and speak their truth, which included anger that Donna had turned her back on them. When I encouraged them to tell her their stories, some were incredulous and scared, but all agreed to try. Donna's key to success would be to listen well, express her genuine caring for the nurses in as natural a way as possible, and play her part in developing a solution. The individual meetings with Sarah before the meeting with Donna were a good example of the benefit of caucus sessions. I spent a good amount of time coaching her to feel ready and able to meet with Donna. Initially, Sarah said she would only go in if a union rep was there with her, but she decided at the last minute to go unaccompanied.

Caucus sessions provide people with the opportunity to say things that they would ordinarily not say, since they are assured of confidentiality. People quickly recognize that mediators are there for everyone's benefit and that holding back would work to their detriment. It was in these caucus sessions that I was able to help people get comfortable enough to forge ahead.

There's an aphorism that came to mind when I was preparing the nurses for mediation: The more we know each other for who we are, the less we treat each other for what we are. "The CNO" had become a clouded symbol that prevented the nurses from trusting her. That needed to change in order for her to take charge of the situation and be an effective leader. Viewing Donna as "the CNO" also prevented the nurses from seeing her as a real person with real feelings. While normally that might not be important to change, it was now, because she had to be much more than a symbol if she wanted to repair ruptured relationships and help people back down from extreme positions. By helping the nurses talk about their feelings toward Donna, I was helping them take a risk, be real, and be open to a real response from this person – this "CNO." When done properly, nudging people out of their comfort zones and encouraging them to reveal something very personal helps them to be more open and less defensive. It helps them feel closer to the other person.

I had to prepare the other partner in this dance – Donna – to let down her guard and see real flesh and blood individuals sitting next to her and thus be ready to feel and express her empathy. The point of not "over-coaching" Donna beforehand (e.g., not answering her questions about what the nurses were going to say to her) or scripting what she should say, was to ensure that she was fully present in the moment and not too much in her head. I trusted her intuition and her ability to know what to say, as long as she could demonstrate by her presence that she was open and receptive to whatever they would say to her. It could have killed the entire dance if Donna appeared to be dancing rehearsed steps, or if she became defensive.

The apology itself was also part of the dance that required choreographing. When conflicts escalate to the degree this one had, apologies are often not heard or not taken seriously. A perfunctory or rhetorical, "I'm sorry," is ineffective at best and may actually make matters worse. Donna's steps were successful because the apologies were genuine and heartfelt.

The shift in tone and attitude during the mediations was palpable. As often happens when people are mistreated, they need to feel respected and receive a sincere apology. Levi wrote, "An apology is worthless unless the required gestures are filled with meaning" (p. 1178). According to Barbara Kellerman's outstanding Harvard Business Review article on managers' apologies, a good apology has four parts:

1. An acknowledgment of the mistake or wrongdoing,
2. The acceptance of responsibility,
3. An expression of regret, and
4. A promise that the offense will not be repeated.

Donna had instinctively hit all of the essential elements.

Shifting from Private to Public Apology

As successful as everyone felt those individual meetings between Donna and the disciplined nurses had been, there was still much work to be done. The nurses would now be talking about their individual meetings among themselves and with others. We needed to bring them together, because there were things said in the individual meetings that everyone needed to hear. We decided that David would facilitate a meeting between Donna and the disciplined nurses as a group. To keep the mediation moving and on track, we scheduled the group meeting for the next day. We hoped the two nurses who had refused to talk to either of us would now feel ready to take part in this group meeting.

We decided to invite two other constituent groups to participate in the meeting. One was the union reps who were originally involved with the disciplined nurses; the other was a group of the new leaders in the ED (a clinical head nurse, the interim manager and the interim director). We wanted the two groups to participate for a strategic reason: we wanted to involve, in some fashion, anyone with the potential to derail the progress of the mediation, as well as anyone who could lend a hand in promoting it. We were hopeful that all of these additional players were in the latter group.

Stepping into the medium-sized conference room, I (Donna) could instantly feel the difference in tone between the way the individual meetings ended and the way this one was beginning. Here, there was a thick heaviness and a feeling of challenge, as in, "We're here to see what you have to say." I tried to shake that feeling and instead focus on the fact that we were all there to move forward together.

I knew I had to repeat my apologies to everyone, especially those who hadn't yet heard them. I tried to find the same feeling and energy I had before, but it wasn't easy. I felt like an amateur performer among veteran critics. If this was a choreographed dance, as David analogizes, it was a like a line dance with too many Rockette wannabes. Perhaps not surprisingly, when I did apologize, there were mixed reviews; some of the nurses were supportive, others skeptical, and some unsatisfied. The less-than-satisfied nurses wanted to know what more was going to be done and how soon. A few threw barbed comments my way. My immediate goal was to avoid responding defensively; I had to stay open. I could see David working to stay neutral and connected to the nurses. To that end, he occasionally challenged me himself. Fortunately, he had warned me that he might need to do that. He made sure that no voice was lost. I think we all felt relieved that he was there working hard to shift the atmosphere of the room from adversarial to collaborative. After people spoke, often in hurried, anxious or harsh tones, he would restate or paraphrase their words slowly using less confrontational language and much more moderate tones.

D.G.: At moments like this, the best thing one can do is trust the process. I accepted that some people in the group were not going to surrender their hurt and anger, not yet at least. Especially with these individuals, I had to avoid the tendency to be impatient or ask too much. Their pain had been accumulating for a long time and they had waited months for this process. I reinforced all of the positive sentiments I heard, while at the same time I made sure that Donna heard their observations and complaints. Donna did a wonderful job of not slipping into a defensive posture. Whenever I could get away with it, I added an ounce of levity to cut the heaviness in the room. The least sign of fear would have sent a terrible message and levity is the best way I know to show fearlessness and confidence, especially when one is feeling a little weak in the knees.

It's not surprising that the group meeting was very different from the individual meetings. While Donna apologized in as sincere a manner as she could, there were only modest expressions of forgiveness. The group meeting needed to happen and was not without merit, but "group psychology" was certainly in play. Levi calls apology a delicate interchange, and wrote, "Like other important rituals, apology requires not only the right symbolic act but also the right people, the right time, and the right place," (p. 1180).

Had the meeting been longer, we might have seen a shift in tone and attitude similar to what had happened in the individual meetings. Whereas a number of the nurses in the individual meetings responded with some expression of forgiveness, only a few of them took that risk in the meeting. I had wanted to have a co-mediator for that meeting but, given the short notice, none was available. In such meetings, with so much going on and so many people with different agendas, two mediators managing the process have a better chance of success. Preparing individuals in advance also would have helped. The involvement of the union reps and supporters probably left the group still clinging to the "claiming" stage. Having advanced to that stage (i.e., claiming their rights), it would have been difficult to return to the earlier naming or blaming stages, when an apology would have had its best chance of producing results. There was too much support for holding on and being "strong," so no one was willing to take the risk of speaking for the group about reconciliation and forgiveness. They believed there was still too much to be done to repair the damage and, unfortunately, they didn't trust that Donna was fully committed to doing it.

The forgiveness I was hoping for was less for Donna's sake and more for the nurses. For them to really let go of the pain and anger, a lot needed to happen on an organizational level. However, the first step was for them to feel some forgiveness on a personal, emotional level. Their fear was that forgiving (prematurely) would jeopardize change, leaving open the possibility that another autocratic manager would get hired, and they'd find themselves back in the same boat as before. In addition, they worried that the promises to right the wrongs would go unfulfilled. For example, even though Donna had promised that all of the letters would be removed from their files, they knew that, as of the day of the group meeting, HR had still not done that.

One of the Sarah's supporters was sitting next to her during the group meeting and she talked about Sarah's humiliation in the face of their colleagues in the ED. Even after being reinstated and starting to work again on a different unit, the nurse explained, it was extremely difficult for Sarah and she remained humiliated.

Donna responded by saying that she and I would hold a series of meetings in the ED and talk to as many of the staff as possible. We would begin with a meeting at 3:00 a.m. for the nightshift, and have morning, afternoon and evening meetings, plus another on the weekend for the weekend staff. Donna said she would present a very different view of what had transpired than management had ever acknowledged, and she would reiterate her apology for not having intervened sooner. She would also outline the steps she was taking to ensure that nothing like this would ever happen again – in the ED or elsewhere in the medical center.

The Letter of Apology

When I (David) went to bed that night, I couldn't stop thinking about Sarah's humiliation. The psychologist in me was trying hard to understand it and think of what more we could do to help her and all of those who had been disciplined inappropriately. Aaron Lazare, in his excellent book, *On Apology*, describes the distinct psychological needs that have to be satisfied in order for people to feel ready to forgive (p. 45). Some of those needs – the restoration of self-respect, assurance that both parties have shared values, assurance that the offenses were not their fault, assurance of safety in their relationships, and reparation for harm – were legitimate needs that we had to strive to satisfy so healing could occur.

I awoke at five o'clock the next morning with the realization that the best way to move this mediation forward was for Donna to write a letter to everyone in the department. Even with all of the meetings we were about to hold, given the realities of the ED, we would be lucky to reach half of the people in person. A letter would reach everyone and help dispel the misperceptions about what had occurred; it could also address Sarah's sense of humiliation. It was the only way to ensure that all of the people who knew some version of the story – many of them incorrect – would ever hear a corrected official version.

When I spoke to Donna later that day, she agreed and we immediately went to work on writing a letter in which she would briefly describe what had happened and apologize. Over the course of writing the letter, I remembered reading a *New York University Law Review* article entitled, "The Role of Apology in Mediation," by Deborah Levi. I re-read it and discovered that many of the examples about which Levi wrote pertained to medical mistakes. This situation was slightly different. We had a management mistake in a medical setting. Nonetheless, what Levi wrote about apologies in mediation was extremely helpful. For example, she wrote, "Apologies ... alleviate tensions that lie at the core of public disputes and eliminate the fiction of translating emotional pain to dollars. Aside from directly compensating specific emotional harm, [researchers] have argued that apology can transcend discrete disputes to 'repair ... frayed relationships,'" (p. 1166). Using apologies to help "repair frayed relationships" aptly described what we were attempting to do.

D.R.: I had felt trepidation about the individual meetings and then again about the group meetings. I was beginning to get used to the feeling. But making it a habit didn't make it any easier.

I had no recollection of anyone at the medical center ever writing a public letter of apology for a mistake he or she had made. It felt like uncharted territory. Still, it felt like the right thing to do. I knew there wasn't a technician, secretary or doctor in the ED who had an accurate impression of what had transpired, so they all needed to get the letter. A letter, though, felt very public. A letter of this nature, to everyone in the ED, was essentially an open letter to everyone in the medical center. A letter like this would travel fast. I felt exposed just thinking about it.

In her article on apology, Kellerman wrote, "A public apology is always a high-risk move." That's exactly how this felt. I'm not the type of person who likes being "public" but being a CNO means being public. Since this letter would be public and since it involved events that had spawned grievances and lawsuits, I knew I had to run the letter by the medical center's counsel before I sent it. I never imagined the emotion and resistance an apology could stir up!

I received a call from counsel, with whom I had always been on cordial professional terms. Nothing prepared me for the emotion on the other end of the line. Suffice it to say, he thought the letter was a colossal mistake. He told me that sending this letter would be the equivalent of committing "professional and political suicide." He warned me, "If you persist in trying to send out this letter, I will go to the Dean to stop you." I asked him to meet with David and me at his earliest convenience. David sent him a copy of Levi's law review article and suggested it might help him understand the letter and what we were trying to accomplish.

I considered the letter and counsel's threat to block my public apology in the following manner: it was obvious that people had been harmed. I knew in my heart that an apology was warranted. Did I worry that my apologies could be used against me? Definitely. Did I worry that my apologies could be used against the medical center? Certainly. But I believed more in people's inherent goodness – at least the inherent goodness of our staff – and that, if I was honest with them, they would be honest with me and not punish me for it. I also believed that if I equivocated out of fear, I would be lost. They would know it and find me dishonest. We'd all be lost!

If doing what was right was going to put me in jeopardy professionally or politically, so be it. If it would put the institution in jeopardy to acknowledge a mistake by a manager – something that happens every day in institutions – then we would have to deal with that, too. At that very moment, I was leading 2000-plus employees on our Magnet Journey, encouraging them to work hard to change the work environment and establish more collaborative relationships. Part of the Magnet designation and recognition of nursing excellence revolves around nursing leadership being transparent and fully accountable. I could not reconcile striving to make our culture more open and accountable on the one hand, and being afraid to apologize for fear of being sued on the other.

D.G.: I understood that the center's counsel believed he was doing his job, namely keeping the center out of trouble. I also knew that most attorneys representing corporations and healthcare institutions act conservatively. They are paid to protect their client, not to worry about the employees' psychological well-being. Whereas Donna and I were focused on healing interpersonal and inter-group relationships, his focus was on legal realities. Being wary of litigation makes one loath to do anything that smells like apology.

It wasn't long ago that apologies were routinely forbidden activities in both medical and organizational contexts. The reasoning was that apologies were tantamount to acknowledging culpability and admitting liability, and thus were believed to encourage lawsuits. However, in recent years, there's been a shift toward a more enlightened approach, one which recognizes that silence, in the face of situations where apologies are in order, is at least as dangerous a strategy as an actual apology (Cohen, 2004, pp. 21-24).

Evidence is mounting that suggests leaders are wise to reject the traditional, conservative stance that apologies are dangerous for organizations. Researchers at Georgetown University found that the folklore surrounding the legal consequences of leaders' apologies is simplistic and misleading, and that apologies can indeed help organizations, even from a legal perspective. Furthermore, their findings suggest leaders can actually get themselves into trouble by stonewalling, refusing to accept responsibility, and not apologizing when situations warrant apologies.

The meeting with the medical center's counsel was frosty to say the least. He asked why the letter couldn't be "two paragraphs" instead of the three pages. We assured him it could be trimmed, but we could not reduce it to two paragraphs and still achieve the many goals we were trying to achieve. We explained that we needed to clear up misperceptions and misinformation, apologize for mistakes that were made by numerous people, try to heal both individuals' pain and damaged relationships, and begin to chart a course toward a culture that would be more open and transparent. The last goal was important, we explained, to ensure that this type of calamity would never happen again, in the ED or anywhere. When he remained unconvinced, we asked him for the specific wording that he found particularly problematic and told him we would work on that. We asked if he had read the law review article. He hadn't.

D.R.: A few days later, after sending him a slightly revised and somewhat condensed letter, he told me he would no longer try to stop it from going out. My guess was that he had read the article and better understood our goals and the need for an apology.

The letter of apology was now ready to circulate. But before it could go out, we had to inform and prepare the directors and nurse managers throughout the medical center. They needed to be briefed for three reasons. First, the letter gave a very brief description of a very complex situation involving their colleagues. They were sure to have questions, especially given the fact that the letter would present a very different account of events in the ED than they may have heard from Lisa or the director. Second, the managers and directors would be the first to field questions about the letter, so we needed to help them be ready. Third, because the letter suggested a new way of communicating and operating together going forward, we needed them to be onboard.

It was crucial to carefully time and coordinate the meetings and sending the letter. We planned to read the letter at my regular weekly meeting with the directors, followed by a special meeting with the managers the next day. The letter would go out when we were in the meeting with the managers.

None of the directors knew of the meetings that had been held during the previous two weeks, except for the interim director of the ED. So I filled them in after we finished our planned agenda. Then I told them I'd written a letter to go to everyone working in the ED.

Now came the moment of truth: I read the letter aloud to a group of people for the first time. When I finished, no one said a word. You could hear the proverbial pin drop. For this group to be speechless was quite a new experience. The letter clearly stirred up a lot of feelings, though I wasn't quite sure what feelings. As we sat in silence, I waited for David to jump in. He waited longer still, and then asked for each person to share his or her reactions and feelings.

A couple directors were quite surprised to hear a radically different story of events in the ED. Having only heard about it from the former director of the unit, it wasn't easy for them to suddenly hear such a different perspective. Some were taken aback by the apology. They thought apologizing seemed excessive. "Was it really necessary?" someone asked. I explained why it was. The manager in the ED and her director were gone. One or both of them should have apologized, and maybe they would have if they had stayed. What had become clear to us was that I had to do it. David and I shared our thinking and the experience with counsel.

One of the directors was somewhat offended by the implication in the letter about the way they and the nurse managers and I operate. What I heard from her was, "We have to operate differently going forward? We operate pretty darn well. What happened in the ED was an aberration. It couldn't happen in my unit." I explained that, even though emergency departments are different than other departments, the human dynamics that caused the problems in the ED

89

could happen anywhere. Besides, it was the gaps in communication that had allowed the problem to escalate to a crisis.

I told them I was taking responsibility for what happened with my apology, but now we all had to take responsibility for ensuring that it never happened again – anywhere. I told them that they had to keep me much better informed of problems they encountered and that we – the Executive Leadership Team – had to be much more willing and ready to discuss our respective problems; for example, problems that arose with individual managers. Too often, I said, we discussed people problems only in private. The group then started discussing for the first time the subtle competitiveness that existed among some of the directors and how it tended to squelch serious discussion of management problems. I told them that we had to shift from being an executive leadership group that simply shared information and made decisions, to one that trusted one another enough to openly discuss our biggest challenges and, most importantly, our mistakes. I argued that we couldn't expect our manager to be open with us about their mistakes if we couldn't be honest with ourselves about ours.

That letter was a much-needed shock to the system. It was shocking to them because they saw themselves as a high-functioning team with good relationships among themselves and between them and their nurse managers. That directors' meeting heralded the start of a six-month program to shift the culture of the Nurse Executive Leadership Team. At that time, they couldn't see how this related to what had happened, or the fact that we needed an outsider like David to help us. Part of the awkward silence after I read the letter to them, I later learned, was David's presence in the meeting. (He had only been there once before.) Belatedly, I understood that they missed the point that David was there to coach me, not analyze them. It would take some more effort to help them understand that we were about to set a new expectation for functioning at a higher level.

The meeting with the nurse managers was scheduled for the following day, the day the letter would be sent via e-mail and hard copy to everyone in the ED. They knew it was a special meeting but didn't know the agenda. A number of them had known Lisa and tried to help and support her initially. The problem was that Lisa had been their only source of information.

The meeting followed a similar format to the one we had held with the directors. I commenced with an overview of the situation in the ED and briefly updated them on the individual and group mediations, as well as the ED staff meetings. Then I read the letter aloud. Having been at the medical center for many years, I knew many of the managers quite well and they knew me well, too. Clearly they could see, hear, and feel my emotions as I read the letter. I had to pause a few times to collect myself before continuing. I had always felt the need to be strong and maintain my composure for them as their CNO, though it was difficult at that moment. As I finished, there were several tearful eyes, but no one said a word. Once again, we allowed time for people to take it in. As I scanned the room, some were fidgeting or looking down, while others were looking around furtively, as if to say, "What's next?" As I noticed the knot in my stomach, I thought to myself, "This should be getting easier." It wasn't.

As I waited, I realized that, even though I believed I had a great relationship with my nurse managers, discussing this type of situation was really hard. It became clear that the work I needed to do with my directors was also work that I (and my directors) needed to do with our nurse managers as well. We all needed to learn to deal more openly with tough issues.

Fortunately, David jumped in again with the same request for each person to share his or her reactions and feelings. Some chimed in with their reactions to what had happened in the ED, but David politely stopped them and asked them to first describe their reactions to the letter. After some hesitation, they spoke and I was quite moved by their responses and comments. They thanked me for being so open, courageous and caring. One person thanked me for my leadership. One of the male managers said I was the best role model he'd ever had in nursing. Most importantly, a number of them thanked me for being human, saying that I made it more possible for them to contemplate admitting their own mistakes.

We then went on to discuss how we needed to change the environment, the way that we all handled problems, and the way we talked about them. They acknowledged that they didn't talk to their directors about many of these things and weren't even comfortable talking in their own peer groups about them. Some said they would only talk one-on-one with individual managers they trusted. That, I said, robbed them of the opportunity to learn from everyone and experience the power of the group.

The letter was going to draw attention to a manager's behavior; understandably, they wondered how this would reflect on them. *"If she was inadequate, will others think that I am, too? Will this become a case of 'guilt by association'?"* One manager confessed that he had heard things from time to time and thought about informing me but hadn't done so. He and others had assumed I knew – the same assumption the staff had made. Some said they had believed the story that there were "troublemakers" in the ED because, in their experience, it wouldn't be unusual to find one or two troublemakers in such a large unit.

I said we needed to make it our modus operandi to address problems more openly, and for anyone to come to me if he or she was unsure that I was aware of a problem. I could see fear in their eyes in response to my telling them we needed to discuss their thorniest management problems in the managers' group. I didn't let their reaction deter me, though. I went on, saying that we had to break down all of the barriers to talking openly and engaging in joint problem-solving.

It was a great meeting and another turning point. When the managers returned to their units, the letter was there waiting for them. It had gone out to them, the directors and everyone who worked in the ED.

The Letter of Apology

Donna L. Reck, MSN, RN, CNA
Department of Nursing
ABC Medical Center
P. O. Box 1234
Anytown, USA

December 7, 2004

All Emergency Department Staff
ABC Medical Center
P. O. Box 1234
Anytown, USA

Dear ED Staff Member,

I am writing this letter to inform everyone of our progress toward making the Emergency Department a better department. The focus of this communication is on one aspect of that progress, namely the resolution of certain conflicts within the department. The conflicts upset the nursing functions in the ED for months, worsening in the spring, and then subsiding during the intervening months after the change of nursing leadership within the unit. However, there were still serious issues to be examined and "healing" that needed to occur.

Over the past few weeks, I've had the chance to meet individually with most of the nurses who were disciplined in one way or another as a result of the conflicts. We had in-depth conversations. I needed to understand what had happened, and they, in turn, needed to be heard. These conversations helped me to learn some important things.

In my meetings, I learned more about what actually occurred in the spring. Without going into great detail, it is important to understand that a meeting with the nurses was interpreted, or characterized, negatively. From my conversations with the nurses involved, I have come to believe that those who participated in the meeting never intended anything but a show of support for a colleague. While each of the nurses recognized the meeting was not the best way to handle the situation, I do not believe their actions justified the negative characterization or the related disciplinary actions that followed and therefore we are correcting the problems that resulted from the misperception.

I also learned from the meetings with the nurses that they felt it was too risky to speak up about what they perceived to be the central problems in the ED. They tried various avenues to address the problems without success. In the process, they learned it was not safe to voice their thoughts and feelings about the problems they witnessed. In their attempts to be heard, they came to believe that their jobs were in jeopardy if they dared to voice their concerns openly. Several nurses with years of dedicated service were described as troublemakers for speaking out. Two nurses were not allowed to continue working in the ED. Other nurses left positions in the ED, believing the situation on the unit would never improve, or would take too long.

In retrospect, I wish I had intervened sooner to resolve the conflicts. For that, I am very sorry. As a result of the meetings with the nurses I have identified a real opportunity, and a need to improve communication within the leadership chain of command in nursing, particularly related to the nursing managers, directors and me. It is my responsibility to know what is going on in each unit. In this regard, I will be taking specific steps to ensure that the nursing directors and nurse managers understand their responsibility to keep me fully informed. For my part, I will be vigilant in ensuring that they are providing me with the level of detail I need.

When I first asked the nurses to talk with me about what had transpired, I discovered they still thought it was risky to talk openly and candidly. I found the nurses' deep reservations about speaking to me very troubling, to say the least. Each of them explained that they feared that speaking openly might result in negative consequences and they described the fear of open communication as part of their experience in the ED. I found this type of fear very disheartening.

My philosophy is that the way to deal effectively with problems is by raising them, acknowledging them, and working together to resolve them. If people feel afraid to talk about what's wrong, situations will only deteriorate, people will become demoralized, and everyone will suffer. Stifling discussion is not a leadership strategy; it's a prescription for disaster.

We cannot allow this type of situation to ever happen again. The nurses I talked to each agreed to come to me if the normal chain of command breaks down again. I assured each of them that I personally want to be informed any time they believe the chain of command is not working properly or if they think I am not being kept fully aware of what is happening. There will be no repercussions for people who come to me with problems they believe nurse managers and directors are not addressing satisfactorily. We all have to work within the chain of command. However, all of us have to speak up when we see problems that are not being addressed. None of us should tolerate a working environment in which raising issues responsibly and asking questions honestly is viewed as anything other than positive.

I understand the circumstances made people very unhappy and am determined to never have that happen again – anywhere in the medical center or college. It is critical to acknowledge what happened, understand what went wrong, and build a workplace environment that will not allow this level of mistrust to develop.

In August we asked for expert assistance from BMC Associates to help turn things around in the ED. These individual conversations over the past few weeks with the nurses who were disciplined were one part of the healing process.

To continue to correct a situation that had gone far askew, I invited all of the nurses involved in the conflict in the Spring to a meeting to let them know, as a group, that I now understand that there was no attempt on their part to be intimidating. As a result of this understanding, I am removing all letters of concern and discipline from the personnel files of those people involved.

I recently held three meetings with the staff of the ED to reintroduce the two nurses who were not allowed to work on the ED for the past few months and a third nurse who left the unit on her own accord. They are excellent, dedicated nurses who desire to work again in the ED. To no one's surprise, they were welcomed back with open arms and great relief.

I know true healing takes time. My sincere desire is that reintroducing them and removing the disciplinary documents from personnel files will help heal the pain and rebuild trust. I am grateful that all of the nurses I've spoken to wish to be part of the healing process. Many of them have made a commitment to be actively involved in trying to make the ED, not just what it was before these unfortunate situations occurred, but a place everyone truly enjoys to work, where patients receive the highest quality care, where staff support one another and day-to-day challenges are handled respectfully and collegially.

We all know there is plenty to do to achieve these goals and that the only sure way to achieve them is by working together as a team. I hope we can now all join together in this important effort.

Sincerely,

Donna L. Reck, MSN, RN, CNA, BC
Chief Nursing Officer

After the letter was sent, I held my breath. Luckily, it did travel fast. People responded favorably and warmly. I felt grateful that the letter struck a chord in a lot of people. People stopped me in the halls to thank me; others left voice-messages. Staff who had never e-mailed me suddenly did so, thanking me for recognizing that a mistake had been made and an apology was needed. The following three e-mails are characteristic of the many I received:

(1) [From a former clinical head nurse in the ED] Hello Donna, [...] I am sitting here at home recuperating from surgery going through my emails and just read [your letter]. I would like to personally thank you for writing such a letter to the ED Team. I am sure it means a lot to them, as it does to me.

Your letter brought tears to my eyes. I cannot tell you how gut wrenching it was for me to read and recall much of what you had written and also memories of what other issues transpired. I am sure that you have had your plate quite full these past few months, with the ED and your other CNO duties. Your job has not been an easy one when it comes to the rebuilding of the ED. But I do feel that the staff is ready to turn it around if they are given the proper tools & leadership to do so. The ED has been through the worst walls of the hurricane, have sat thru its eye of stillness to heal, and is ready to face the winds of change that are ahead of it. Just do what you do best Donna, listen to them and lead the way. You are a great leader.

I just wanted to say thank you, and to let you know that I still care immensely. My heart will always be in the ED [...].

Take Care, Kelsey

(2) [From an ED technician] My name may not be recognized as one involved with the E.D., but I, too, was involved with similar circumstances that you have described in your letter. As an EDT, I enjoyed my job but regrettably moved on because of something that happened personally. My reason for writing is not to seek recognition but to thank you for taking the time to fully understand what has happened in the department. I now have a better appreciation for staying in the department [...].

Thank you for taking the time to get to bottom of this. It makes the rest of our efforts more worth-the-while.

Thank you, John

(3) [From an registration associate] Donna, I wanted to … thank you for the letter you wrote. As you well know, I am not clinical staff. However, just by virtue of my position, and working in such close proximity with the excellent nursing staff on third shift in the department, I felt the pain along with them. My coworkers are part of my family.

The issues the nurses had to deal with since last summer affected me daily. Not in a specific way, as specifics were not discussed, but in that the prevailing atmosphere was one of a greatly demoralized crew. One of the reasons I got involved with the BMC effort is that I believe a sincere effort is being made to change things for the better. Already, lines of communication are wide open compared to a few months ago. That alone is reason to feel heartened. […]

Your writing this letter has alleviated my concern over the stewardship of the new vision and value of our ED. I do believe that I have fairly realistic expectations. I do not have a utopian vision. There will always be concerns, and issues, however, I now have a foundation of belief that this institution will listen and give them the attention they deserve.

Thank you. Bonnie

Epilogue

The letter was the culmination of the first phase of working in the ED. The broader work in the ED was just getting underway. Two weeks before the letter went out, BMC Associates, the Chairman of the ED and I coordinated a three-month strategic planning process involving approximately thirty representatives from all eleven constituent groups in the department. I wanted BMC to lead the strategic planning because they had met with most of the key players and were trusted by them. With the general level of distrust as low as it was at that time, having someone everyone trusted was important. A week after the letter was sent, nearly everyone in the ED participated in one of two all-day strategic planning retreats. The representatives polled every member of the department for their concerns (collecting 113!) and then proceeded to categorize, prioritize, and create detailed action plans (DIPs, for short) for the most pressing issues.

This ground-up strategic planning process culminated in the formation of the Emergency Department Interdisciplinary Council (the EDIC), a twelve-person group comprised of representatives from every discipline and group within the ED. The charge of the EDIC is to help facilitate communication among the various groups within the ED and be the principal forum within the department for addressing issues that affect more than one group or discipline, hence its *interdisciplinary* nature and composition. It is a collaborative forum for addressing issues, including those uncovered in the strategic planning process, and providing solutions and resources for projects and initiatives. It is also charged with holding people and groups accountable and assisting in the resolution of conflicts within the ED, and between the ED and other departments, groups, or entities outside the department. The EDIC was the first such departmental interdisciplinary council of its kind in the medical center. Subsequently, other departments have followed its lead and are taking steps to develop their own councils.

I wanted to give the ED's next permanent manager a fighting chance of success rather than just a fight, so I also committed myself to work closely with the interim manager and director. It would be months before the ED would be healed sufficiently to accept regular leadership that could replace them. But we were slowly getting the ED back on track and my continued level of involvement was important to re-establishing trust.

The letter turned out to be the stepping-stone from the work in the ED to the work throughout the Department of Nursing. The work throughout the department began when I read the letter to the directors and then to the managers. Then, over the course of the ensuing six months, David and I held a series of half- and full-day retreats with the directors. We also co-lead a series of discussions with the managers, and then brought the two groups together to focus on communication, specifically among the directors, managers and me.

The week after the letter went out, David and I also met with most of the approximately eighty clinical head nurses in the medical center. By going to the clinical head nurses, we were taking the message of responsibility and apology one more level down in the organization. We wanted the clinical head nurses to also feel the need for greater openness and transparency. We wanted to make the whole story real for them so that they, too, could learn the lessons and help work to change our culture.

At these meetings with the clinical head nurses, I read the letter and relived part of the experience and the emotion, which helped make it real for them. The discussions were often moving. One CHN raised her hand and asked me, "Why did *you* apologize for what happened? You didn't do it."

That issue certainly kept coming up. The idea behind it seemed to be, "You shouldn't have to apologize for something somebody else did." That may have been the most significant lesson for many people, including me. I told them, if you're going to lead and accept the kudos when things go well, you have to be ready to take responsibility when things go wrong, even if "somebody else did it." Hiding because someone else did something doesn't make it right; it diminishes you as a leader. Besides, I had made mistakes, too. By stepping up to the plate, we give the people we work with a gift – something very human and something we all need.

So, there you have it. Just like Detective Joe Friday used to say, "Just the facts, Ma'am." And perhaps a little more. After all, that nightmare did become my Buddha.

References

Cohen, J.R. Toward candor after medical error: The first apology law. Harvard Health Policy Review, 5:21-24, 2004.

Felstiner, William L. F., Abel, Richard, & Sarat, Austin. The emergence and transformation of disputes: Naming, blaming, claiming…, Law & Society Review, 15 (3-4), 1981.

Grigsby, Kevin. Managing organizational pain in academic health centers. Academic Physician and Scientist, January 2006.

Kellerman, Barbara. When should a leader apologize – and when not? Harvard Business Review, p. 73 – 81, April 2006.

Lazare, Aaron. On apology, New York, Oxford University Press, 2004.

Levi, Deborah L. The role of apology in mediation. New York University Law Review, 72(5), 1997.

Acknowledgements

The authors would like to thank Kevin Grigsby, Eileen Barker, Melinda Ostermeyer, Edward Kopf, John Gromala and Adam Twersky for their wonderfully helpful thoughts and suggestions in reaction to earlier drafts of this chapter. We hasten to add that any shortcomings are most definitely our own and, yes, we do apologize for them

Donna Hart Reck, MSN, RN, NE-BC

Donna Hart Reck is the Chief Nursing Officer at Penn State Milton S. Hershey Medical Center. Ms. Reck's accomplishments while at Hershey include establishing an organization-wide nursing department; championing and overseeing the implementation of Connected, the medical center's clinical information system; and leading the organization in its successful efforts to achieve the elite Magnet designation.

Ms. Reck graduated with a Bachelor of Science in Nursing from The College of New Jersey and earned her Master of Science degree in Nursing at The University of Pennsylvania. She is currently completing her PhD studies at Penn State University. She is board certified in Nursing Administration and has received several national awards and recognitions. Ms. Reck has written numerous articles, is a frequent speaker at national conferences, and occasionally consults on collaborative management, nurses' shared governance, working collaboratively with unions, and conflict resolution.

David Gage, PhD

David Gage is a clinical psychologist and co-founder of BMC Associates, a multidisciplinary team of professional mediators with backgrounds in psychology, business, law, and finance. BMC was started in 1990 to prevent and resolve conflict in the workplace and among business owners. BMC works in diverse settings to help people resolve their differences. Their work in organizations includes all levels, from staff to managers and executives, to boards of directors and business co-owners. They work across all industries ranging from manufacturing to retail, and technology to healthcare.

Dr. Gage received his B.S. degree from The University of Wisconsin at Madison and his Ph.D. from Catholic University in Washington, DC. He is currently an adjunct professor at American University's Kogod School of Business and has previously taught at the University of Maryland Medical School. He is author of The Partnership Charter: How to Start Out Right with Your New Business Partnership (Or Fix the One You're In) and has written numerous articles related to conflict resolution in the workplace. His mediation work has been featured in the New York Times, Fortune, The Wall Street Journal, and The Washington Post. He is a frequent presenter to many business and professional organizations, both locally and nationally.

PEARLS ON
THE STRING

CHAPTER 6

Different Pearls – Different Strands (Gender)

by Margo Karsten, MSN, PhD

Courage: mental or moral strength to venture, persevere, and withstand danger, fear, or difficulty – Merriam-Webster's online dictionary. My belief is that, as nursing leaders, the virtue we need to strengthen is outward courage. I have been in healthcare since 1984, starting as a staff nurse working day/night shifts on an orthopedic floor. I decided quickly that I needed to move into a position where I could influence the work environment. It seemed to me that "whoever was making the rules" couldn't be a nurse. Working 8-hour shifts, alternating between days and nights, and not having any voice in how the unit was lead just didn't feel right to me. So I started my leadership journey and soon became an assistant "head nurse" then a head nurse. At age 25, my officemate (who had been a head nurse for many years) told me, "You'd better keep your nursing cap on and stay close to the bedside, because I don't think you are going to make it in leadership!"

I thought to myself, I literally don't have a nursing cap and I actually think I do have what it takes to be a leader. She may have objected to that fact that I was addressing practice issues directly with physicians, challenging clinical practices, establishing unit-based competencies, and acknowledging that we needed to have frontline staff involved in decision-making. But that seemed to me to be the direction nursing needed to take. So I thanked her for her advice, quickly dismissed it and continued on my journey. At the end of my head nurse tenure working with the team, we ended up presenting research-based protocols (specific to pain and low-back pain patients) at nursing conferences - and it was only 1985.

I continued my quest, finished my Master's in Nursing Administration, and enjoyed a variety of leadership opportunities. In one healthcare system, they were in a leadership transition and asked if I would co-lead as the CNO until they could find a permanent CNO. It was a great experience and I realized that, in that role, I could influence the way in which nurses practice. Just as importantly, I could influence the nurse leaders. So, from 1990 to the present, I have been a CNO, COO or CEO. I have a passion about assisting nurses into the executive suite. The numbers vary, but according to the latest figure I read, only about 18% of CEOs in Healthcare are women. I could not find current figures on how many CEOs are nurses. I know that, when I was a CEO, I was the only nurse at that time in the region of Colorado and Wyoming.

So what I have learned and where do I see our work heading? It centers on having outward courage - the courage to ensure that our voices are heard, no matter what roles we play. More importantly, we need to be aware of the challenges that still confront women as nurse leaders. In the spirit of influencing nursing leaders, I want to share various stories that reflect the reality of the issues still facing women in the workplace and how we need to lead with outward courage in order to overcome these obstacles.

For a Fat Girl, You Don't Sweat Much!!!

You may think that statement was made by someone in middle school or high school. The fact of the matter is that it was made during an executive meeting to a female executive who was 39 years old and pregnant with her third child. It was uttered in front of the Chief Information Officer, the Chief Financial Officer, the Vice President of Strategic Planning, the Chief Operating Officer and the Chief Nursing Officer. The female executive said she was speechless; however, there was a greater tragedy to this story. The tragedy was no one said anything; uncomfortable laughter was the only response, coupled with my statement, "Stan, I can't believe you just said that." The three other women at the table sat silently and gave no verbal support. The males in the room laughed and said nothing. One person came up afterward and said that he was uncomfortable with that comment, but had no courage to stand up for his convictions during the meeting. This story is one of many examples of gender bias that still occur - even in the 21st Century.

My second example concerns an organization that had, after many years, achieved the bond financing they needed to expand the business. One of the brokers created shirts and handed them out at the "black tie affair" that was held to commemorate this achievement. The t-shirt featured an image of "Charlie's Angels" with the heads of company officials in place of the faces of the regular actors. "Charlie" was depicted as the male CEO of the business, while the "Angels" showed the heads of three female executives, including the CFO and the VP of Planning. These shirts were distributed to over 100 people at the bond finance celebration. Board members were in attendance and, again, silence was the only reaction. Two days later, the CEO distributed the shirts as gifts at a leadership retreat. Although one of the woman featured on the t-shirt was unaware of the shirts, the other two women (who were aware of the altered image) said nothing when the shirts were distributed. Silence reigned.

Sometimes the situations are not as bold, and yet the same pattern of reaction continues: silence. In one discussion at an executive meeting, the CEO pounded his fist on the table and encouraged the other senior team members to start using the same forceful leadership style he was demonstrating. I voiced the only dissenting option when I said, "I am not motivated by that type of style and I do not think this is how we should lead in this culture." Again, the rest of the room remained silent.

In nursing, there are many examples where we, as nurse leaders, could all take an active role. Consider this: our executive team was discussing open visiting hours. The CEO was adamant that we should restrict visitors. Since I had been a patient, and I have very strong beliefs about this topic (in addition to having read plenty of literature that supports open visiting hours), I spoke my opinion. Although there was another nurse executive in the room, she made no effort to support my position.

There are countless other stories with the same theme. As we reflect on these stories, I believe lack of courage (or possibly fear) plays a huge part in motivating people to remain silent. However, we can look back in history and find a woman who did not allow fear to silence her convictions. On December 1, 1955, Rosa Parks boarded a bus after a hard day at work. She looked around and did not find many open seats, so she took the first one available. When the bus driver requested that she give her seat up, she refused. She did what was right; she was tired of being treated without equality. We can all find inspiration by remembering her own words, "Our mistreatment was just not right, and I was tired of it. ... The only tired I was, was tired of giving in. ... I have learned over the years that when one's mind is made up, this diminishes fear; knowing what must be done does away with fear." Imagine what could happen if we, as nurse leaders, did not allow fear to stand in our way, but made up our minds and allowed the fear to diminish!

Embracing the simplicity of Rosa Parks' ideals is critical for our success as nursing leaders in today's hospitals and healthcare settings. Imagine how very different our world would be if she had just given up her seat on the bus that night. The next time you are in a meeting and there is an insulting comment, do not let silence reign if you have an opposing view that you believe would benefit patients or families, or if you feel that humor has been taken to an inappropriate extreme. Break the silence and speak up for whoever is the target of the inappropriate comments. When you do, organizational change may occur. The change may not have the same magnitude as that sparked by Rosa Parks. But, given the number of various challenges faced in the healthcare environment, your lone comment could improve the condition for one patient or family member - or even influence an organization's culture.

Equal Pay for Equal Work!

Last, but not least, we continue to have work to do in regard to how women in healthcare are being paid. Overall, women continue to earn only 77 cents on the dollar paid to their male counterparts. For most women, the "Equal Pay" date usually occurs in April, meaning that a woman would need to work from January 2008 to April 2009 in order to match a man's earnings for 2008. According to economist Evelyn Murphy, president of the WAGE Project (www.wageproject.org), this creates a huge gap over the lifetime of the average American fulltime woman worker, costing her between $700,000 and $2 million.

I read these findings in disbelief, until it happened to me. As I mentioned in the beginning, I worked my way up the corporate ladder, beginning as a Chief Nursing Officer, progressing to a Chief Operating Officer and then to Chief Executive Officer. During all the promotions, I found myself feeling grateful for my pay and responsibility. Feeling like I was worth $300,000 never entered my mind. Therefore, I never questioned my pay in relation to that of others. It wasn't until a counterpart CEO was hired that I started hearing about potential equity issues. One brave woman shared with me that she had heard that the new CEO had received a $50,000 sign-on bonus. While this may be a common practice, I hadn't received such a bonus. Having been with the organization for over five years, and having a track record of achieving business results, I began to question whether or not I was being paid fairly. I sent an email to the system CEO and inquired about my pay; he reassured me that he would, "Never bring someone in," above my pay range.

Fortunately, there is a company called GuideStar that lists salary information for healthcare and other non-profit organizations right on the Internet. After I had left that organization, the local newspaper decided to run an article comparing healthcare salaries in the region. Imagine my surprise when I read the following exposé: "In 2004, the last year IRS forms were available, Karsten was paid $293,062. That was less than her counterparts at five similar hospitals within 60 miles of Poudre Valley."

Although I felt betrayed and angry, I learned I was not alone. As I share my story with others, I learn about similar experiences. For example, a female executive helped her company go public. As part of this process, their company was required to file the salaries of the executives. She learned that she received significantly fewer stock options than her peers. She explained how she methodically went through the subsequent negotiation discussion with her boss. She stated that being objective, with comparative data, was critical to her success, and that removing any emotion and subjectivity is the best strategy in such situations. I would agree with her insight. As I negotiate salaries, I try to keep current on the base pay for comparable positions. In addition, negations include benefit packages and such elements as sign-on and retention bonuses. Since I have become a "fair pay" activist, I'm finding that activism is common for women assuming leadership roles, such as CNO or COO. After I shared a national comparison on CNO salary ranges, I heard from a CNO colleague that she, too, found out that she was being paid about $40,000 less than the databank average.

As Martin Luther King Jr. stated, "Our lives begin to end the day we become silent about things that matter ... I have made a commitment to never become silent again about things that matter. When I do, I am supporting the inequity that abounds, and we'll never make a difference if we stay silent." Reflecting back, I should have been courageous earlier in my career. I believe I was in denial about possible gender bias and that's the reason I didn't question the situation or ask for objective wage and benefits data. What would I have done if I had discovered that I was getting paid significantly less than every other male in the state? I perceived that, "I needed the money, whatever the salary was; I was in no position to leave." So I never asked. My advice is to 'ask' such online information sources as pay-equity.org and empower yourself to negotiate wages with resources like Ellen Bravo's book, "Taking on the Big Boys." Learn to use effective tactics, such as being assertive and understanding the 'what' and 'why' of your own situation.

Do your own research and gather your own objective data from credible resources. In addition to GuideStar, www.salary.com, www.HotJobs.com and cliniccareers.cpcs.org all offer information and advice on Salary and Benefits and other assistance. After you gather your own data, make an appointment with your boss; however, make sure you understand what you are willing to put at stake. If you present your case and you have objective data that shows that you are not being paid equitably, be willing to walk away if management isn't willing to make any changes. I talked with my husband and shared with him the current status of women making 77 cents on the dollar. Then I asked him what a man would do if this situation was reversed: what if men made 77 cents to a dollar, compared to women. He was clear, "I would find a new job." He didn't hesitate; men know their worth and are confident in their ability to walk away from an inequitable situation. It is time for women to find the courage to do the same, or the tradition of women receiving lower pay will continue.

Have Courage!

In closing, I believe that we, as nurse leaders, must find our own truths and take courageous steps to insure that our voices are heard - wherever we are and in whatever position we find ourselves. I feel as though I will always be a work in progress. Right now, I am trying to move toward a more authentic life for myself, a more conscious awareness of the voice and courage that lies within. At each challenge, we have to give ourselves permission to grow, evolve and change. Maria Shriver has a great message, one by which I am trying to live my life: "It's passing on what we have learned and creating meaningful change through these experiences. That's the kind of power that truly matters." Understanding this inner power, and having the courage to express it to influence the lives we lead, is our work.

Margo A. Karsten, MSN, PhD
Vice President and Chief Operating Officer,
Exempla Saint Joseph Hospital

As Vice President and Chief Operating Officer, Margo Karsten is responsible for day-to-day operations for Exempla Saint Joseph Hospital. In addition, she also coordinates the strategic planning process.

Margo is an experienced health care administrator and consultant. Prior to joining Exempla, Margo was president of her own consulting firm and helped organizations improve their work environment, achieve employee engagement and prepare for the Malcolm Baldrige National Quality Award review.

Margo served as President and CEO of Poudre Valley Hospital, a not-for-profit 295-bed tertiary regional medical center in Fort Collins. Prior to that, she was Chief Operating Officer and Vice President of Nursing for Poudre Valley Health System, a multi-hospital system serving Northern Colorado, Wyoming and Nebraska. Margo also served as Chief Nursing Officer at the Medical Center of Aurora and was Director of Nursing Management Services at Presbyterian Healthcare Services.

Margo completed her PhD from the Graduate School of Education at Colorado State University in Fort Collins. The focus of her dissertation was on Physician Job Satisfaction. She received her MSN with an emphasis in administration from the Graduate School of Nursing at the University of New Mexico in Albuquerque. Margo received her BSN from the University of Minnesota.

Margo's professional affiliations include the Colorado Nurses Association, the American College of Hospital Executives and Colorado Performance Excellence. She has served on the boards of Larimer County Food Bank, Mountain and Plains Girl Scout Council, Fort Collins Advisor Board for the Junior League, Colorado State University Advisory Committee and the Poudre School District Foundation.

CHAPTER 7

Baroque Pearls - When Teams Become Gangs

by Beverly I. Keyes, MS, RN

The year was 1996 and I was working as the Director of Emergency Services in a small rural hospital. The talk of the healthcare community was a small urban hospital in the neighboring county. This hospital terminated the employment of all their managers in one day as part of their strategic plan to develop a model of self-directed work teams. Their model was designed to save millions for the nearly bankrupt hospital district and provide a high quality of patient care. Their new mantra for staff was "see it, do it, own it." There was a general belief among their Senior Leadership that staff would instinctively "do the right thing". Never did I imagine that six years later I would become the Chief Nursing Officer (CNO) for that District and the leader of their self-directed work teams.

I was excited to be the CNO of such an innovative organization. This was my first CNO position and an opportunity to put into practice all I learned from the coursework in my recently completed Master's Degree. The concept of teams and the change was abundant in the literature at the time. Healthcare was making a move and I was about to be a part of the forefront, or so I thought.

The Senior Leadership team quickly shared their philosophy. They started by having me read the policy on organization accountability. This was an elaborate policy that was very academic in nature. I read many more academic team concept policies. Nobody seemed able to articulate the philosophy other than the aforementioned "see it do own it" which was translated by the staff as "don't see it, don't do it, or you will own it". Once you owned "it", the problem was yours to solve.

I was also told shortly after my hire that I was part of a group, The Culture Club, where the Senior Leadership Team and a few selected others decided the organizational culture theme for the year. The current year's theme was the fish philosophy developed by John Cristensen based on the culture of the Pike Place Fish Market. The Culture Club was convinced that staff wasn't "getting" the philosophy. This group decided they needed a new "gimmick" that would get staff to behave and give good customer service. Brightly colored fish were hanging from ceilings and on shelves everywhere yet something else was needed. Senior Leadership was aware the organization was not functioning well but did not understand what builds a culture. This leadership team would have a big roll out party, tell staff what the prevailing culture should be and expect that culture to appear. There seemed to be big disconnect with Senior Leadership, expectations and the need to lead by example. The Club decided on the "give 'em a pickle" theme for the year. This is a very well thought out customer service and leadership training program by Bob Farrell of Farrell's Ice Cream Parlors. The next few months were spent showing the pickle video and handing out plastic dill pickle pins and dill pickles. The culture became focused on pickles instead of the intent of the program. Within the organization the culture deteriorated in direct proportion to the increase of dill pickles handed out. Staff would dart into patient rooms when the pickle wagon came by. Visitors looked askance when offered the dill.

At this point in my career I made a conscious decision to take a stand. I refused to participate in the "Culture Club" any longer and challenged the Senior Leadership team. My reason was that I could not stand by and watch proven programs like John Christensen's or Bob Farrell's, improperly implemented, watch the programs fail, and then blame the staff for the failure. There had to be leadership accountability. I drew a line and my career path was tenuous at best. I had to step up to the plate and lead, not follow the "Club". I would have been remiss in my duties as a CNO to allow this non-clinical group to lead the clinical services. My role was to set expectations and develop our culture through best practices and evidence based medicine.

My first action was to develop a strategy for the clinical staff. What I knew was that I had at least four patient and family complaints a day, I never heard discussions about patient care among the staff and the physicians were not treated with respect. The staff informed visitors, law enforcement, and anyone else that would listen that they did not have bosses, "they were in charge of themselves". The RN's relinquished their duties such as IV starts, rhythm recognition, and assessments to the Nursing Assistants. The MD's came in at noon to round with the Nursing Assistants because the RN's didn't know their patients. Staff worked their schedules around calling in sick and covering for each other on triple time then bullied the staffing coordinators to comply. It was clear that with 180 employees reporting directly to me I had to identify the informal leaders and identify them quickly.

I reflected upon the unprofessional behavior by staff and the acceptance of poor quality of care and customer service given patients. I could not help but wonder what happened to all the wide eyed, energetic nurses that this staff had once been. There was a phrase that some of the staff used over and over, "I keep beating my head against the wall and nothing happens. Now I'm only coming to work, doing my job and going home." The high achievers had quit achieving, the bullies had taken over, and the team sank to the lowest level. It suddenly became clear. The nurses were no longer practicing the art of nursing. They were professionally empty. The low achievers had taken over and the bullies ruled. Teams had become gangs.

By then I had been on the job about four months. The bullies, or informal leaders, had certainly identified themselves. They wrote emails to me telling me what they would or would not do. This group was confrontational towards the CEO and would march into his office, yell at him and walk out. These informal leaders even went so far as to go to a board meeting and tell the board how the District was going to do business. These people were never challenged on their behavior. The saddest part of all is that the demands were personal for their benefit and again, patients were never discussed.

One by one I added names to my list of leaders. There were the quiet leaders that had given up and the bullies. I identified first that the biggest bullies were the long time employees. I also looked at my turnover statistics. What I noticed was that the turnover staff was short term employees and the few I knew had been skilled and had good attitudes. I also realized I did not even know that some of these employees had left the organization. The system was that without managers the teams hired and fired and the CNO was not notified. There was no such thing as an exit conference.

My next task was to enlist the aid of the Human Resource Director. My plan was three-fold; identify why people left, address behavior issues with the bullies, and set new clinical expectations for staff. At first this seemed a monumental task.

The Human Resource Director and I talked with former employees and identified the reasons they left. The main reasons were poor patient care and bad attitudes among staff. Former employees described how they were treated, threatened by staff, and they used the word bullied. These former employees relayed to us that they were told not to "rock the boat or they would pay". This group also quickly identified areas of clinical concern so I did not have to start from scratch. A little digging on my own revealed all they shared and more.

The first year I was involved in 89 written progressive disciplinary actions with primarily RN staff. Many were with the same staff, just moving along the progressive discipline path. I started by having a conversation with the individual and set my expectations. After that if the behavior continued, I went to the next step of discipline. This was an interesting process because we have an in-house Union. Each employee that received discipline was accompanied by a Union Representative so I essentially was able to make my point with two people of the same behavior at once.

I think one of the most important actions I took was spending the majority of my day out on the units with staff rewarding good behavior. My goal was again to lead by example. I looked for what was done right and made sure I verbally acknowledged that behavior immediately in front of others. When call lights went off I too answered them, when the phone rang I answered the phone, and when family came to the desk I made eye contact and asked "may I help you?" My clinical skills have always remained current and I was able to work side by side with staff. I was able to get to know the staff personally and talk to them about their personal clinical goals. Many staff did not have goals other than to get through the day.

What happened next was fulfilling and exciting to me. The quiet high achievers that had been bullied into changing their behavior because they made the low achievers "look bad" started to change their behavior. They started taking risks by making suggestions. When someone made a suggestion, I responded with a positive comment. I put their suggestions on our meeting agendas. We talked about barriers to success and what was the worst case scenario if we failed. I worked hard to build a safe environment where if a process failed, we could look at the cause of the failure, learn from the mistake and try again.

As time went on, the hospital facilitator, education coordinator and I worked hard to champion the development of a Professional Practice Council. The Professional Practice Council (PPC) is a multidisciplinary group that included not only the clinical departments but diagnostics, facilities, IS, materials, and physicians. The three champions of PPC met monthly with the group. We had an identified agenda that included an education component, quality issues, organizational updates, safety concerns, infection control issues, and clinical changes to name a few.

There were interesting outcomes from this group. First, the other Senior Leaders with the exception of the CEO did not value the work this group performed and did not participate. The group became quite close over the first year and routinely communicated with each other and problem solved outside of scheduled meetings. This team performed clinical tracers together teaching each other their departments and performed pre-survey activities across the organization. They also learned about statistical analysis and made monthly reports to the committee about quality initiatives they were working on by using statistical measurements. The Professional Practice Council achieved one hundred percent compliance from the Joint Commission for every initiative and process they had undertaken.

Once the high achievers felt supported by the CNO and had the PPC to work with, many things changed. Many of the Registered Nurses achieved certification in their area of expertise. I was able to work with staff and develop career ladders for the non-licensed staff. Most of the staff became cross trained to another area. As the staff became more professional, felt supported, and were not afraid to take risks to make the work environment better, patients and patient satisfaction became a top priority. As of today, all of our patient satisfaction scores have risen from the twentieth percentile of completely or very satisfied five years ago to an average of 84.8 percent completely or very satisfied in the clinical units today.

Through early identification of the bullies, holding people accountable for behavior, rewarding positive behavior, recognizing the need for clinical renewal of staff, and working hard on communication and relationships, staff now takes pride in the job they do. As time has passed the culture is cohesive, collaborative and patient focused. There is a clear strategic plan and vision for the future that staff is able to articulate. The mantra now is "do the right things, at the right time, for the right reason." The gangs are gone now and the teams are focused and purposeful.

In retrospect the dollar savings that was desired with the termination of all the managers was reached in the short term, but in the long term, much more was lost to poor patient care and low satisfaction, lack of staff, turnover of staff, and manipulation of the time and attendance system. The analogy is to imagine a professional sports team without managers or coaches and expecting them to succeed.

Beverly Keyes, RN

Beverly Keyes has over 35 years of extensive and progressive experience in healthcare administration, quality and regulatory compliance, and academics. In addition, she has years of participation in government affairs and a as council woman and town ombudsman. Ms Keyes is also a skilled negotiator, having negotiated city employment contracts with the teamsters as well as having negotiated healthcare union contracts.

Ms. Keyes held leadership positions in organizations throughout the Pacific Northwest in addition to her hospital Senior Leadership positions, including Chief Nursing Officer. She was appointed by the Governor to a position on the North Region Executive Trauma Board and was selected by the Department of Health to work as an educator with Directors of Nursing Teaching Leadership skills.

"Education and Quality" is a priority for Ms. Keyes. She taught Nursing at the Associate Degree level. Ms. Keyes was also an Affiliate Faculty of the American Heart Association, teaching ACLS, PALS, and CPR to instructor candidates and students. She is known for mentoring staff and encouraging them to achieve clinical certifications and obtain higher education. In addition, Ms. Keyes authored a recovery room text book for the Nursing Program in Bhutan. Ms. Keyes has been a consultant for over 25 years. She has actively assisted others to achieve successful regulatory compliance in addition to the stellar achievements of her own facilities.

CHAPTER 8

Lining Up The Pearls: From Behind Closed Doors To The C-Suite

by Veronica A. Maras, RN, BSN, MAOM

For me, nursing leadership wasn't a planned career path, but rather the result of the interplay of a series of interesting events. I am, I think, what most people would call a late bloomer. While I try to instill the skills of thinking about goals and planning for the future in my children, it took me a long time to figure these things out for myself. My career as a nurse was the result of a series of defining events in my life, not because I was a devoted person who wanted to become a nurse in order to help people.

I became a nurse for two reasons. The first was because my dad was in a very bad car accident when I was about eight years old. He was in a hospital in a different town, so I couldn't visit him very frequently. I distinctly remember talking to him on the phone and feeling bad that I couldn't be there. He said not to worry; the nurses made everything all right. There was one nurse in particular that he said made those first few days after surgery tolerable. He said that, if it hadn't been for her, it would have been impossible to go on. I thought it was wonderful that someone he hardly knew could make such a big difference in his life.

The second reason was because I was raised with a strong Catholic background and even named after a saint. My parents basically gave me two choices: I could become a nun or a nurse. I chose 'nurse' and that's how my career path began.

I graduated with a diploma from Saint Vincent School of Nursing. While I was in school, however, I married and became pregnant with my first daughter. So, when most of my friends were beginning their nursing careers, I was busy being a new mom and figuring out the challenges of motherhood. I stayed home for as long as I could, but frankly, we had to eat. I tried to find a job that wouldn't require me to work all the shifts and weekends that were typical of a new nursing graduate just starting out in the work force. Although this may not have been a very professional way of thinking about nursing as a career, that was my mindset at the time.

Because I was looking for day shift only job, my very first position as a nurse was in private duty. This was a shocking experience for a new young graduate. My colleagues were what I considered to be very old. Some of them had children my age and they seemed past the point of having a passion for the nursing profession. They were just working for the paycheck. They were nice enough people, but none of them were what I envisioned as any kind of role model that would inspire me to do great things. As a matter of fact, I was quite smug, because my education was current and I know I was more influential returning my patients to health than were some of the staff with whom I worked. Although I loved going to work everyday and I always had an interesting assignment, the job just didn't seem very fulfilling.

However, my best friend from nursing school, Patty, and I and our husbands would sit down every Friday night and play pinochle, watch our babies and eat chips and dip. Patty was on call as a perioperative nurse. She had really great stories about the operating room and I thought that job sounded really exciting. How great it would be to be the one they called when someone was in a bad accident or was really in trouble. So my friend suggested that I become an operating nurse, too. I said, "OK," and switched jobs! Again, not a lot of thought went into changing jobs. In retrospect, it seems rather embarrassing that I had no career plan, but simply followed the suggestion of a good friend to join her in the operating room.

In spite of my lack of planning, though, I really had a very good experience being new in the operating room. I had very good preceptors who wanted me to succeed and, as I moved from service to service, I loved the job more and more every day. I could make extra money by being on call and I didn't have to work a lot of off hours (not true of today's perioperative nurse). I remember going home every night and writing down what I had done that day so that, the next time I had to set that case up, I would remember how to do it. A lot of things made sense immediately and some things never made sense, but I knew I loved the excitement of it.

Being a perioperative nurse was an adventure every day. When I first started, the nurses were both scrubs and circulators. For me, the easy part was learning the procedures and equipment; the hard part was learning how to work closely with physicians. I will never forget some of the cases in which I participated: the sad events, the unbelievable experiences, and the horror of accidents that people survive.

The job was very exciting and challenging, and I began to figure out that how I managed myself and the other people in the room had a direct relationship on how well the procedure went and on how well my day went. I discovered that I liked organizing the case flow and making sure we had the supplies we needed to prepare for the next day. It was a source of pride to me when my colleagues would say, "You are so easy to follow; we know everything will be done correctly when you are on duty." That felt good.

I soon realized which services I preferred and which doctors I preferred, as well. I remember there was one doctor whom I didn't particularly like; it took four years before he would actually call me by name. For him, I was just a face behind a mask. I began to wonder what you had to do to become more than just that. In fact, we once handled the case of a woman with an acoustic neuroma. At the time, it was a really big deal: the patient went to sleep in June and woke up in July. I scrubbed for the surgery and it ended up being a seventeen-hour case. When I saw the surgeon the next day, he wasn't even aware that I had been in the operating room. It was then that I decided I needed to do something different.

So, do you know what I did? I moved to Ohio and took a job in a long-term care facility. By this time, I had two children and my personal life was kind of messy, so this was a great job. For me there was considerable personal satisfaction during this part of my career. Every day, when I went to work, I knew I made a difference. The residents loved me (as they did anyone else who paid attention to them). For many of them, the nurse was the only person with whom they had daily contact. That part of the job felt so good. It began to dawn on me, though, that that's what mattered - making a difference in the lives of the patients. I liked that feeling and I wanted it to be there every day. Selfishly, I began to think about how I could get that feeling every day. As my personal life got messier, I left the long-term care facility, moved back home and went back to the operating room where I had worked before.

This time around, the dynamics were very different. The leader, a very long-term individual, was leaving, so every one moved up a notch and the nurse manager position came open. I knew all the other applicants were much more seasoned than I was. However, I had a lot of energy and self-confidence, and I was given the opportunity to become the nurse manager for a twelve-room operating facility. Since I had no idea how budgets worked or staffing decisions were made, I often wondered how that decision was made. I knew things from a very clinical perspective and it seemed to me that I had been given this opportunity by chance. But it was the beginning of my career in nursing leadership.

At that point, I began to realize all the things I did not know. The first thing I did was enroll in school. Although no one was really pushing me to do it and I was paying for it myself, I knew I had to get my college degree because there were just so many things I did not know. I spent many a night at the computer, with my kids falling asleep on my feet. It took me eleven years from start to finish to get my bachelor's degree in nursing. I do not recommend this, but it is what I did.

As I began my leadership career, I soon discovered that the hardest part was building relationships with staff and physicians. I figured out that, in order to get people to do something that they didn't really want to do, they had to respect and trust me as a leader. There is no easy path to trust and respect, though; both must be earned over time.

Being in the operating room had been a much more isolated role than that of being a nurse manager in other nursing areas. And, since I was always working with physicians and anesthesiologists, I did not have a ready nursing role model. It was hard to fit it, because I felt like I had to be in scrubs every day in order to gain credibility and respect, so I also looked different than my counterparts with the same title.

Going to nurse manager meetings made me crazy. The other nurse managers talked about things that didn't apply to me, like order sets and nursing assessments. They dealt with awake patients and pain; even their documentation was completely foreign to me. It took me a number of years to recognize the value of networking with other managers during those meetings. Once I learned how to use the other nurse managers as networking resources, the world opened up.

I began to change my focus. It wasn't all about me; rather it was about listening to what the other managers talked about and applying that to my own environment. I also got comfortable contributing my knowledge to the network. I began to be recognized very differently among my peers. My reporting structure changed and I acquired my first real professional nursing mentor. While things were not perfect all the time and I still had a lot of learning to do, she was a great cheerleader and let me know when I was going down the wrong path.

Along the way, I also began to network in professional organizations. AORN (Association for Operating Room Nurses) is a phenomenal organization for both young and seasoned leaders. The resources that were available through that organization provided specific insight into both management and leadership, and I began to make friends at a national level. I wrote several articles that were published and, through this experience, I met several influential women. I created relationships both online and in person and soon was offered the opportunity to become a consultant for a woman I met through AORN. I kept my 'day job' and did the consulting as a side job.

Although becoming an operating room consultant was a wonderful career move, it again seemed almost as though it happened by accident, rather than by design. Ultimately, it was all about networking and developing relationships and being given a chance by someone much savvier than I was.

For a number of years, I worked both as a nurse manager and a consultant. While my title never changed in my perioperative role, my responsibilities kept expanding; soon I had created a structure that supported many of the functions that used to depend solely upon one person. But by this time, the environment in the operating room had become very complex. Gone were the days when a nurse made money on every surgery. The med-surg line item in the operating room budget alone exceeded the entire budget of most of the businesses in our town.

It was time to go back to school. This time there was no wavering. I was ready to commit to this course of action when a rather unique opportunity arose.

The facility where I worked had begun a relationship with a rural community hospital, which just happened to be across the state line. The hospital needed a director of nursing who could support both the interests of the main campus and this satellite facility. It was a thirty-two-bed hospital that had just become a wholly-owned subsidiary, so there was fear and trepidation on their part and almost no one wanted to go from a big hospital to a small rural community hospital.

I am not really sure what it was about the situation that intrigued me. But I had a strong infrastructure in place in my current environment; I knew my job cold, what I could do and what I couldn't do. I knew and understood the pitfalls and the politics of where I was, so I volunteered.
Again, I am not sure why I was given the opportunity, but I took it. And it was the best leadership move I ever made. In a thirty-two-bed hospital, my leadership style and my decisions made an immediate impact. It was scary at first. I was from the system that just purchased this facility: although they were fiercely independent and their community had supported them completely, they had just been unable to make it alone.

I went from running an operating room to being second in command. The CEO was a woman who was as tough as nails, but she knew her job and the community loved her; so did I. My first week on the job, we had our department of health review and it was all my responsibility. I found out quickly who could be counted on. It was actually a great way to start a new job. They had to admire anyone who could handle the DOH during week one, so I gained credibility right off the bat. And by this time, I knew how to work with people and build a team. I made it my number one priority to learn my new environment and try to fit in.

Being a leader in this small facility provided more experience than I could ever have hoped for. I became all things to all people. Not only was I in charge of the operating room, but I also ran the lab, cardiac rehab, infection control, billing and coding, and the cafeteria. I could see the results of my decisions immediately, whether they were right or wrong (very unlike the impact of decisions in a larger environment).

This was an incredible learning experience for someone who was interested in learning how hospitals actually run. The process was complicated by having two administrators, who were both struggling with what to do next with this facility. One was the CEO of the big hospital and one was the CEO of the smaller hospital, and I reported to both. It took awhile for everyone to be on the same page.

I spent three years in this environment and I was hoping to be the next CEO of the smaller facility. But one of the stipulations for that job was local residency. So when the CEO of the small facility retired, I knew I had to do something different. I understood that the new leader would have to put his own team on the field in order to achieve maximal success, so it was time for me to go.

So as luck would have it, a new surgery center was being built n my home town. They had already hired an administrative director, but they needed another person to help them get up and running. I thought about this long and hard, because it meant I would have to accept a considerable pay cut. But it was also back in my hometown, so I would no longer have to make the long commute to my current job.

I decided to apply for the position and was given the job. The person who hired me was not the person for whom I worked, but we clicked immediately. She was the out-of-town expert and I supplied all the local knowledge; it was the best team effort ever.

In the past, I had only been responsible for renovating or refreshing existing organizations. I had never participated in building something from the ground up. I began to learn about limited liability corporations and how to write by-laws for a joint-physician hospital venture. I learned how to stage purchases so that everything we needed would be there on opening day, instead of the orders still being processed. I learned about architects and builders, and the unexpected issues that arise in a big building project. I also started and finished my master's degree.

I chose to get my master's degree online. This allowed me to keep working while going to school on my own time (without wasting time in my car driving to and from a classroom). For me, it was a very good decision. Again, I learned about how you can either forge relationships or offend someone through the written word. It was amazing to me how powerful a tool writing had become. Through the online coursework, there were many team projects. It was quite challenging to do a team project online, with a group of people I had never met whose skills were unknown to me. I did not get a master's in nursing, so my networking expanded to a completely different world. My favorite class was economics. I had a professor who was an ex-senator of Alaska. The team to which I was assigned also contained the vice-president of a big electric company in Georgia and a resort owner from Puerto Rico. I am not sure what they said when they found out I was a nursing administrator, but it worked out great. We all learned from each other and it I was amazed how differently each team member thought.

Eventually, the surgery center was up and running. Because it turned out to be a very successful project, I was moved back to the main hospital campus. The main hospital was doing some restructuring by this time and was moving to a paired leadership model (physician administrator and a business administrator). I was fortunate to become a part of this. I was paired with a very savvy physician administrator who was also a general surgeon. My background in the operating room was the perfect complement and we were able to be very successful together.

Ultimately, though, this organizational structure was revised and the paired leadership model was dissolved. I was asked to take on the additional responsibility of nursing and became the Chief Nursing Officer, while also retaining my responsibilities for the surgery service line. This has been the biggest challenge of all.

I love what I do and I am happy in my profession. Although it wasn't exactly a career path by design, everything turned out well in the end. My advice for anyone starting out is to:

1. Seize your opportunities as they arise. The jobs might not be exactly what you are looking for but, if you wait for the perfect opportunity, something else may pass you by.
2. Trust and believe in the value of networking. Learning that lesson early can help you make a difference for our profession both nationally and internationally - probably in ways that haven't even been invented yet!
3. Take chances outside of your comfort zone. Look for ways to participate in areas that are not your expertise. It is all about working with people and creating relationships.

I have such a great sense of pride when I tell people what I do. Being a nursing leader affects the lives of many people in such a personal way. My influence will be felt for years to come. While it is a daunting responsibility that I take very seriously, I would challenge anyone to find a more rewarding career.

Veronica A. Maras, RN, BSN, MAOM

Veronica Maras has served in progressively more responsible leadership roles during her tenure as both a nurse and an administrator. Most recently, she served as the senior vice president for patient services and chief nursing officer of a 450-bed facility in Northwest Pennsylvania. She is adept at managing and leading perioperative services, emergency services, rehabilitation and neurosciences, as well as nursing. She has developed expertise in the area of physician and hospital relationships. In addition, she is a resourceful leadership mentor.

She has also served as the COO of a rural community hospital and provided project management for several multi-million dollar building projects.

In addition to her leadership roles, Veronica is also active in professional nursing venues and has served on both local and national nursing boards. She has written several articles for publication and has served as a perioperative consultant. She is active in her local community and volunteers for multiple organizations.

CHAPTER 9

Selecting the Best – Creating a Vision for Nursing

**by Laura F. Sittler, RN, MBA, BSN, CNA-BC, CNOR
and Jane McCurley, RN, MBA, BSN, CNAA-BC, CNO**

"God has always led me of Himself... the first idea I can recollect when I was a child was a desire to nurse the sick. My day dreams were all of hospitals and I visited them whenever I could. I never communicated it to any one, it would have been laughed at; but I thought God had called me to serve Him in that way."
– Florence Nightingale, Curriculum Vitae, 1851 [1]

As Nurse Leaders, we have had inspiration in some fashion from the words and thoughts of Florence Nightingale, the founder of the Art and Science of Nursing. She remains an enigma for all of nursing, and an example of the dedication and the leadership that the calling of nursing instills in each of us. Ms. Nightingale had a keen interest in leadership, using her strength and experiences to set a path of wisdom and vision for nursing.

Being a nurse leader in today's environment calls for executives who believe in the power of caring for others and who have a vision for nursing. Today, we are challenged with so many competing needs that, at times, we fail to remember the wisdom taught to us by Ms. Nightingale all those years ago. At its core, nursing still maintains the same basic tenets: the Art and Science of Healing and Caring.

Joining the staff of our organization as the newest members to the senior nursing council, we felt it was paramount to ascertain the foundations of belief held by the other members. Most of the team had been with the organization for many years, and did not visibly demonstrate a clear pathway built on a vision for nursing. Other nursing managers were fairly new to the organization, with either multiple years of progressive management experience, or just beginning their leadership careers. Our initial assessment of the leadership team was that its members were unable to clearly vocalize a unified philosophy of nursing focused primarily on patient care, an attitude which we felt should have permeated not only the leadership team but the entire organization itself.

Instead, expectations were unclear, as if everyone were waiting for someone else to define a direction and provide an energizing vision for the whole nursing team. Understanding the ramifications of vague leadership on our frontline caregivers led to the realization that we needed a nursing leadership retreat to create the foundations for an explicit and unified doctrine of nursing for our organization.

We realized that we shared a similar vision for nursing and that we both had a strong belief that the patient was being lost in the day-to-day routines of both staff nurses and managers. So we decided to work together to form a unified approach to professional nursing goals for our leadership team and the role that we wanted to play in the organization as futurists and visionaries. Our goal was to help the team focus on the fact that patient care is why we became nurses in the first place, and to remember the words of Florence Nightingale in order to regain that timeless feeling of compassion and the nobility of nursing. It was easy to see that working together would enable us to guide our nursing team to realize that the wisdom we find in Florence Nightingale's words is still very applicable in today's health care setting.

To develop the proper nursing focus for our organization, we decided to look for a model that would help us influence the grass-roots nurse to take the time to be compassionate with the patient, and to use the basic foundations of nursing practice and the other techniques that we all learned in nursing school. After researching several theorists, we chose a model we wanted to bring to our hospital. Although relationship-based care was our ultimate goal, we realized the constraints within our current environment and knew we needed to begin with the basics. We thought that Jean Watson's CARING model would provide the building blocks for a sound model based on a foundation of the nurse theorist.

The CARING model centers on the basic acts of the bedside nurse that combine to give the patient a sense of humanism in the health care setting. We knew that this model would demonstrate to our patients that the timeless touch of nursing is still present in modern healthcare. This focus on patient care reflected the ideals that we find the most powerful. This model paralleled the acts of kindness and compassion that Florence Nightingale instilled in her team all those years ago and provided the foundation upon which we wanted to build our own leadership for our staff and management team.

Jean Watson's model puts the nurse at the bedside with the patient and the family, and crafts a method that inherently lets the nurse use the acts of touch and compassion in her everyday care.[2] In order to deliver this philosophy, we first had to create a Mission and Vision statement for our nursing organization - and it had to be one that was simple and achievable. The entire group of nursing professionals had to realize the benefit of being there for the patient and the importance of the simplest of human mechanisms, touch and compassion.

"... holding another's life in our hands ..."
- Jean Watson's ethical foundations [2]

As the nurse executive team, we are charged with establishing the tone of our organization, serving as role models for professional excellence and energizing our staff of nurses to feel compassion in the simplest of tasks every day. In order to accomplish those goals, we felt that the nursing department needed its own Mission and Vision statement. One which would be compelling enough to stand in tandem with the Mission and Vision statement of the hospital and still propel the philosophy of nursing to the core of the entire organization.

This vision of driving nursing excellence through the Magnet Journey provided the groundwork for planning an event to serve as a learning session for our nursing team. We held a daylong, off-site retreat, which gave our nursing directors a unique forum that allowed them to be away from day-to-day interruptions. It also gave them an opportunity to interact with each other in an informal setting and to network more closely while we mentored them in the energy that we saw as the future of the nursing team at our facility.

The group consisted of the Nursing Directors, Managers, Nursing Educator, Nursing Administrative Supervisors, and the CNO and Assistant CNO, all of whom, at times, acted as leaders of the nursing team for the organization. We felt it was important to include and recognize the importance of all levels of management and leadership in our nursing organization, as they would need to live and demonstrate the end product (our new Mission and Vision statement) for the entire nursing team.

We started the day with brunch and an opening session where we discussed our agenda and the ground rules for the day. Those rules emphasized the need for everyone to participate, to be kind and courteous to each other, and to stay focused (keeping pagers and phones on 'silent'). In addition, we wanted to reinforce that we are all here to make a difference in the lives we touch. As the session leaders, we started by giving our thoughts about nursing and about our love of nursing. We talked about the stories that we carry in our hearts about patients who have inspired us, made us cry, or have shaped our lives and careers. As we began this new journey as the new senior nursing leaders to the

135

organization, our task was to compel a new modality of nursing philosophy in the organization. So we rounded out our opening remarks with a poem that we thought would set the tone for our event. We chose one to remind us how we had all been called to nursing to provide care to our patients. One that reinforced our feeling that this would be a day to reinvigorate our beliefs in nursing, our professional pride and our commitment to our patients.

As a nurse you head into the storm of people's lives to make a
difference with your hands, your words, your eyes.
No time to dwell on what can't be done in the sea of challenges.
So much to do that is yours alone to ensure.
Paid by smile, tear, extended hand, questions in the night, you make a
difference that folds into their whirlpool of change.
Buoyed up by startling courage and endurance, grateful to share
in birth, in death, in trying - and always trying.
You feel the pain but show the hope.
Now laugh, now listen, hands flying, face calm.
And they know they are special to you, different every one.
- Unknown

As one reads this poem, it seems that it could have been written many years ago by a patient who was touched by a nurse in some way that remained unforgettable. And this was the pattern of inspiration that we wanted for our day's events.

The Work of the Day

The task for the day was to dialogue on the need for Mission, Vision, and basic philosophy statements and a nursing-driven business plan for our Organization, one that could lend itself to our desire to join the journey for Magnet Status.

We began by leading the group in a session about building a Mission statement - what a Mission Statement means. We also discussed how a Mission Statement should proclaim our essential nursing beliefs for the rest of the hospital. It should contain our ideals, along with statements that describe "who we are" as a nursing group. The Mission statement should define our core purpose and explain why we exist within the Hospital Organization. We needed a statement that would define us, and would also be inspiring, long-term and natural, as well as easily understood and easily communicated. For example, we talked about the history of our Hospital, what the Organization stood for in the community, and the role that it plays. We discussed our Hospital Mission, and how it defines our Organization as a whole, and how it was never constructed to be the end-all in healthcare, but is specifically tailored for our Organization. This lead to discussions on what is really important to us as a Nursing Team, how we envision our Mission, and what defines our Core Competency.

The exercise was followed by breakout sessions, where groups of six worked separately to identify key words that would define our reasons for existing. We used flip charts to capture what each table discussed and then collectively talked about the commonalities and wrote down key words and phrases shared by all the groups. During this process, the group became visibly more cohesive. It was fascinating to watch how comments by one participant led others to expand on that idea, and to start to see that our collective love of nursing was shaping our thoughts into what we considered to be a statement of "who we are" as a nursing Organization. Remarkably, we were able to draft a statement that included wisdom and words grounded in the Art and Science of Nursing philosophy founded by Florence Nightingale. [1]

Additionally, a key part of our education plan for the group was to teach the participants the foundations of why we were crafting a Mission and Vision statement. We wanted to help them understand, at an individual level, the necessity for a Nursing Mission statement within the hospital because, ultimately, these were the people who would "hard-wire" this new set of values into the organization. We wanted to make clear to them that The Mission and The Vision statements are tools that help the organization identify "who" the nurses are and "who" they aspire to be.

We then used brainstorming sessions to identify, as a nursing team, what we believe in and who we are, and to discuss our various thoughts and ideas. We used the flip charts again and encouraged team members to just toss out key words that they felt defined nursing excellence and commitment. It was really inspiring to see our team embrace this session and begin to talk and break down barriers between themselves. They began to get to know each other and to dialogue about why they each had a calling to nursing and how that shapes our identity as a nursing organization.

We discussed with them the aspects of Jean Watson's model [3] and why the CARING model was important to us. We explained that, as the nursing executive team, we felt a strong belief in empowering our nursing teams to bring the human touch experience back to the bedside. We talked about our belief that the patient should be the focus of everything we do in the organization and we, as the nursing team, have the important job of modeling that philosophy for the entire organization on a daily basis.

The five basics of the CARING model are these ideals: [3]

- As the Registered Nurse, I will introduce myself to my patient and her family and explain my role in her care today
- I will call the patient by her preferred name
- I will use touch appropriately
- I will sit at the bedside for at least five minutes each shift to plan or review care with my patient
- I will use the Mission, Vision and Values of this Nursing Organization to guide my care of my patient

These are the key elements for "getting back to patient care" at the most basic levels. We had a strong desire to ensure that all our patients had these five basic rights when they interacted with a Registered Nurse in our Nursing Organization. In order to provide these simple gestures, we had to continue to define our Vision of ourselves and craft our Values statements.

A Vision Statement is different from a Mission Statement, in that it describes the focus we have for "tomorrow." It tells the public, our audience, who we aspire to be! It is inspirational, and provides a clear picture of the desirable future for our team. We wanted our team to focus on the key words of "aspiring" as we knew at the time that we had a lot of transformation coming up, and that change was imminent. It was especially important to have the team think beyond the here and now, and to think of the great team we could become if we all worked together on achieving something more powerful as a group. This led to many conversations within the group; some people verbalized a sense of loss, of having to endure a changing environment, while others were visibly eager to make those changes and to progress toward a new day.

So, what was the result? It was transformational, to say the least! We were mesmerized and astonished as our team, with ourselves as its newest members, crafted and created an amazing statement of our Nursing Mission and Vision for our organization. It was incredibly pleasing to accomplish this amount of work in a single day, with active participation by each and every member of the team. At this point, the team was freely discussing important principles and we continued our conversations during our lunch.

Our retreat was held in an old Victorian home that had been converted to a day spa and retreat. The afternoon was sunny and slightly warm for a December afternoon. While we enjoyed our lunch in the main portion of the mansion, we talked eagerly about the ideals that are the Hallmarks of our Organization. As we sipped tea and ate sandwiches, we defined the essential characteristics of our nursing professionals, which each of us held in principle. Over lunch, we crafted ideological philosophy statements and values that we felt were paramount to our nursing organization, words by which we could live permanently. We agreed on words we could record in a document, words that would describe, as a whole, the beliefs that would shape our professional lives and our interactions with our staff and patients back at the hospital.

After the Mission and Vision had been formulated, it was time to look at the "State of the Union for Nursing" at our hospital. We once again brainstormed about the current situation, as well as the future. We identified the top critical issues and created the strategic direction for nursing at our hospital. Our group constructed 1-, 3- and 5-year strategic plans. Since it was a beautiful sunny day and we had time to relax a bit, we did this exercise at the pool of the retreat home. We discussed our business objectives and strategies for the next year, how to write a business plan and how to incorporate a 5-year plan into our daily working life in the hospital. It would take time and energy, but the momentum that we gained from our work at the retreat, combined with our gentle approach with each other and our commitment to better patient care, was inspiring for all of us. We now had a direction and a look at what tomorrow would bring; it was energizing to say the least! Since the day was coming to an end, we concluded this session by developing the tactics needed to drive the strategic plan with measurable outcomes to evaluate success.

As a special treat to our nursing team, we had prearranged to have each team member select a spa treatment at our spa retreat. We had a mini wine bar and snacks set up in the common area of the spa. While we relaxed with wine and cheese, we laughed together and continued to build our team cohesion in this informal and relaxed setting. It was a perfect end to a day of incredible team building and goal setting, a wonderful way to conclude our journey toward a direction for a new nursing executive team coming into the Organization.

We knew when we left the retreat that day that our team had 'owned this process.' They had embraced the ideals and had put on paper more than words. The inspirational philosophy created by our nursing team was both heart felt and sincere!

Here is the Mission Statement they developed that day: [5]

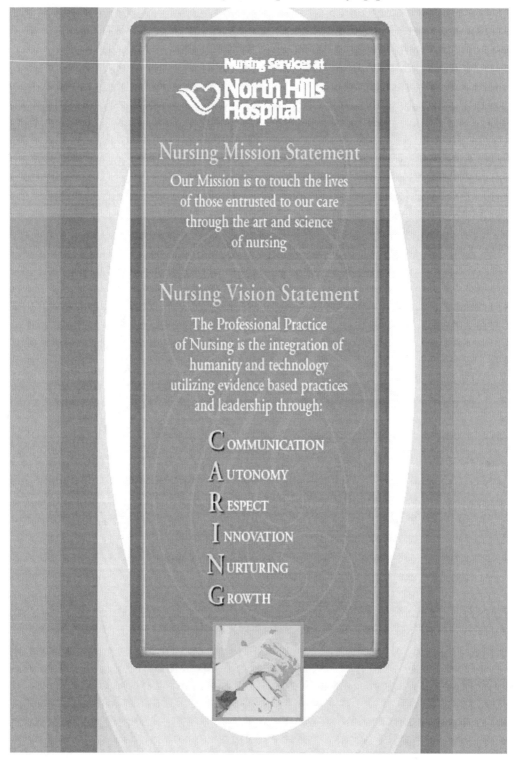

"Caring is a starting point, a stance, and attitude, which has to become a will, an intention, a commitment, and conscious judgment that manifests itself in concrete acts".
- Watson, 1988 [2]

As you can see, the usefulness of creating a nursing-based Mission and Vision statement that has sound buy-in at all levels is elemental to the success of the CARING model as described by Jean Watson. The nurse understands her purpose and uses her vision to aspire to bring an extra touch of compassion to the patient. We felt it was imperative to recognize also the wisdom of Florence Nightingale and re-instill the nature of nursing as an Art and Science, as it is based in the humanness of each of us.

"To all of you who CARE deeply, not only about what you do, but also about how you do this work in the world, I thank you. We are forever grateful, we are forever changed...."
- Cheryl, a grateful patient [4]

The goal of our retreat day was to build a team that had a strong belief in why nursing is so noble and a focus on how we prepare and care for our patients is more than singular tasks and modalities. How it is constructed of much more, how it is based in a centric model of nursing beliefs:

"The model creates a culture change for our organization, in that it prepares us to find the inspiration of nursing in our values and aspirations. To create and work in an innovative learning organization "renews" & "rejuvenates" the SPIRIT of Nursing" [3]
It's about Profession and Passion!

Critical Issues and Business Strategies

Our team identified these issues as the key obstacles that we would need to overcome as we went on to build our business objectives. There were 10 critical theme areas that we felt nursing in our organization needed to address as we progressed toward our goals and strategies for the future [5]:

- Retaining our bedside nursing staff
- Promoting a healthy work environment for our nursing staff
- Developing a nursing-based Mission, Vision and Strategy approach for our Organization
- Developing a Nursing-based Philosophy for our Organization

- Implementing a Nursing Delivery Model of Professional Practice at the bedside and beyond
- Promoting culture shifting in our nursing services population
- Communicating and executing drastically-needed improvements in our nursing leadership team, as well as improvements the skill levels of the team members
- Ensuring nursing leadership development to promote a high-performance leadership team
- Focusing on patient-centered care and on improving patient-centered satisfaction

The Nursing business plan is used to create top priorities based on our assessment of our strengths, weakness, threats and opportunities (SWOT). It is used to provide improvement priorities for our nursing services team and to demonstrate to the entire Organization what is important to nursing with respect to patient care.

Based on our research, we knew from the literature that "the patient's reaction to and satisfaction with nursing care is the MOST important predictor of overall satisfaction with hospital care!" [6] Knowing this, it was obvious that our targeted critical themes would have major impacts on nursing care, satisfaction, work environment and, most importantly, the way our patients see us as nursing professionals and view our hospital in the community. All extremely powerful motivators for the work that needed to be accomplished with our nursing business plan.

Lessons Learned & Next Steps Beyond our Retreat

The days and months ahead proved to be more challenging than we anticipated with regard to the work we had accomplished at our retreat planning session. With the springtime coming, we decided to incorporate a nursing forum-type rollout of our Mission and Vision work and the CARING model. During Nurses Week in May, we designed programs built around professional growth and planned for a nursing 'town hall.' We talked with our bedside nursing staff about the Nursing Model of CARING. We used testimonials from patients and caregivers to role-play how the nurse really impacts the patients and the experiences that they have while in the hospital. As a further step, we designed a commitment statement for each one of our nurses to sign after attending the town hall presentation, in which they agreed to utilize the five elements of the CARING model at the bedside.

We also held hour-long sessions, which were attended by both our nurses and the nursing leadership team, to discuss the theory of Jean Watson and demonstrate how the power present in nursing from the days of Florence Nightingale is still a noble way to serve our patients. We used a PowerPoint presentation to take the nursing staff through the crafting of the Mission and Vision, Philosophy and Business Plans for Nursing Services, how and why they were created and what the usefulness of each of the products is to them and their patients. We diagrammed the CARING model and role-played how to use those simple gestures at the bedside for the greatest impact with their patients.

"Nursing is a noble profession,
but it is up to you nurses to make it noble ..."
– Florence Nightingale, 1859. [1]

The take away message for the nursing staff at this forum was to understand that the CARING model preserves the relationship of the nurse to the individual patient, and that it allows the nurse to provide basic elements of human care and compassion. These ideals are at the core of nursing and the basic instincts related to why nurses choose this career. We explained that these are critical steps to providing patient-centered care and to improving the dynamic in which patients evaluate us as care givers. We discussed how this allows patients to see us as professional nursing staff and not "task masters" and how it imparts the ability for each nurse to stop and interact one-on-one with our patients in a non-hurried fashion. We stressed how it is important to us as nurse leaders for our staff to understand that this philosophy is our hope and desire for them. Our goal at the nursing forum was to instill a sense of rejuvenation related to nursing, and to engender the spirit of pride and professionalism that is reflected in our Organizational Nursing Mission and Vision Statements.

Patient "Satisfaction with nursing care is largely based on the perceptions of
the nurse's affective behavior toward the patient." [6]

Where We Are Today

Now, almost a year later, we are still pulling our team together. We intend to continue our journey with the Magnet foundations; our accomplishments during the last year serve both as lessons learned and building blocks for the future. We have taken strong steps toward our goals of "hard-wiring" the values we defined during last year's retreat, but we have also endured some unexpected changes in our nursing leadership team over the last year. So we continue to build our team, looking and searching for individuals who want to lead a dynamic nursing staff and who believe in the tenets of Florence Nightingale's words and works. We continue to foster a nursing team that is committed to patient centered-care and to using the CARING model in their everyday work ethic. Our next steps are to create best practices related to teaching and role-modeling the CARING model to the bedside nurse, and to instill in our nursing staff a pride for our noble profession. We are well on our way, but still have loads of work to do and, in the end, we know in our hearts that our mission and vision is to touch our patients in a special way. To leave a legacy with each of them that a nurse cared about them and for them during a time when they were most vulnerable. This is our legacy and we have a Mission and Vision to pursue!

References

[1] Florence Nightingale, Mystic, Visionary, Healer : Barbara Montgomery Dossey, 1999.
[2] The Philosophy and Science of Caring: Jean Watson, RN., PhD.1985.
[3] Caring Science as Sacred Science : Jean Watson, RN., PhD. HNC., FAAN., 2005.
[4] Anonymous; Patient Compliment; HCA, inc., North Hills Hospital, 2006.
[5] North Hills Hospital, Nursing Executive Work Session, December 2006.
[6] HCA, inc. CARING Model, ATLAS Intranet documents & Power Point, December 2006.

Mrs. Laura Sittler, RN, MBA, BSN, CNA-BC, CNOR &
Jane McCurley, RN, MBA, BSN, CNAA-BC

Mrs.Laura F. Sittler, RN, MBA, BSN, CNA-BC, CNOR
Chief Nursing Officer
CHS, Inc.
Woodward Regional Hospital

Mrs. Laura Sittler serves as the Chief Nursing Officer at Woodward Regional Hospital. Mrs. Sittler's professional experience is based in cardiothoracic nursing and Perioperative Management; she has also spent a considerable amount of her career working in Service Line Development and Professional Consulting. Her role in the facility is to guide the Magnet journey for the organization and to provide strategic work streams for achieving the nursing business model and professional practice of nursing under the tutelage of Ms. McCurley. Mrs. Sittler enjoys nursing as a career, as it provides avenues to mentor and foster teams of individuals. She enjoys the ability to provide inspiration to other nurses as they develop in their love for patient care, and thoroughly believes in the nurse as the most noble of professionals and the advocate for the patient.

Laura is a member of many nursing professional organizations, such as AONE, NTONE, TONE, ACHE, and AORN. She holds reverence for the work of Florence Nightingale, and positively believes in the passion and power of nursing, as well as a belief in lifelong learning and the need for nursing-based research and the call to evidence-based practices and leadership paradigms in nursing. She is a staunch supporter for bedside nursing and holds dear the philosophy of mentoring and coaching the aspiring nurse leader for the next generation. You may contact her by either email or phone:

lffoltz@earthlink.net
Laura.Sittler@hcahealthcare.com
214-629-1965 (cell)
Woodward Regional Hospital, Woodward, Oklahoma 73801

Jane McCurley, RN, MBA, BSN, CNAA-BC
Chief Nursing Officer for North Hills Hospital

Mrs. Jane McCurley serves as the Chief Nursing Officer for North Hills Hospital, a 176-bed community-based facility in the DFW, Texas Metropolis. Ms. McCurley has been a Registered Nurse for more than 28 years, with a clinical background in Emergency Nursing and Critical Care, as well as Management and Leadership in Acute Care hospital settings. Ms. McCurley joined North Hills Hospital in June of 2006 as CNO; prior to that, she served as CNO and VP of Inpatient Care for a sister facility at Las Colinas Medical Center.

Ms. McCurley knew she wanted to be a nurse as a little girl and shares her passion of the profession not only with the bedside nurse, but with the community at large. She is able to speak of nursing commitment with such passion that she re-ignites the nursing flame that may have started to die down in others. She is considered a "natural nurse's nurse" and is greatly respected by her staff and leadership team for her devotion to the noble enterprise of nursing and to always putting the patient first.

Both Jane and Laura Sittler belong to many nursing professional organizations, such as AONE, NTONE, TONE, ACHE, and those of their respective clinical professional practices. They both hold reverence for the work of Florence Nightingale, and positively believe in the passion and power of nursing, as well as lifelong learning and the need for evidence-based practices and leadership paradigms in nursing. They are staunch supporters for bedside nursing and hold dear the philosophy of mentoring and coaching the aspiring nurse leader for the next generation. You may contact them by either email or phone:

Jane.McCurley@hcahealthcare.com
Laura.Sittler@hcahealthcare.com
817-255-1100

CHAPTER 10

A Pearl Tie Tack

by Michael D. Skinner, RN, BSN, MBA

Being the President of a community hospital for seven years has given me insights into senior executive leadership that may prove helpful to those of you contemplating increasing your own leadership responsibilities. I have had the benefit of association with many fine colleagues, mentors and confidants who supported my professional aspirations and were crucial assets to my education and perseverance during critical and stressful times. Accordingly, this chapter is designed primarily for those in management who are planning to advance their organizational influence and leadership to a more senior level and who seek, through the written word, some form of mentorship from one who has been in a similar position.

I am an advocate of revealing past professional decisions and behaviors that ended up being counterproductive; I believe those revelations to be powerful motivations to learn. So I will model that which is most difficult for young leaders to do: be open with others, including subordinates, about mistakes made and lessons learned, with a degree of self-deprecating humor. In the past, leaders felt they could not show vulnerability or be perceived as less than omniscient. In reality, just the opposite is true - those you lead want to know you are human and, therefore, are in a position to learn from mistakes just as they are. As I outline each of the key lessons in this chapter, I will note areas where I have stumbled, recognized the mistake, learned from it, and moved on. Hopefully, that will encourage you to do the same as you learn and grow in leadership.

Most of us in leadership could spend hours telling stories about our management and organizational experiences. However, I have focused this summary on seven distinct factors that I believe, were you to incorporate them into your daily leadership behavior, would make you a superb senior leader in hospital management.

1. First and foremost, focus on building successful relationships

I am only speaking, of course, about my experience in not-for-profit hospitals. I can't vouch for this being a top element of successful senior leadership in the for-profit world, but I would be surprised if it didn't occupy a top spot in any successful organization.

When I was a middle manager at various hospitals, I understood that the accomplishment of several critical objectives, stated and unstated, would signal to others that I was successful. To me, these objectives included:

- Exceeding budgets
- Having very good consistent employee satisfaction scores
- Keeping union activity at bay
- Preventing "Type 1's" on JCAHO surveys in my department
- Willingness to forgo time-off to demonstrate commitment and loyalty to the organization
- Maintaining physician happiness
- Treating hospital and management colleagues as a surrogate 'family'

In most of the organizational cultures in which I worked, I knew that meeting these objectives was essential to being seen as capable of taking on larger roles and departments. Those cultures were revenue producing and had large staff; size mattered.

I would like to offer a perspective on success that is quite contrary to those measures. Today, I would be very critical of a manager who espoused only those objectives to achieve organizational success. In fact, I would suggest that the number one leadership success factor for those aspiring for senior leadership positions in hospitals is this: relationships with your stakeholders (or, as some would say, constituencies), first and foremost. I will give you my simple definition of 'stakeholder' shortly.

Let me give you a couple of examples why using the cultural success factors stated earlier may be harmful to your career. First, all managers want to exceed their budget expectations. I have found that those who consistently exceed their budgets are often far too conservative during their budget planning time, and are much too averse to taking risks. They plan their budgets so that they can be exceeded. However, there are legitimate times when budgets can not be met, never mind exceeded. Typically, budget planning takes place a full 18 months before the final results are known the next year. In health care, there are too many variables to be able to predict an outcome. In fact, there are times when some of these variables can legitimately produce a negative variance and, if a manager was slavishly concerned with exceeding budget, he or she might make short-term decisions that would have adverse long-term consequences for the organization (which does not add to one's ultimate success).

As for obtaining and maintaining very good employee satisfaction scores, we want to be liked and respected, and good satisfaction scores give everyone a nice, warm, cozy feeling. These scores are also visible to every leader in the organization. But consistently positive scores may, and I want to emphasize may, indicate a paternally led department. Staff members want security in their job, and any change will put pressure on them, which will increase their fear and anxiety. My experience is this: change is necessary for an organization to adapt, change causes stress, and stress of staff is often reflected in lower satisfaction scores. In other words, consistently high satisfaction scores may mean the manager himself is resisting the need to change and acting paternally to the staff.

Finally, the objective of demonstrating loyalty to the organization by forgoing time off can also backfire. Young leaders are understandably eager to show their capabilities and their capacity for hard work. They can be caught up in working very long hours, working weekends, and taking little time off for vacation. I see this all the time. And I hear how proud young leaders sound when they say how late they worked, or talk about how they sent emails from home to coworkers at 2 a.m. But to refrain from taking time off for personal growth, rest, and most importantly, family, is a recipe for personal and professional disaster.

So, if I have been successful in raising the possibility that older cultural objectives for leadership success may be false indicators, how is my theory about relationships, first and foremost, any better?
I will outline a concept for leadership success, one that is deceptively simple but also one of the most difficult to obtain consistently. This method is often disregarded in leadership development education because it is not quantifiable, but is seen as 'soft' and obvious instead.

The following process will enhance a manager's opportunities to become a senior leader. First, identify your stakeholders (or constituencies). Stakeholders are those who could affect either your job satisfaction or career. Because this list will include an entire group, it should be relatively short, in order to be managed adequately. At a minimum, it should include the person to whom you report and the members of your staff.

Once that list is created, the next step is the most challenging, and essential. You need to determine the general values and interests of each stakeholder or constituency. For example, your boss says, "I appreciate it most when my staff takes the initiative on an issue first, and only come to me as a consultant."

Then you know not to approach him or her frequently with problems to solve for you, since that would create a lot of dissatisfaction with your leadership potential (no matter how much you exceed your budget or how late you work to show loyalty to the company!). I urge you to discover what leadership values your boss appreciates and then attempt to demonstrate those values while interacting with your stakeholders.

Another example might be how a leader participates in meetings. Your leadership colleagues, and the unstated organizational culture, may appreciate directness in dialogue during meetings. So, if you sit back and don't participate, it will be interpreted by your constituencies as the undesirable trait of passiveness. Identify some of the successful senior leaders whom you admire; watch how they conduct themselves and see how they meet the needs and values of their stakeholders.

Developing positive relationships, first and foremost, with your stakeholders, will be one of the most beneficial factors in your career growth. Develop that list of stakeholders, establish what they value most (recognition, autonomy, security/safety, power, etc), and work hard to attain those goals.

2. Thank stakeholders in public, critique in private

The senior leaders I have admired most have always demonstrated courtesy and respect to everyone in public and private, even to those who might be loudly disagreeable or lack social skills.

One of the first senior vice presidents for whom I worked took this concept to the extreme. She would not tolerate any other senior VP criticizing my work publicly. She protected me and her other subordinates almost to a fault. However, if I made a mistake, or did less than quality work in her eyes, she would slam her office door behind me and then bellow out, "What the hell were you thinking? What went wrong? This will not happen again, will it?!"

She had the concept correct about public versus private criticism, but her style was intimidating to her staff. Although this style would not, or should not, prevail in today's leadership environment, she taught me a very valuable early lesson about leadership.

My expectation of those in senior leadership is that they should always, without exception, recognize the effort and success of every individual in public and only critique or criticize someone in a private conversation. Public humiliation is not a tool to be used in contemporary hospital organizations; it is not a viable tenet for any successful senior leader.

It is essential that a person's integrity be maintained during a private discussion of any mistake. I can think of many instances where a private and powerful conversation is necessary as a means of discipline and guidance; I simply can't imagine an occasion that would require the public chastisement of a subordinate.

During my tenure as President, I accidentally violated this tenet once, and I continue to regret it. My leadership quotient when down significantly in the eyes of those who witnessed it. Fortunately, several of those witnesses spoke to me in private. They showed how much they cared about me by telling me I was wrong to publicly criticize someone, and explained how disappointed they were that I had violated the tenet I had long espoused. It was a humbling experience.

This leadership rule may not need further embellishment; I have found that most leaders would say it is obvious. However, it is easy to be seduced into reacting and giving criticism in public. And self-righteous indignation expressed in public has a nasty after-taste.

3. Always Consult Before Deciding

Roger Fisher and Scott Brown highlighted this idea in their book, Getting Together: Building Relationships as We Negotiate. I have freely adapted it to my use since I first read about it a couple decades ago. I find that it is a close cousin to the concept of Relationships, First and Foremost, because it acts as a tool to explore the values and interests of those you serve.

Early on in every young leader's career, he experiences the euphoria of having a great idea and knowing that, if this idea were implemented, his organization would be improved. But, inevitably, the young leader will encounter immediate resistance from others in the organization when trying to implement this wonderful concept. This happens even though others may have concurred initially that the idea was commendable. This situation leads to understandable confusion on the part of the young leader.

The problem that surfaces over and over when a new project is started is the conflict between the good idea of an individual and the consequences to others and the potential impact on their organizational responsibilities. The new idea causes conflict because it will require other staff to change their behavior. Although the project will demand the time, resources, and energy from others, and will advance the career of the young leader, others in the organization do not believe the project will advance their values or interests. It is equally unsatisfying for a young leader to advance his or her idea by saying, "It is best for the organization." This rarely gets others excited about the new project and for good reason: the 'organization' has no head, no brain, and no feelings. It is simply a compilation of many individuals with similar interests and values. It is unclear from that kind of statement what value the new idea has for each of those many individuals.

The way to prevent this potential conflict is to always 'consult' others before deciding. This is one of the best communication vehicles around for leaders. Rather than focusing on, "what is best for the organization," (that headless, heartless entity), identify the stakeholders (those who are important to advance your idea, job satisfaction or career), clarify their intrinsic values and interests, and then design a proposal that meets their interests in addition to your own. It is best to know ahead of time which elements of your proposal will be well received and what factors may cause others to create barriers to its implementation.

It costs nothing but time to seek opinions, challenges, affirmations or assumptions. You don't have to act on what you learn, but the process of sincerely seeking the thoughts of others impacted by your decisions will let them know that they have been heard. It is generally known by most of our constituencies that, as leaders, many decisions are ours alone to make, but they do appreciate having had their perspectives heard.

4. *Trustworthiness in leaders is very difficult to achieve and unbelievably easy to lose.*

The issue of trust and trustworthiness can be a slippery virtue to understand or explain. Many hospitals have the value of trust embedded in their Mission Statement or Operating Principles. We want our constituencies to trust us; being trusted makes us feel good, and allows our decisions to be accepted with less resistance and to become more durable.

However, trust (or whatever we want to call this elusive value) is very difficult to attain, yet very susceptible to a slip of the tongue or an innocent facial expression. One way I felt I could create trust in my leadership was to always do what I said I would do or, if I was unable to follow through as promised (which can happen), to explain myself in a timely way with an apology. As it turns out, that is only part of the trustworthiness building formula. I have found that asking any constituency to completely trust a leader is inappropriate. No one should be asked to simply put their profession, their job, etc., in the hands of someone else who has his/her own values and interests. Rather, senior leadership should always strive to build a 'trustworthiness bank' with their stakeholders. This means consistently behaving in ways that continue to encourage the trustworthiness of the relationship.

I frequently counsel young leaders on this critical issue of trustworthiness. I caution that trying to solve a conflict or a problem with someone with whom the trustworthiness level is low almost always produces a long negotiation, and concludes with an outcome that is shaky and likely not durable. Lack of trust is an impediment to good long-lasting decisions. I advise leaders that, if time allows, they should first work on the trustworthiness issue with the person with whom they are in conflict, then move to the actual issue to be resolved. This is especially important if that person is a stakeholder.

Over time, I have added a second benchmark (in addition to following through on any commitment or promise I made). I ask myself the following question, "Does what I say about you face-to-face (as a constituent of mine) match what I say about you to others?" For instance, if I tell you that you are a wonderful and trusted colleague at work, and then criticize you to others when you are not around, I have failed my own trustworthiness test. Basically, if I have nothing positive to say about a person in public, I do not say anything at all. All those in senior leadership positions whom I have admired have demonstrated this attribute.

I have, unfortunately, failed this test myself in the past; I viewed it as a shameful and cowardly act on my part. I have found that, at the least, it is an immature and adolescent behavior and, at the most, it can be disruptive to the development of positive and trusting long-term relationships with those who affect your job satisfaction or career.

5. *Whenever something is not going well, I understand that things will probably get worse before they get better, and that I must act Presidential in any case.*

Of the seven leadership lessons I have learned as President, this was the most troublesome. As a young leader, I was taught to solve problems in a timely fashion. Find an issue, gain insight and counsel from others on the issue, strate-gize various solutions, and test out the most promising plan. All very deductive, very linear, very clean: "Bring on the next problem, please." Unfortunately, only the most simple of hospital management issues can be processed in this way. Most of the problems dealt with at the middle and senior management levels are much more complex, and sometimes they can never be fully resolved.

In my experience, solving a complex management challenge can create a very interesting phenomenon. Unlike the resolution to a simple issue, which can justifiably be drawn out on a timeline as relatively straightforward, with some-what predictable points of positive results after a management action, a complex problem may seem to worsen after an intervention, before the situation actually begins to improve.

The young leader probably cannot imagine the successful resolution of a complex issue may mean that the problem gets worse after she takes action. This is, however, a common plight. This is so because people have to believe that any change they are asked to make meets their values and interests, or they will resist making that change (which would solve the problem). That is

155

natural. So, a leader attempting to make any major change in an organization (which is headless and heartless, and a compilation of many people with differing values and interests, remember) will find significant resistance and, initially, any change will cause stress and anxiety for staff affected by the solution process. This resistance will slow down the intervention results, and some regression may occur. The research of Elizabeth Kübler-Ross on the grief process of death and dying exemplifies how a situation can feel worse before it gets better. She explains how denial, anger, bargaining, and depression take place until, exhausted and out of options, a grieving patient acquiesces to the stark fact of impending death and is finally able to move on. In much the same way, people asked to make significant behavior modifications at work can pass through the same stages of resistance while coming to accept the inevitable benefits of the change.

But a senior leader learns to appreciate the value of patience and perseverance during the implementation of problem solutions. She comes to understand that complex hospital issues cannot be pushed to resolution simply by more, or more forceful, management actions. Complex issues have their own pathway to resolution and their own timeframes, during which denial, anger and bargaining must take place. Although a sense of regression may be prominent during this time, the patience and perseverance of a senior leader almost always has huge payoffs. You must know when to hold off on more management actions and to sense when staff are ready to move on.

Believe it or not, the understanding that problems may feel like they get worse before they improve, that the stages of a change process can be similar to those of grieving, and that one must have patience and perseverance during change is not the major lesson I have learned. To be sure, these elements of wisdom were significant, but I believe a senior leader needs one more skill in order to deal with organizational changes.

I once had a hospital system leader give me advice which, at the time, seemed simple, but turned out to be very important. He said (and I am paraphrasing here), "When someone gives you a compliment, take it graciously - even if it is unearned. Because there will be times when you, as a leader, will be held accountable for the actions of others and, guess what, you will need to be gracious then, too!" In other words, I had to act Presidential, no matter what the situation. People want their leadership to act like Leaders at all times, even when things seem to be getting worse. During times of stress and anxiety, leaders at all levels must remember to act Presidential. Others will remember more about how you acted during stressful times than about the actual problem itself.

6. *Learn to love challenges*

Most of you have likely heard this over and over, and it may start to sound like an old cliché. However, it bears repeating that there is an endless supply of challenges. They keep a senior leader employed, and will ultimately help the senior leader stay sane in the arcane and irrational world of healthcare policies and financing.

Remember, you are not being paid to solve a limited set of problems. Your job is to provide a working environment in which the staff can accomplish the mission of the hospital. And a hospital is arguably the most complex work setting in the world, one that can be dangerous and fraught with potentially deadly mistakes. If you go to work every day with the idea that solving one big problem will improve your life for quite some time, you will ultimately wake up one morning suffering from job burnout - because two more problems will pop up for every one that you solve. Since a hospital provides an endless stream of issues for senior leaders, I recommend you cultivate an attitude of, "I love challenges!"

As much as I love a challenge, though, and as much as I wanted everyone to think I had an endless supply of energy, focus and optimism, I ultimately learned one of my most valuable lessons. I was forced to admit to myself, and finally to others, that I had limits to the sheer number and complexity of challenges that I could tackle effectively by myself. Sometimes having too many challenges drained my resources faster than I could replenish them. And admitting to that turned out to be okay. You can survive this confession because everyone else is in the same situation.

I don't pretend to have answers that would be relevant to all mangers who aspire to senior leadership. But I have discovered a partial answer to this dilemma. What I have found most helpful is to find a mentor (or a leadership confidant), someone you admire and trust who can devote time and energy to helping you with your career growth. Admit to yourself and others that you are about to cross a threshold that will make you less effective and then seek out others with whom to discuss the situation. This is a mark of a mature senior leader. Although it may be, "lonely at the top," having a trusted member of leadership with whom you can discuss the persistent stress of continuing challenges is a wonderful way for a leader to feel less lonely. If you don't have a mentor or leadership confidant, get one! Having a mentor, and ultimately being one, is a very enriching experience.

7. *Middle management is the most difficult role in hospital leadership, by far.*

I have outlined some of the lessons I have had learned that I feel will help managers take on senior leadership roles in hospitals. One could expect that, as a result, I would be suggesting that the higher management roles are more difficult. There is no doubt that the role of a senior leader is very difficult and complex, but only because there are more environmental variables for which they are held accountable that can go wrong. And senior leaders should always remember to be gracious, even when held accountable for actions they did not take. However, I believe there are no more difficult roles in hospital management than those of Supervisor, Coordinator, Manager, Director, or Vice President (which are euphemistically categorized as 'middle management'). Middle management can be either a purgatory for those unwilling to understand the limitations and boundaries of their position and power, or it can be one of the most rewarding roles and experiences a person will ever have.

Hospitals and their leaders literally change lives. Patients and their families are directly affected by the work done by hospital staff and, in turn, staff are directly affected by the work environment created by their leaders. Middle managers are leaders because they have earned that right. They have proven they can, and do, change the lives of their constituencies for the better. Their leadership is where the rubber hits the road, where strategic proposals and operating plans are finally implemented. The grand visions of Presidents and senior leadership are worthless without middle management to put them into action. Middle managers have to cope with all of the grieving process of change discussed earlier, and they are the ones who work most effectively on the trust-worthiness issues. They are the first to remind senior management (those who dream up visions and plans) that, in the end, everything centers on relationships, first and foremost.

Middle management is not for the faint of heart. These positions can be the most difficult to fill, in part because the staff, from which middle managers are typically recruited, see the enormous challenges faced by managers. Staff members typically say, "I wouldn't want a management job for all the money in the world." Yet, managers are the very folks who change the lives of their staff. What a responsibility!

Why would one want such responsibility? It can't be for power. The limits on authority can be very frustrating to one who yearns for it. It can't be for the money. The typical pay structure for middle managers is sometimes barely higher than that of their staff (and sometimes less than that of many senior staff members). The acceptance of a middle management position must stem from a wish to be more influential in the direction of the hospital, to add more voice to its future, and to participate in and influence long-term planning.

Most of all, however, managers want to change the lives of staff, colleagues, patients and families in significant and necessary ways. That responsibility is enormous, and that is reason why middle management positions are the most difficult roles in the hospital.

Let me end this chapter with one quick anecdote, which I use to highlight the ultimate test for leaders. Right after basic training in the U.S. Army, before I began medic training, I was 'volunteered' to get a military license to drive trucks and jeeps. Two weeks of training in Texas was supposed to prepare our group of young soldiers for the ultimate challenge: the Convoy. Sergeant Kelly, our teacher, was a retired soldier; he was short and wiry, had no sense of humor, and was prone to using interesting language. He had given each team of two the task of driving a two and one half ton truck. Our objective was to hold a tight formation in a convoy. Sergeant Kelly and his driver sat in the lead jeep, upon which there was a big white sign that said, "Convoy Following."

Needless to say, the convoy exercise was designed to scatter us all over the Texas countryside, which proved successful. The ten trucks, with panicked teams, finally each found Sergeant Kelly, patiently waiting for us, sitting peacefully in his jeep on the side of a local road. One by one, we all pulled up sheepishly behind him. When the last of the trucks had arrived, he jumped lightly out of his jeep, called us out of our trucks, had us stand at attention and had this to say: "Boys, it's very embarrassin' to be sittin' in a U.S. Army jeep, with a big sign that says "Convoy Following," and there ain't no convoy! Now, here's what we are gonna do….!"

The lesson I learned from that experience was this: if you are a leader and see no one following you when you look behind, you are a leader in name only. I submit that, if you follow the seven leadership concepts outlined in this chapter, you will be on your way to becoming someone others will want to follow freely.

Bibliography

Fisher, Roger, and Brown, Scott. Getting Together: Building Relationships as We Negotiate. Penguin Books, New York, 1988

Kübler-Ross, Elisabeth. On Death and Dying. Simon and Schuster/Touchstone, 1969.

Author: Michael D. Skinner
              1228 Surry Road
              Surry, Maine 04684
              207-667-4803

Michael D. Skinner, RN, BSN, MBA

Michael D. Skinner began his career as a medic in the U.S. Army in 1971. He attended Fitchburg State College in Fitchburg, Massachusetts, receiving his BSN in 1977. After several years working as an RN in both critical care and mental health, Michael began his management career at Eastern Maine Medical Center in Bangor, Maine. He earned a Masters of Science in Business degree, with a concentration in healthcare financial management, from the University of South Carolina in 1985.

Mike was a Vice President of Medical and Oncology Services at Dartmouth-Hitchcock Medical Center until 2001, when he accepted a position as President, Baystate Franklin Medical Center, a 100-bed community hospital in Greenfield, Massachusetts, a part of Baystate Health of Springfield, Massachusetts.

Mike retired from BFMC in 2007 and is now living in Surry, Maine with his wife, Pam.

CHAPTER 11

Polishing the Pearls

by Terryl Kendricks, RN, MSN

Timeline

2002

The facility is a 320-bed acute care facility in North Texas. The hospital provides service to the adult population. The hospital sits in the cultural district of the community, along with three other competing facilities and one pediatric facility. We were all competing for the same employee, physician and patient base. Quality patient care was imperative for an organization to succeed in this competitive environment.

In September 2002, when I accepted the position of Chief Nursing Officer, I immediately began to question what had I gotten myself into and why in the world would I accept this position. Having held a previous position in the same facility, I was familiar with the organization's shortcomings and reputation in the community.

Financially, we were a stable organization, but there were some hurdles to overcome related to the perceived quality of care - particularly related to nursing care. In spite of the low perception of care, the quality indicators and patient outcomes were positive relative to national benchmarks. With that being said, patient, physician, and employee satisfaction were at an all time low as compared to national benchmark data. Patient satisfaction scores ranked in the 4th quartile, 185 out of 192 hospitals. Physician and employee satisfaction scores also ranked in the 4th quartile. Nurse staffing benchmarks placed us at the bottom 25%. As if this wasn't enough, two months into my tenure as CNO, the hospital's Chief Executive Office (CEO) announced that he would be retiring within the next six months.

So why did I accept this position? I knew Plaza had the potential to excel in this community. While I knew that all the surrounding healthcare organizations were committed to providing quality care to a diverse population, I wanted Plaza to be different. My objectives were to continue pushing the quality agenda and to be part of a culture where people (employees, visitors, patients, and physicians) were treated with dignity and respect. The ultimate goal was to improve the image of Plaza Medical Center internally and to the community at large.

During my immediate tenure, I developed a strategy to turn this sinking ship around. Theoretically, I was aware that I could not make changes for the 300+ staff members who reported to me indirectly, but I could affect the twenty direct reports. The million-dollar question was - will this be the team to move nursing forward at Plaza? The challenge would be to get those twenty to embrace my vision and goals for nursing and to use them as vessels to share the vision and motivate others on the clinical team.

My assessment of the situation was that I had taken charge of a nursing organization that worked in silos. In my mind the system facilitated the "silo mentality." The nursing organizational chart was structured into three divisions, medical surgical, critical care and surgical services. Each division held separate meetings with what seemed to me to be separate and conflicting agendas. I thought this model only fragmented the organization and did nothing to promote teamwork or collaboration.

2003

In keeping with my mission, I restructured our nursing department into two areas of focus: operations and quality. I removed the division lines and instructed all nursing unit directors to report to me. In addition, I recruited two directors – one to push the quality agenda and the second to focus on budgeting and other nursing operational issues. Since these were new positions in the hospital, it took some time for the positions to evolve. For a while, it was difficult for the new directors to get comfortable in their roles and to develop a clear grasp of their responsibilities within our organization.

Was there resistance to change? Absolutely, there was! Secret division meetings continued to occur, but more for staff comfort than out of spite, I'm sure. I did not interfere with their meetings, but I implemented mandatory monthly Patient Care Services (PCS) and monthly Nurse Executive Council (NEC) meetings. They soon found that these meetings were duplicating the material covered in their 'secret' meetings, and that attendance at the PCS or NEC meetings was not an option. It wasn't long before the team figured out whose agenda we would be following. There was a certain amount of discord, however, and some people simply did not board the 'turning ship' but chose a different course.

That summer produced even more organizational upheaval. In June, our CEO retired and the CFO was reassigned to another facility. In July, a new CEO was assigned to our facility. This news was bittersweet for me. I had participated in the interview process of the new leader. I felt he was a visionary leader and someone who could move Plaza forward, but I wondered whether or not he would accept the changes I had implemented in the nursing department. I was relieved to find that, not only did he accept my reorganization strategy, we had the same goals and vision for the organization. I remember vividly him explaining to me that the, "best hospitals have the best nurses who provide the best nursing care." That was his vision for nursing. He asked me what was I going to do if this did not happen at our hospital. I sat quietly for a moment before I answered. I think this surprised him; he probably was thinking I was weak or didn't have a response. In actuality, my response was that failure was not an option and was not even being considered. Given the support, resources and right nursing leadership in place, nursing would put Plaza on the map.

That fall, our nursing leadership team developed the nursing strategic plan that would be included in the hospital's business plan. During one-on-one meetings with medical staff members and board members, our new CEO had been informed that his focus should be on improving both facility aesthetics and nursing care. When the business plan was presented to and approved by our hospital Medical Executive Committee and our Board of Trustees, board members, medical staff committee members and other members of the executive team all commented that it was comprehensive and well conceived. This plan would guide the course of our organization for the next five years.

The business plan included ten strategies, but strategy number eight, the nursing business strategy, was most important to me. This was my opportunity to prove my leadership ability in successfully executing my plan. Our strategic goals included improvement in the patient, physician and employee satisfaction indicators, nurse staffing benchmarks, and a focus on leadership development. During the next six months, we held several nursing leadership retreats to develop objectives designed to help us meet these goals.

2004

This proved to be a year of success, in terms of moving the organization forward and meeting our strategic goals. Employee satisfaction ranking moved from the 4th quartile to the 2nd quartile. Patient satisfaction ranking moved from the 4th quartile to the 1st quartile, which was the highest score ever achieved in the history of the hospital. Physician satisfaction improved from the 3rd quartile to the 1st quartile. Nursing benchmarks were increased from the 25th percentile to the minimum of the 50th percentile ranking, which resulted in thirty-four additional registered nurses joining our nursing staff. This was a significant turnaround for an organization in the space of only one year. But the executive team wondered if we could maintain that level of performance.

2005

In order for the Plaza to continue on this road of success, I realized I would have to develop a strong, forward-thinking leadership team. I partnered with the nursing leadership academy to assist with assessment and development of our leadership skills. During this time, there was a fifty percent turnover on the nursing leadership team. I did not take the turnover personally and actually welcomed it. In my heart, I acknowledged that some leadership changes needed to occur if I was going to change the face of this organization. There were various reasons for the increased turnover, including retirement and general frustration with nursing management. I believe that some staff simply could not transition to the new role expectations and the demands placed upon them to be successful leaders in our organization.

Due to the turnover and recruitment of new managers by the end of 2005, the nursing leadership team became fragmented again. I might add that, during this time, the community was also faced with the sudden closure of an acute care hospital. Our facility, like others in the community, was challenged with absorbing this new patient population, recruitment of new hospital employees and partnering with new physicians. Because we were just not prepared to handle it, this influx caused additional stress on the organization. It caused workflow inefficiencies, intra- and inter-departmental infighting and a regression to the 'silo' culture. One of my leaders even termed it the Fort Worth Tsunami. I found myself with an immature leadership team that needed to acquire some skills in team building, interpersonal relationships and crisis management.

I began researching the literature on programs that promoted team work and conflict resolution. The programs weren't quite what I was looking for and didn't meet the needs of my team at that time. I was looking for something that wasn't a canned, high-tech presentation; but instead allowed the group to interact in real-life situations and problem-solve together.

You know - some people just enter your life at the right time. I began mentoring a graduate student from University of Texas at Arlington. She began to assist me in my research into training programs for my leadership team. As luck would have it, that student and I were scheduled to meet with her instructor, Dr. Sharon Judkins, for a student evaluation. After our meeting, Dr. Judkins and I began discussing the success of nursing at Plaza and our future plans. I explained how proud I was of our success so far, but also how concerned I was about the well being of my management team. My priority at that time was to assist my leadership in controlling their stress level and maintaining a positive work environment. The last thing I wanted or needed at that point was for any of the negative attitudes or dispositions of the nursing management group to be recognized at the staff level.

Dr. Judkins told me about the hardiness training program. Initially, I was skeptical - only because I was unfamiliar with the term and its relationship to the work environment. After weeks of discussions with Dr. Judkins, feedback from nurse managers at a previous facility who had been through the training and my own research on hardiness, I made the decision to have my managers go through the training.

2006

I planned the nurse executive retreat for early 2006. The focus of the three-day retreat was the hardiness training session. I started with a small group of only 14 managers and directors. During the first four hours of training, the group seemed uninterested and thought they already had the answers to all of their problems. By the end of the first day, the group became more engaged in the program and, by day two, they had become active participants. The training continued for the next eight months with this small group. A second group, which consisted of managers and second-level nursing supervisors (team leaders), completed the training later in the year.

The feedback from the training sessions was phenomenal. Participants told me that this training was the best thing that I could have ever offered them. It helped with their peer relationship communication difficulties. Some of the trainees said the program gave them a sense of empowerment. The group was so excited about the training and its effects on them personally, that they wanted it to be mandatory for everyone.

I witnessed a major transformation in my group right before my eyes. It was like a new beginning. The group began to mature in the way they managed conflict and how they communicated with other departments. They became perceived as more helpful and less offensive. Prior to the training, the group relied on me to solve their problems; now they only come to me for advice on their proposed solutions. The nursing leadership formed this incredible bond of support for each other. Not only were they supportive of one another, but they also held each other accountable for their actions. It was at this point that I knew I had "turned the ship around."

2007

Plaza satisfaction and quality results continued to show improvement. Employee satisfaction ranking moved from the 2nd quartile to the 1st quartile (number 4 out of 192 hospitals). Patient satisfaction ranking continued to be in the 1st quartile. Physician satisfaction remained in the 1st quartile. The quality indicators showed Plaza to be in the top 10% nationally in core measure performance. The organization also received the Texas Nurse Friendly designation and is currently on the journey for Magnet.

2008

This new year will bring a new set of challenges. The face of the nursing leadership has changed. With turnover, successful recruitment and organizational chart changes, the players have changed. The role and expectation of the nursing leader is expanding and becoming, unfortunately, more demanding. But our organization cannot afford to step back; we must improve continuously. Now is the time for our leadership team to renew our commitment to the to the coping skills learned in the hardiness training and to continue on our road to success.

Terryl Kendricks, RN, MSN

Terryl Kendricks is the Chief Nursing Officer of Plaza Medical Center of Fort Worth, a 320-bed tertiary care hospital. She oversees patient care by with the leadership of nursing staff of over 400 employees.

Ms. Kendricks has a Bachelor of Science in Social Work from Chapman College and a Bachelor of Science in Nursing from Texas Christian University. She holds a Master of Science in Nursing Administration from University of Texas at Arlington. She is a. 2005 Johnson and Johnson Nurse Executive Fellow from the Wharton School of Business.

Ms. Kendricks serves on the Foundation Board of the University of North Texas Health Science Center and on the Board of the DEW Hospital Council. In 2007, she was named as one of the Business Press Great Women of Texas and one of the Great One Hundred Nurses of the Metroplex. She is a member of the Sigma Theta Thu Nursing Honor Society and the Texas Organization of Nurse Executives.

CHAPTER 12

The Pearl in the Center

by Rebecca Lewis, RN, MA, MSN

In my first management position, I desperately sought instructions on how to be a good manager. I ordered lots of management books, read articles and attended numerous seminars. I thought that someone had to have the answers for which I was looking, or at least an instruction manual. I found lots of management theory, good and not so good role models, and trial by error experience.

My first management experience was in a unionized Veteran's Administration Hospital. I had the right initials (M.S.N.) after my name and no management experience. I had the Nurses Union President and the AFGE (American Federation of Government Employees) President in my "shop." It wasn't long, however, before I had a grievance filed against me! I made lots of mistakes – not malicious or intentional, just out of ignorance. For example, I made workload assignments based on skills of the staff who could/would give the best care to the sickest patients. As a result, the "best" staff got the hardest assignments day after day after day – until they confronted me and asked why I was picking on them. They felt as though the assignments were really like that proverbial slap in the face. Although I was honestly trying to see that our patients got the best care, I wasn't taking very good care of the staff – not the staff with the best skills, and especially not the staff who needed development.

My "pearl" to a new nurse manager would be to care for and develop your staff using the same skills you use for patient care. First and foremost, you have to "care" for the staff in the same way you want them to care about patients. Your staff will know if you care sincerely about them, that you care if they have problems at home, that you truly want to assist in their careers, that you will support them if they are going through a divorce or death of a child, or if they get cancer. I personally feel that nursing managers are not "wasting" their clinical skills by going into management - they are just extending those skills by caring for the staff who cares for patients. Your span of influence expands from concern for one nurse's workload to concern for the entire work unit.

Have you noticed that some physicians have truly outstanding surgical or diagnostic skills, but have terrible communication skills (what we used to call bedside manner)? Conversely, some physicians are very nurturing and caring, and both nurses and patients love them. Which type of doctor do you think gets sued more often? It's like the adage says, "They need to know you care before they know how good you are." Nurse managers are no different. Would you rather have a manager who is not the best educated or experienced, but who truly cares about you, or have one with all the right credentials who is eager to advance, but is too busy to spend much time getting to know the staff?

Use your nursing assessment skills to individualize the "care" you give your staff. Find out what do they need from the job - and from you. Develop a plan to help them meet their goals, whether that is to advance, remain a staff nurse who feels appreciated or transition to retirement. Don't make the mistake of being "fair" and treating them all the same. Like your patients, they are individuals with different needs. Develop and implement your plan, continuously monitor whether or not goals have changed, and evaluate what you can do to improve outcomes.

It sounds easy, but what about those staff who are lazy, incompetent, or generally a pain in the rear? We all know them. I like to rationalize that, if you managed to get rid of the ones you have, you'd somehow inherit two or three more by osmosis. The secret is to figure out the best way to utilize them. What do they want? What are their strengths? What if they really have a legitimate problem? For instance, one of the 'bizarre' staff members back at the VA actually had a brain tumor! And we know that our nursing workforce is aging and will develop more and more health issues. We are going to need to be more creative in the future!

Finally, "Nurse, heal yourself!" Do you go home at the end of the day feeling proud of "your" staff and the care you gave through them? Is management right for you? Ask yourself these questions:

- Can you manage conflict by realizing that there is strength in differing viewpoints? If you are able to listen/discuss/debate the merits of everyone's input and get the team to consensus (even if they don't all agree), you'll rarely be surprised by something you didn't anticipate. As a young manager, I was concerned when it seemed our Senior Leadership team appeared to bicker with each other. When I got up the courage to ask the CEO about it, his answer was that he intentionally recruited a team who disagreed on everything. That way, when they discussed an issue, he felt confident that they had analyzed everything. They had agreed to thoroughly debate the issues upon which they disagreed, but to leave the room in agreement on how to implement their group decision. The point is you'll have a stronger team if you agree it's okay to disagree, as long as you support each other.

- Are you sensitive to subtle staff cues – are you feeling the pulse of your people? Can you take criticism to heart and express your weaknesses? Upset/hurt employees may react exactly like grieving/angry patients and family members. Do you get mad and give patients and families the cold shoulder? No matter how experienced or how old your staff are, everyone has a basic human need to be acknowledged and appreciated. Like any family, your team will get upset with you and each other. They need to know that you may not always agree with their style, but you still care for and appreciate them as individuals. Sound like a "family"?

- Fake it until you make it! Try to be warm and approachable, even if your staff are getting on your last nerve. Listen to that irritating person (even if it's killing you) – she is trying to "tell" you what she needs. How would you handle a demanding patient? What strategies do you use for "high risk" patients? We rarely get to pick the patients we want and, unless you are opening a new unit, you probably won't get to handpick your staff either. So you "inherit" some "parking lot" people. Imagine if the entire organization was called out to the parking lot and, like drafting a ball team, you got to pick your team. Think of the hurt feelings of the "misfits" left standing outside in the parking lot! Like in a Disney movie, you could build one heck of a team with a misfit members if you gave them the right coaching and motivation.

- Be modest/humble. Give all the credit to the people. Build up your staff; praise them to each other. Remember that, if you badmouth one of them to the others, they will expect you to badmouth them, too, if and when they fall out of your favor. Show appreciation for a hard job, even if the outcome wasn't perfect. Think about your children playing sports. Do only the talented kids get to play? Does the coach berate the child who struck out or dropped the ball? Do you want your team to think of you as a coach who builds up the team – or criticizes the players? When you need to "coach" or counsel people, cut the session in half and then in half again. Even though you may think you are being so weak that the person being counseled will not get the point, he may feel like you are stabbing him in the heart. Be kind and sensitive – always.

- Give them hope. Everyone wants to be on the winning team. Engage your team in strategic issues and keep them informed of management information. Discuss the "what ifs" of the organization's future. Remember: if you are discouraged or negative about the future, the staff will also be apprehensive. They want you to give them a compelling vision and hope for the future, even if things are "tight" at the moment. They will be able to handle future bad news if you include them in the discussion and plans on what must be done right now. Just like terminally ill patients and families, your staff need hope and they need to be included in planning.

Ultimately, everything you need to know to be a good manager, you learned in nursing school. Use the same skills, just with a different group of people!

Rebecca Adams Lewis, RN, MA, MSN

Rebecca (Becky) Lewis is currently CEO of Knox County Hospital in Barbourville, Kentucky. Becky's prior experience has included being a staff nurse, educator, Director of Surgical Services, Vice President of Cardiac Service Line and Interim Management. She also is a nurse surveyor for the Commission for Collegiate Nursing Education (CCNE).

Becky has a BSN and MA in Education from Spalding University in Louisville, Kentucky and an MSN from the University of Kentucky.

CHAPTER 13

The Same String - An Entire Career at one Place

by Linda Knodel, RN, MSN, MHA, CNABC, CPQA, FACHE

In 1954, I was born the third child of Anne and William Carns of Williston, North Dakota. Regular and ongoing healthcare was an integral part of my life. The first two children did not survive and this was due to the fact that Rhogam was not available in the late 1940's; survival due to mother-child incompatibility was non-existent. Due to these complications, the local physician recommended that my mother have her third delivery at the University of Minnesota, as they would have the support necessary in the event complications arose during the birth. The University of Minnesota was over 1,000 miles away form my parents' hometown. Mother took the train by herself, to the University of Minnesota, two weeks prior to my birth. She stayed in the hospital the entire time prior to the C-Section. There were no incompatibility problems with my birth and all went well. Two years later, my brother, Bill Carns, Junior, required a full body transfusion immediately after his birth. The family story is that an urgent plea for a blood donor for my brother's blood type went over the local radio. A local resident donated the necessary blood and a positive outcome resulted. I also recall my mother undergoing numerous surgeries while I was growing up. Visits to the hospital and physician clinic were frequent. The smell of these two environments remains vivid in my mind. More often than not, those smells were offensive, but I never thought so. Hospitals and clinics always intrigued me. The science behind caring and curing was fascinating. At the age of three, I requested my first "nurse kit." The "kit" consisted of a white plastic purse that contained a nursing cap and an apron (with a large red cross on both of those items), a plastic stethoscope, candy dots (to be used as pills), a plastic syringe and a reflex hammer. If, for some reason, I couldn't find my nurse outfit, I would take one of my mother's tea towels and wrap it around me while performed nursing duties.

When I was in fourth grade, I heard about the opportunity to be a Candy Striper at our local hospital. When I asked my parents, they did not approve of this and said, "You need to come straight home from school." As an individual who doesn't do well with an answer of "no," I did not follow their directions. Instead, two of my girlfriends and I would rush over to the local hospital after school, put on the pink and white candy striper aprons and deliver fresh water to the patients, answer lights and be of assistance to the staff. There was one patient in particular, Mary, whom I will never forget. Mary was 109 years old and a resident in the hospital. She was blind and very frail. It was through my work as a candy striper that my call to nursing was validated. I became the only person who could get Mary to eat. She rarely ate breakfast or lunch, but waited for supper at 4:30, when I would arrive. She would eat her entire meal for me! I knew I was making a difference in Mary's life and found this so gratifying. This affirmed my desire to continue the ministry.

As a junior in high school, I took an elective class called "Health Careers." This class provided exposure to the duties of various health professions, both in the classroom and in practical settings. This class continued to affirm my desire to become a nurse. During the summer between my junior and senior years of high school, I was chosen, along with 60 other students, to take part in a trial project at the state technical school, the Whapeton State School of Science. This 6-week, residential on-campus experience exposed us to multiple trade occupations. Again, the nursing program appealed to me the most. As a high school senior, I realized that resources would be vital for me to go to college. I applied for every scholarship that I could find. I also applied to five schools of nursing. During the application process, I found two-year, associate degree programs, three-year diploma nursing programs (which were often associated with hospitals), and the four-year baccalaureate degree. According to my high school guidance counselor, I should select the baccalaureate degree program if was interested in teaching. If I wanted to focus on bedside clinical care, I was advised to choose one of the associate or diploma programs.

Literature indicated that St. Luke's School of Nursing (in Fargo, North Dakota) had very high ratings and had very strict admission criteria. In fact, the required entrance exam took an entire day on their campus in Fargo. I shared my dream of attending this school with my guidance counselor, who indicated to me that it would be unusual for someone from Williston, to be accepted at this prestigious Fargo school. He indicated that most of the St. Luke students were from the eastern part of the state.

I accepted this challenge with great optimism and was successful; I was accepted into St. Luke's and graduated on August 16, 1974. During my college tenure, I was active in the school governance council and held various offices and positions. The local Catholic Church was only one block from the school dormitories, so I was able to participate in church events, as well. I have always participated in community, professional and academic opportunities … any activity that I could get my arms around - just to learn more and to be engaged.

My mother was a college graduate and a role model for me. She graduated from teacher's college and taught for several years. I believe that I was one of a handful of grandchildren on either side of my family who graduated from college.

Upon graduation from nursing school, I was offered a job in the intensive care unit at St. Luke's Hospital (now known as Merit Care) in Fargo, North Dakota. I was also offered a job at St. Alexius Medical Center in Bismarck. Making the decision was difficult because I greatly enjoyed working at St. Luke's, yet Bismarck was half way between Fargo and my hometown of Williston, North Dakota. The one and only person I knew in Bismarck informed me that St. Alexius was the hospital to work at. I chose not to apply at the other facility in Bismarck, received an interview at St. Alexius and was offered a full-time night position on the medical floor.

In retrospect, this was probably the most important step in my career. It was during that period of working straight nights that staff nurses and other colleagues that told me that they would take me under their wings and make me the best nurse ever. And I can tell you from the bottom of my heart, that is exactly what they did. There is a culture at St. Alexius of empowerment, and the nursing staff at St. Alexius worked very hard to embrace a non-punitive learning environment. This created a safety net for nurses who made mistakes and were willing to learn from them. As a new nurse, I was met with optimism and a forgiving attitude.

I had been working on the medical floor for a year when my supervisor, Laurel Sullivan, asked if I would be interested in filling in for a nurse in the dialysis unit who was going on maternity leave. In nursing school in the early 70s, I was taught about the renal system and renal failure; I had not been educated about dialysis. This was new, foreign territory! The artificial kidney and its associated technology, and the management of a chronic patient population, combined to create a very new nursing experience, which I embraced. Truly, the assignment to the dialysis unit made a major impact in my career, because the physician who was the medical director of the dialysis unit, Doug Miller, really embodied the team concept.

He would work and speak in terms of teams, even before teams became fashionable. His attitude was empowering and provided our whole multidisciplinary team with the ability to provide proactive (versus reactive) patient care.

Dr Miller viewed the staff as experts in the care of end-stage renal patients and their families. Our critical thinking skills were challenged, just as he would challenge the skills of those residents on his service. Dr. Miller acknowledged the vital role that we played as nurses in developing care plans, and working with transplant agencies and the community. We were taught to be prepared for patient care conferences and to know what interventions and outcomes we would recommend for our patients. Dr. Miller was a Harvard graduate who was fellowship-trained in nephrology at the University of Colorado.

I remember one day visiting with Dr. Miller and saying, "Dr. Miller, we have a patient who travels 250 miles one way, three times a week (1500 miles a week) for his dialysis treatments. We really ought to go to that community and see if they would be interested in a collaborative arrangement." The facility in that community was another Catholic health care provider. We were met with open arms and we opened a chronic hemodialysis unit at Mercy Medical Center in Williston, in 1985. I also approached St. Joseph's Hospital in Dickinson, North Dakota with the same opportunity. Today these two hemodialysis units continue to be very successful. St. Alexius was the first to provide satellite dialysis in North Dakota; we were also the first in peritoneal dialysis. Another phenomenon that really came out of this was that we were empowered not only by the medical director but by the organization, St. Alexius, to be innovative, be creative, and to partner during a time when partnerships were not in vogue. Building these kinds of relationships allowed us to become a highly respected healthcare center for western and central North Dakota. Working in this kind of an environment only one year out of school, I thought this situation was the norm. I was naïve. Little did I know this attitude was the exception and not the norm – and I am grateful that I chose to become part of an organization with this progressive attitude.

I had the opportunity to build a new dialysis unit at St. Alexius in 1986 and, before we moved into it, the CEO approached me and asked if I would assist in improving our compliance with JCAHO standards related to quality assurance and the medical staff. Again, I dug back into my toolbox of having gone to a diploma school in nursing and did not recall learning about tissue and transfusion review, surgical indications review, medical staff quality assurance and the like. I seized this new opportunity with enthusiasm. And, at the same time, I realized I needed further education, since I was not familiar with this kind of work. Once again, I was empowered, given lots of opportunities to learn, to grow, to organize many medical staff committees and organizational efforts. It is reassuring to look back and recognize that many of the systems and processes that were implemented are still in place today and are anchored by even greater systems and processes for organizational success.

As the director of quality review and risk management, I also initiated the very first pre-admission program in the state of North Dakota for insurance authorization and pre-admission certification. I developed a pre-admission office and also assisted with the concept of a pre-surgical admission process. In addition, I had responsibility for Infection Control, Utilization Review, the dialysis unit, and the women's and children's inpatient units. I realized during this period of my career that the healthcare system is very interdependent and that each department within the medical center plays a vital role for our patients and community.

In 1987, I decided to go back to school to get my Bachelor's degree in Healthcare Administration. For several summers, I commuted to St. Joseph's College in Windham, Maine. I had three small children, all under the age six and my husband, being the wonderful man that he is, supported me in this endeavor. I graduated June 1991 and, in July 1991, I entered the ISP, Master's in Healthcare Administration program at the University of Minnesota. During this period of time, again, I was overwhelmed by the support that I received from my leadership and management team at St. Alexius. While I was getting my degree, we added several new services (including a hospital-based skilled nursing facility), developed a home care agency and durable medical equipment company.

We also decided to have nursing educators on each and every unit within the medical center, supporting all of the ongoing practice challenges and changes. We implemented the very first bedside computer charting system in 1991, which was virtually unheard of during those days. Our Chief Executive Officer (CEO) had great vision and allowed the organization and leadership to try out new and innovative solutions, thus ensuring that our medical center remained on the cutting edge healthcare strategies.

In 1989, our Chief Nursing Officer (CNO) resigned and moved away. I was asked by the CEO if I would assume that responsibility. I felt ready for this new and exciting challenge. As Senior Vice President and Chief Nursing Officer, I have had the opportunity to truly focus on patients and patient care, and the important individuals who provide this care. It has also been an opportunity to build a leadership team that is second to none. Our succession planning and top-notch clinical staff earned St. Alexius the distinction of Magnet status in 2006. Nearly 30% of our staff nurses are certified at the national level.

Receiving distinction does not come without pain! In 2004, the Magnet standards were revised to note that the Chief Nursing Officer must be prepared at either the bachelor's or master's level in nursing by the year 2008. I had neither degree! So, once again I donned the student "hat" and obtained my master's degree in nursing. In fact, my whole leadership team went back to school. It was great sitting next to my team as we forged ahead to meet this organizational goal. In 2005, our leadership team boasted 23 master's graduates.

St. Alexius is sponsored by the Sisters of St. Benedict of the Annunciation Monastery. In 1885, they started the very first hospital in the Dakota Territory. This pioneering attitude continues to this day, and every day at St. Alexius. It is about tradition and about service.

Other great influences in my life have been June Warner and Marie Manthy. Marie Manthy called me on a very cold February day in 1991 and asked, "I don't see your name on the graduate roster for your MHA." I replied that I had not and that I was planning to attend a different college. Marie said sternly, "You need to go to the University of Minnesota." Had I not listened to Marie, my life would be drastically different than it is today. I am proud to say that I received my degree from one of the finest Master's of Heath Care Administration (MHA) programs in the United States. Another key influence in my life has been serving on the Boards for the American Organization of Nurse Executives (AONE) and the American College of Health Care Executives (ACHE). These fine professional organizations provided me with enormous personal and professional growth opportunities. Pam Thompson, RN, MSN, FAAN, CEO- AONE, and Tom Dolan, PhD, CEO-ACHE have provided me with outstanding mentoring as well as professional growth opportunities.

Just like the staff nurse who came up to me in 1974 and said, "We are going to take you under our wing and make you the best," numerous others have stepped up to the plate to help me grow and influence healthcare for our families, friends and communities.

In closing, I'd like to say that one's profession is very important, because it truly becomes one's identity; however, the real identity becomes embracing and upholding one's family and their distinct values. When family supports you during an entire career and lifetime, that is far more meaningful than anything else. I am honored that our three beautiful daughters have chosen healthcare paths; Kristen a prosthodontist, Kendra a women's healthcare nurse practitioner, Katie a healthcare mediator and dispute resolution specialist, and son-in-law, Andrew, a physician. My husband, Ken, truly carries the banner of distinction for all of us. If you see a door, open it; if a call comes in, answer it; if a voice is heard, talk and if a page is turned, honor it. I owe so much to all those who have influenced my life.

Linda J. Knodel
RN, MSN, MHA, CNABC, CPQA, FACHE
Senior Vice President Chief Nursing Officer

Linda J. Knodel is the Senior Vice President/CNO at St. Alexius Medical Center, Bismarck North Dakota. Linda has held this position since 1989. Linda's nursing experience has been solely at St. Alexius Medical Center. She has served in such roles as the director of quality and risk management, the director of the renal dialysis and aphaeresis unit and staff nurse on medical floor.

Linda has a masters in healthcare administration from the University of Minnesota, and a masters in nursing from the University of Mary; she also completed a Wharton Fellowship at the University of Pennsylvania. Linda is an active member of the American Organization of Nurse Executives and served as past NDONE President, former AONE Region 6 Board member, and former AHA Regional Policy Board member. Linda served on the nominating committee for the American College of Healthcare Executives and held positions as past Regent for North Dakota and past president of the North Dakota ACHE Chapter. She currently is on the ACHE Board of Governors. She also serves as a member of the North Dakota University System Southwest Region Workforce Training Board.

Linda speaks at the local, regional and national level on numerous topics including leadership, patient safety and informatics. She is recognized and published in several journals and manuscripts.

RESTRINGING - PEARLS WORTH USING AGAIN

CHAPTER 14

A Broken String: My Position is Gone!

by Karen O. Moore, RN, MS, FACHE

If you asked the general public about their perceptions of job security for nurses, they would say it is very high. That is probably why nurses, their families and communities are shocked when nursing jobs are eliminated, whether those jobs are positions at the bedside or one of the many nursing leadership positions responsible for keeping hospitals in motion every day. However, there is an incredible amount of change happening in health care, coupled with growing financial challenges and the increasing complexity of systems required to deliver patient care. This will undoubtedly prompt hospitals to eliminate even more nursing positions in order to achieve efficiencies or bring in the different skill sets or technology needed for patient care delivery.

There are many situations that result in jobs disappearing. As a nurse and senior hospital administrator, I have actually been involved in some of these decisions to eliminate nursing positions in response to organizational restructuring, divesting or developing clinical programs or the inevitable circumstances that require one style of leadership to be replaced by another. This article will describe my personal experience with such a transition. The importance of the skills and insights gained from being on the receiving end of this change not only helped me to build inner resources but also made me aware of how organizations can manage the dynamics the transition created by such job elimination. I am grateful for a number of things I learned from my situation, but will discuss that in more detail later.

Prior to my own situation, I had read articles about leaders in transition (often written in the third person or by the consultants or coaches who worked with those whose positions had been eliminated). Based on that information, I had a file drawer of critical documents in my desk, which I planned take with me if I was given no advance warning of my elimination or time to vacate my office. My 'vanishing position' situation began when our CEO left and the governing corporation decided upon a different approach to organizational structure for the hospital. Everyone was watching and waiting as the organization started through a transition during these circumstances, to see whether the corporation would demonstrate core values while executing these changes. They decided that my position as Chief Operating Officer in our 95-bed community hospital would be eliminated and the focus of the site administrator role would be changed to build business partnerships and grow our market share. The senior leaders wanted an outsider to lead this change in organizational culture and the transformation of the hospital; I was not viewed as a candidate for that role. On the positive side, I was given advance notice that my job was being eliminated, prior to the rest of the organization being informed, which allowed me to process the news first.

According to the literature I had read on leaders in transition, there are basically three "official" phases in the process: Endings, Neutral Zones and New Beginnings. My own experience fell into four categories:

- Why is this happening to me!?
- What do I need?
- How do I want to leave?
- Now, what do I want?

Why is this happening to me?

When your job is eliminated, it is natural and appropriate to react with fear, shame and/or the need to control the situation. But these feelings may derail you from taking the right action or knowing what you need; you must work through those feelings first - not go around them. While a friend, sympathetic colleague or family member can be supportive with good intentions, it may be difficult for an outsider to really help you through this transition. I found that the assistance of professionals skilled in executive coaching and career counseling was critically important. These specialists are objective, have seen many others through transition, and are passionate about helping you get through it with new skills and confidence. The "team" I assembled included an executive coach with whom I had worked, legal counsel and trusted experts such as recruiters and outplacement counselors. The message here is don't try to get through this alone. You cannot rely solely on a supportive spouse, sibling or friend, who may feel helpless and has no real power to assist you. Your job actually becomes making it through the transition and, if you are like me, this will be uncharted territory and you will be a novice. Just as you would not set sail across a body of water without knowing how to sail a boat or having a crew, supplies or the technology to manage the trip, you will want to assemble a crew of experts to help you navigate through a job transition.

A big challenge during your transition may be the fact that, while your new job has become to manage your transition, you may not have left your old job yet and the organization may expect you to stay fully engaged in your role, as if you were not leaving. Working with a transition team will require the same dedicated time and focus that all new learning entails. But having others to work with you during the change enables you do your existing job while allowing you space to work through your feelings, plan your next steps and prepare for the inevitable questions and opinions that will come from colleagues. At this point, it is important to negotiate time away from work to engage in these transition activities while still fulfilling your obligation to be present at work to provide support and lay the groundwork for a smooth change.

You will know what to do in the work situation, but how do you productively use the time allotted to focus on your next steps? Discipline of thought and processing of emotion needs a plan, just like any other change. Rather than just sitting with the enormous pressure of trying to manage your feelings, job, relationships, and new job search (all of which can create fear and confusion), it is important to create a plan (or commitment to yourself) that is anchored in what you really, really want to do. This clarity can only come from reflection, stillness and self-compassion.

There were two things that helped me achieve this state. As a person who was frequently busy "doing" and focusing on the needs of others, I needed to find solitude. I found it on a bicycle. Long road rides got me out into nature, challenged my physical strength and involved me in a new community of people. In addition, the professional support I engaged included an executive coach to assist me with the separation process, and a three-day retreat in a cabin in Maine, on a lake (back to nature again) with another executive coach who's focus was on helping me plan my future. This turned out to be one of the most helpful experiences I had during the transition.

I had been particularly stuck on feeling sorry for myself, which I didn't really understand, given the resources and supports I had mobilized. But I was also trying to manage some particularly draining relationships and they were keeping me from doing the self-work that this opportunity presented. The retreat provided the space and safety to explore some deeply personal issues that were very connected to how I was thinking about the future. I don't think I would have connected those dots without the experience of that retreat. They say that true understanding comes from a place between fact and feeling. Finding that space can be tricky and I can only say I was fortunate to stumble upon this opportunity without looking for it. But I was open to taking the leap and seeing where it brought me.

What do I need?

The clarity gained from the retreat in Maine was pivotal for moving into transition. Transition, by definition, is a time of uncertainty as well as possibility. It is critical to accept that premise and embrace it. Once my colleagues knew I was leaving, I got many questions from well-meaning individuals, such as, "How could this happen to you?" or, "What will you do?" I was also offered platitudes, such as, "You'll be fine," which was, of course, correct but somehow left me feeling shut down - as if getting to "fine" only required that I sit on my couch and meditate.

In fact, real action is needed during this type of transition, but since you might be feeling immobilized by negative emotions, it may be hard to take action. That is why you need a team. For instance, does your organization have a work force transition policy or a separation agreement? At the time of transition, it is common in healthcare for some kind of transition assistance or support, since our business tends to place a stronger value on people than some other industries. However, I still find reluctance in healthcare to provide senior executives with separation agreements as a part of the employment contract. Transition provides an important stimulus to work out such an agreement.

Through separation agreements, an organization shows its support for employees and recognizes value of their service. If the situation arises where such an agreement is needed because your position is being eliminated, but your organization has not provided one, it needn't be negotiated from scratch while you may also be feeling vulnerable. You and your transition team can study industry standards, consult legal counsel and speak with colleagues to find general guidelines. Your organization may have it's own standards and these will be important to understand, as well. Perhaps you can even modify an existing document for your use. Just make sure you are being considered at the appropriate level of the organization and have comparable terms to others of your scope, seniority, and level in the organization.

Questions from others inside and outside the organization can be anticipated. When fielding these inquiries, it is very important to have a scripted statement that reflects your concept of the situation; one that is honest and will be believable to others. No matter what people may be imagining, you can portray yourself in a powerful way in order to manage perceptions of others. People will take their cues from you. If you are feeling like a victim and portray yourself that way, you may get sympathy, but I advise against that approach. Also, if you cannot credibly support the communication strategy developed by your organization, avoid that issue in your script. And avoid lying about the reason you are leaving, even if asked to do so by your organization. You should devise a thoughtful, honest appraisal of your situation that you can state to others with integrity. You can build a foundation of statements such as, "I understand this decision. I am sad to be leaving, but I am looking forward to the future and what's next. I am grateful for ..." As you answer questions about why you are leaving, state your answer not only with words, but also with your heart and your eyes. Because now you are moving onto the next place where you need to be in order to assist the organization through transition.

How do I want to leave?

You might ask, "So, why is it my job to assist the organization with changes that are resulting in the elimination of my position? "They" made this decision. "They" created this situation. Why not let "them" handle it? To some extent, that is true. You do not need to take responsibility for the decision. Likewise, because the decision was not your responsibility, you should avoid shooting arrows at those who did decide on this transition strategy. If you have lived and led others with honesty and integrity, this situation gives you another opportunity to demonstrate those values. I think this is an important point, whether you have a staff position or an administrative job.

You have had the time to work through the feelings created by learning you will lose your job and, hopefully, to negotiate what you needed for the transition. Now, those with whom you work will also need time to process their reactions and emotions regarding this change. Even if they are angry initially - remember, they will remain in the organization and must be allowed to go through their own phases of processing their reactions in order to reach their own conclusions.

In many cases, the elimination of your position may make their jobs more challenging or considerably more difficult. With the help of my management team, we created a 12-page transition plan that identified current job responsibilities, status and key transition points, and accountability issues within the organization. It was an important guidance document that helped me work with my team and with the senior leaders of the organization. Moreover it also served as tangible evidence of the redistribution of my work to others in the organization who may have already been feeling overworked.

As the date of my departure grew closer, my colleagues started to get angry at me for not being at work enough. Our transition plan served as an important reminder to others, especially those who reported directly to me, that helping and supporting them was my priority. It was their job to assume new responsibilities, ask for what they needed and negotiate their new workload within the organization. It would have been unethical for me to hold onto all of my duties right up until the day I left, and then try to wrap everything up with a bow and leave the others to try to determine how to divide up my tasks among themselves. Even so, it is perfectly normal for those staying in the organization to be anxious about the redistribution of duties and be in denial as long as possible before you leave.

What do I want?

Leaving (or an ending) precedes a new beginning. Transition provides a time for you to think about what you really want. If you are fortunate enough to have some time off before assuming another job, you may begin this process while still at your old job. If so, take the time to really create the self-focus that will fuel your decisions about what comes next. As luck would have it, my extended family just happened to have planned a weeklong vacation at the shore just as my old job was ending. I think having an activity like that proved to be more beneficial than immediately beginning the process of dealing with changing routines at home as I adjusted to a new life without work.

Take the opportunity of a job transition to recreate yourself. One of the first decisions I made was to move from my home in the country into a village where I would be near friends, shops, my yoga studio, biking opportunities and my daughter's school. I also decided not to work or even look for work for four months. My first weeks at home without an administrative assistant and high speed Internet access kept me pretty busy. I picked up a weekly planner I found on the counter at my dentist's office. I opened it up to the first date after my job ended and wrote, "begin new life." It was official.

As I look at that calendar now, four months later, it is appropriately full of appointments and open spaces. Thumbing through the days, I can see time spent with family and friends, time with my daughters, and time for bike rides, yoga and music. I can see time for meeting with people, for keeping professional contacts, seeking counsel and being a part of my community. I put steps in place to strengthen my financial planning and goals, reinforce my commitment to fitness and health, and to build my computer skills. I joined a women's writing group and even took hula hoop classes (I have successfully acquired that skill, I am glad to report). I found out I still didn't like to cook. And I turned down calls about positions or work because, although that organization may have really wanted me, I didn't really want to do those jobs. It has become clear to me that I don't want to move again before my youngest daughter graduates from high school. Surprisingly, I was contacted recently about a job closer to home that I may not have otherwise considered previously but would help me to meet my current personal, professional and financial goals.

My retreat coach and I have an exchange going and she ends each e-mail with a reminder to, "Leap and the net will appear." I respond by saying, "I've leapt, but I still don't see the net yet." Although I still don't see that net, I've figured out that my problem was that I was looking for a real net. I was looking for safety born of fear and forgetting that safety didn't move me anywhere and there was nothing to fear. My little planning book is proof to me that I have gone from confusion and fear to doing things routinely that I care about everyday, even though those things may scare me just a little (or a lot).

I am so moved by the poem "The Journey" by Mary Oliver. It illuminates for me the fact that it is not enough to know you have to begin and to stand by the truth you may have known all along, but were not ready to accept. It clarifies for me how I needed to be humbled. How I needed to learn that the fact that others didn't need me did not define me, and how I can use that experience to learn what I really want out of life. I hope you find it as inspirational as I do.

The Journey
by Mary Oliver

One day you finally knew
what you had to do, and began,
though the voices around you
kept shouting
their bad advice--
though the whole house
began to tremble
and you felt the old tug
at your ankles.
"Mend my life!"
each voice cried.
But you didn't stop.
You knew what you had to do,
though the wind pried
with its stiff fingers
at the very foundations,
though their melancholy
Was terrible.
It was already late
enough, and a wild night,
and the road full of fallen
branches and stones.

But little by little,
as you left their voices behind,
the stars began to burn
through the sheets of clouds,
and there was a new voice
which you slowly
recognized as your own,
that kept you company
as you strode deeper and deeper
into the world,
determined to do
the only thing you could do--
determined to save
The only life you could save.

11/30/07

Karen O. Moore RN, MS, FACHE

Karen Moore has been in health care for over 30 years, starting a career as a staff nurse and quickly assuming leadership and administrative positions. She obtained her RN from Boston State College in 1977 and her Masters in Nursing Administration at the University of Massachusetts, School of Nursing in 1989. She has been a senior health care executive for 20 years in academic and community hospital settings. Her work has focused on innovation and change management, strategic planning and implementation, conflict resolution, leadership development, organizational ethics, new program development and monitoring and measuring staffing and productivity models.

Some of Karen's accomplishments include introduction of new patient care delivery models, development of new business partnerships with physicians, creation of a healing environment in a community hospital, interest-based labor contract negotiations and strengthening service lines across an integrated health systems to build clinical services regionally.

Karen is currently the CEO at Kindred Hospital Parkview, Springfield, Massachusetts. Ms. Moore's experience is distinguished by her commitment to patient safety, quality of care, and supportive work environments. She received the Massachusetts Hospital Association Leadership Award for her efforts in partnering with hospitals to create a voluntary compact of excellence with the Patients First Initiative. Ms. Moore also received the Mary B. Conceision Award for Nursing Leadership in 2007 and a 2007 Distinguished Alumni Award from the University of Massachusetts, Amherst. Karen is also the Past President of the Massachusetts Organization of Nurse Executives and Fellow in the American College of Health Care Executives. Ms. Moore also chairs the board of Medically-Induced Trauma Support Services (MITSS) a nonprofit organization formed to support patients, families and clinicians when a medical error occurs.

CHAPTER 15

Valuable Asset: We Are Being Sold!

by Peggy Diller, RN

After the initial stunning announcement, most of our staff was surprised and in shock, trying to understand why this was happening and what it was going to mean to us a team and to each of us as individuals.

The hospital's senior leadership team realized that this was a time when it was critical to rise to the occasion. As the Chief Nursing Officer, I knew that strong leadership was going to be essential to reduce the effects of staff uncertainties on patient care. I had been through this before and I thought I knew some of what was ahead!

One key to managing in this situation would be to increase the level of communication to the staff while expanding leadership visibility throughout the hospital. Our Chief Executive Officer (CEO), emphasized the "business as usual" approach through the upcoming changes. We couldn't allow any decline in quality of care or in patient satisfaction, and we also needed to maintain staff morale as much as possible. Thinking back on the lengthy transition process, it is easy to see that we went through stages of emotion similar to those described by Elisabeth Kübler-Ross in her model of the Five Stages of Grief. Many staff reacted immediately to the announcement with a sense of denial ("No it can't be true."), followed by a feeling of anger ("Why us? We are doing so well financially this year."). This then progressed to the stage of bargaining ("We can show the system that we can make even bigger profits this year and that our very good core quality measures results will continue to improve."). This was followed very quickly by an atmosphere of sadness throughout the organization ("Why try to keep being part of the system and attending their meetings? Why do we have to keep trying?"). Ultimately, most staff attained the acceptance stage, with staff and leaders making decisions to stay on and adapt to the new owner's model, search for opportunities within other hospitals in our current system, or to leave the organization entirely. During this period, many people thought, "Maybe it won't be so bad," "Guess we will live through this – we have overcome adversity before" and "Let's just get this over with!" But, often the question of, "Have you found another job yet?" was followed by, "How soon will you be leaving?"

During the few months after the announcement, we learned a lot more about the process of the sale of a not-for-profit organization to a for-profit entity. Although a not-for-profit organization does, indeed, need to make a "profit", the money/income is reinvested back into the organization rather than used to provide benefit back to a for-profit entity's investors. To our chagrin, we learned that the finalists who wanted to take over and maintain our hospital's operations were all for-profit entities. (The developers and others who were only interested in tearing down the building in order to build houses, condos and apartments were not given serious consideration, in light of the commitment to the community to maintain the hospital as a community resource.)

Non-profit hospitals across the country, and not just in our state, are struggling increasingly for financial stability. In California, payer mix deterioration and seismic upgrades/retro-fitting and/or possible facility replacement lead the way in consideration of the financial future of many organizations. These factors compound the concerns over a shrinking workforce, increased competition for healthcare workers, higher-cost replacement workers to cover position turnovers, and the mandate to meet unfunded nurse staffing ratios. Like any other business, when nonprofit hospitals face severe financial hurdles, there are not many options: they can reorganize, "tighten their belts," and become more efficient. All of these methods had been tried at our hospital over the years (multiple times, in most cases), but we still found ourselves facing the prospect of being sold.

Not-for-profit hospitals are dedicated to a public purpose. They are required to provide charity care and other benefits to their surrounding communities in exchange for local and federal tax breaks. When a non-profit hospital is sold to a for-profit entity, the community has a right to the proceeds of the transition, because the hospital's assets have been transferred to the for-profit hospital's owners or shareholders and no longer exist to benefit the community. One of the most important issues in this type of transition is the question of whether or not the public is getting a fair deal. California law requires the State Attorney General to review and consent to any sale or transfer of a health facility owned or operated by a nonprofit corporation whose assets are held in public trust. This requirement covers health facilities that are licensed to provide 24-hour care, such as hospitals and skilled nursing facilities. The goal is to determine if the selling price reflects the true value of taxpayers' investment in the non-profit institution.

So what was the process?

The "Announcement"

The announcement that the hospital was being put up for sale was communicated to our Chief Executive Officer (CEO) from the corporate organization's leadership. Multiple discussions about payer mix shifts and seismic upgrades had been held over the past few years at corporate and Board levels, but the possibility of sale considerations had not been explicitly shared with employees. As part of the announcement, a communication plan had been drafted, with a top priority of informing the hospital's Board of Directors about the decision to sell. This was accomplished through telephone calls from our CEO. Then prepared press releases were reviewed and the created list of other "important people" to be contacted was immediately assigned. Examples of those contacts included local legislators and politicians, key members of the medical staff, and local professional/healthcare organizations. Meetings were set up for the hospital's leadership management team, followed by open meetings and forums for the hospital's employees led by senior leadership. Department managers/leaders were asked to speak to their staff members who were on duty, providing them with the information and inviting the employees to attend any open forums that were scheduled for either the day shift or the night shift. Drafted written communications were drafted and provided to all the employees and physicians on the medical staff, while press releases were provided to local media outlets.

Communication

As with any major event, all avenues of communication were used, formal and informal, written and verbal. Whatever information was available was readily shared. A hospital intranet site was established through our CEO and public relations department for around-the-clock access by our employees. Employees were invited to submit their questions and encouraged to ask about rumors on an on-going basis. Sections of monthly staff and management meetings were given over to open forum discussions as we strived to ensure on-going communication, reaching out to employees and physicians alike. The question and answer sessions during every staff meeting were very important, although many of the questions initially had no answers.

Visibility

Early on, our leadership team discussed how each of us could increase our existing administrative presence out in the various hospital departments. We were determined to go beyond, "I will visit my units/departments more often." Since our senior leadership team already made regular administrative rounds, staff were used to seeing us out and about together, as well as separately. We agreed that each of us should be visiting across all departments in the hospital, in order to be available for employee questions and to provide information as it became available. In this way, we felt that employees would became even more comfortable with our presence and thus would be more likely to raise issues or concerns in person, or ask for clarification about whatever rumors were circulating.

Keeping focused

We were very proud of our patient care quality. Our core measures results were pretty good overall and those not quite where we wanted them to be were continuing to improve. We felt that professionalism should be the standard for all; it was essential that our leadership and staff maintain a calm, professional demeanor with a focus on compassionate and safe care. Patients often asked about the sale of the hospital and how it would affect them; this question arose frequently on our patient satisfaction survey questionnaires, as well. A basic tenet of crisis management is that a company must demonstrate that it cares and to verbalize and act in a manner that is reassuring even in times of uncertainty. We worked hard to have our staff feel comfortable with the impending sale, and to be able to reassure patients that the hospital was going to continue to be available to them for their healthcare needs.

Morale/team-building

Our hospital followed the communication plan that had been developed in conjunction with senior leadership of the system, and designated spokespersons provided updates to the news media as information became available. But, it was very difficult for our staff when articles were published in the newspaper that did not accurately reflect the current situation at the hospital. When quotes of individuals talking, or speculating, about the hospital sale were printed, it would occasionally send ripples of negative emotion through the ranks, touching off uncertainty and sometimes hostility at the thought that the "papers" might be providing more information about the sale than the hospital leadership team.

Efforts to maintain morale were scheduled and carried out, including such events as ice cream socials, casual Fridays, and special "celebrations" in the cafeteria for all shifts. Also, nursing leadership seemed to be fairly successful in convincing staff not to make rash decisions and to consider trying out the new owner before resigning. And the hospital system had a policy of reinstatement that allowed an employee to return to any hospital in the system within 12 months of leaving or being sold. In addition, we were repeatedly reminded, through actions and conversations, that friends, family and colleagues are very important in sustaining everyone through times of turmoil/transition. So, even though a few nurses decided to transfer to other hospital positions within the system during the first 8 months after the sale announcement, our total RN turnover was virtually unchanged from the year prior for the same period.

Buyer relationships

As the sale progressed toward buyer selection, the "finalist" bidders were provided with an opportunity to conduct their due diligence reviews. Financial and contractual documents were gathered, as well as numerous operations reports and documentation of processes. The buyer candidates were provided with a detailed overview of the hospital and then were given access to senior hospital leadership to explore more specific questions and interests. Hospital tours were provided to each of the three finalists after they were identified.

Once the selection of the buyer was made public, more specific planning and communication was initiated. Details about services to be maintained or possibly not continued were discussed. On-site office space was provided to the selected buyer. A number of meetings were held with individuals at the hospital to clarify benefits and pay practices, billing and business practices, organizational structure and reporting relationships. We designed serious plans for the smooth transition of the operations of every department from the existing owner to the new owner. For the front-line employees and our patients, our goal was to make the transition as seamless as was realistically possible.

Public hearing

In California, the review process includes at least one public meeting and, when necessary, preparation of expert reports. The sale of a non-profit hospital to a for-profit buyer requires the State Attorney General's approval, in order to ensure the continuation of existing levels of charity care, continued operation of emergency rooms and other actions necessary to avoid adverse effects on healthcare in the local community. I attended the public hearing on the sale, and although I thought I was prepared to hear anything at the meeting, it was still a bit disconcerting to listen to speaker after speaker offering negative comments, distorted "truths," and perceptions far different than what I believed to be accurate. On the other hand, it was nice to hear some speakers talk in a positive manner about the hospital and the anticipated buyer, as well as offer comments about good experiences that others had had with that buyer. A consultant's report recommending the conditions for the sale was also provided to the Attorney General, and was available on the Attorney General's web site for anyone to read.

Internal relations

As the nursing leader in the organization, I experienced the divisiveness that occurs when the buyer is opposed by community and by the medical staff. Those supporting the sale often have a much less strident and out-spoken approach than those opposing the sale. When individual physicians decided to "stir up" the employees, much good will and hospital leadership effort were diminished. Even talking one-on-one with some of these physicians did not always result in productive outcomes in terms of stopping the instigation of employee uncertainty and the initiation of false rumors.

So what was the result?

As I stated previously, I had been though the sale process before. During that experience, two public hearings were needed because there was not enough time for everyone to speak during the first session, which consisted largely of speakers opposing the sale. Despite this level of contentiousness, though, the sale was approved by the State Attorney General; it moved forward and was completed. The transition to the new owners even occurred in a more seamless manner for employees than I had anticipated. All senior leadership personnel were retained, except for the Chief Financial Officer and CEO.

But in this more recent case, the California Attorney General's office actually denied the sale of the hospital - about twelve months after sale announcement and less than three days before the expected decision date and three weeks from the scheduled transfer of ownership. According to a local newspaper article, this was the first time that anyone could remember a denial having ever been issued. Since a number of key hospital leaders had already given their 30-day notices (in light of the expected new owner's organizational restructuring), we faced the immediate challenge of lining up interim coverage for all of those positions to ensure continuity of the organization with a minimum of disruption.

The lessons we learned about the impending sale of a hospital:

- Frequent, on-going communication is essential.
- Lack of information gives rise to incredibly interesting rumors.
- Visibility of senior leadership is critical and contributes to the staff's ability to deal with uncertainty.
- Don't make assumptions or invest too heavily into a transition until it is a "done deal."
- Don't "badmouth" those staff who resign, those who decide to stay, the new buyer or the existing owner (It's a small world!).
- Never underestimate the importance of good leadership, or the value of having nursing leaders who continue to talk with staff and model expected professional behaviors.
- It takes a lot of behind-the-scenes planning during any organizational transition to ensure that it goes smoothly and to make it look easy.
- Personal perseverance and a positive attitude are essential to living through a sale!

Peggy Diller, RN
Chief Nursing Officer, Interim
Kaiser – Santa Clara

Peggy Diller is a nursing executive with over 30 years experience. Her background includes clinical bedside positions in Pediatrics and Critical Care; clinical educator positions; and nursing leadership positions covering all areas of nursing, as well as the departments of Pharmacy, Radiology, Food Services, Infection Control, Social Services, Utilization Management and Medical Staff Services.

Ms. Diller obtained her nursing education at Bryan Memorial Hospital School of Nursing in Lincoln, Nebraska. She holds a BS degree from Nebraska Wesleyan University and earned her MS degree from California State University in Los Angeles. She is a founding faculty member of the California Center for Nurse Leadership and teaches human resource management in this week-long leadership program.

In her role as Chief Nursing Officer, Ms. Diller has responsibility for the provision of patient care at the 327-bed Kaiser Santa Clara hospital. Hospital services include, but are not limited to, obstetrics and gynecology, emergency services, adult and neonatal intensive care, telemetry units, medical/surgical units, and inpatient and outpatient operative services. The new service covering comprehensive cardiovascular services, including open heart surgery, began on March 17, 2008.

Ms. Diller has been recognized for her community service as a Girl Scout Leader for the past 25 years; she received a national award in 2005 for outstanding service in her numerous Girl Scout roles and activities. Peggy has also been committed to outreach beyond the boundaries of California, participating in service missions to a hospital in Kenya, a church in New Zealand, and an orphanage in China. She was honored for this work with the Association of California Nurse Leaders' HUMANITARIAN AWARD in February 2008. As an active member of the American Organization of Nurse Executives, in October 2005, she participated in a nursing leadership delegation to hospitals and schools of nursing in Moscow, Novgorod, and St. Petersburg, Russia.

Peggy is active in the Nursing Leadership Councils (NLC) of Southern California, having served as President of the Los Angeles area NLC and as President of the NLC Board of Directors-Hospital Association of Southern California. She has worked with the Orange County Healthcare Collaborative of the Orange County Business Council. She also has been active on the Board of the Association of California Nurse Leaders (ACNL), as well as serving on a number of ACNL committees. Peggy was the 2006 President of ACNL.

CHAPTER 16

Diamond Mining: Adding Sparkle to the String

by Robin P. Newhouse, PhD, RN, CNAA, BC CNOR

Transitioning from the clinical setting to the world of academia was never a consideration for me. It was not one of my career goals and was far removed from my chosen professional track in clinical nursing. The decision was not one of an instant moment, but occurred after working with giving mentors over time and experiencing the joy and reward of teaching. There is an exceptional reward in watching students develop their thinking and expertise as new nurse leaders and realizing, personally, what an honor it is to be a part of that process. To tell the story, I need to go back to the beginning – the specific points of time, events, experiences and memories that formed the foundation for the "tipping point" of my transition to faculty. Back to when I discovered diamond mining.

Taking the scenic route in my educational preparation, my first health care job was as a nursing assistant at Anne Arundel General Hospital in the Emergency Department (ED). I enrolled in a local Associate Degree program at Anne Arundel Community College, returning to the ED as a Registered Nurse (RN). As my clinical expertise grew, along the novice to expert continuum, I added coronary care, intensive care, post anesthesia care and the operating room to my clinical experience. As I became involved in more organizational activities and "quality assurance," it became clear that I needed additional skills, knowledge and abilities available only through further education. I returned to University of Maryland Baltimore for an RN to BSN program. That is when I first heard about the concept of diamond mining.

The RN to BSN program required that I complete a practicum, so I asked my Director of Nursing, Nancy Sheets, if she would precept me. My objectives included helping the organization to develop a quality assurance program in the

Ambulatory Surgery Department. Throughout the semester, she mentored me. Then, one day, she said something that seemed odd at the time - she said that I was a "diamond in the rough." I never forgot that simple phrase; I stored it away as a source of personal affirmation and direction.

Graduation from the BSN program began a trajectory of growth in the clinical arena. After graduation, Nancy encouraged me to assume the role of Supervisor for Ambulatory Surgery. That first leadership position required a steep learning curve, providing my introduction to nursing administration. During that time, I published my first article with Nancy's help. The next challenge was to open a surgery center for the hospital and taking the position of Perioperative Supervisor. Once again, my skills and abilities were challenged and I found myself returning to school for a Masters Degree in General Administration at University of Maryland, University College.

Further clinical and organizational growth would require that I gain experience in other organizations. I accepted a position of Nurse Manager in Perioperative Services at Laurel Regional Hospital, progressing to Director of Nursing. Next, I moved to a Baltimore teaching hospital, Sinai Hospital of Baltimore as Director of Perioperative Services. Throughout my career, I have had the opportunity to deliver nursing care and provide leadership in the delivery of nursing services. I observed and worked with nurses who have such commitment, excellence and competency that I became more confident that nursing processes are directly and significantly related to the quality of care delivered. Understanding and measuring this relationship meant that I needed to return one more time to school - this time for a PhD.

I entered the PhD program at University of Maryland Baltimore under the mentorship of Mary Etta Mills (mentor, friend and colleague) while I maintained my clinical position. During my four years in doctoral study, I also completed the requirements for a second Masters Degree in Nursing. I developed a passion for the study of nursing structures, processes and related outcomes.

After completing my PhD in 2000, I was interested in clinical practice leadership, research and teaching, but still never saw myself on an academic faculty. I moved to Johns Hopkins Hospital as Nurse Researcher in Nursing Administration, with a joint appointment at Johns Hopkins University School of Nursing. I assisted nurses in the conduct of research, and built infrastructure for evidence-based practice. I began teaching undergraduate research through an adjunct position at University of Maryland Baltimore School of Nursing, outcomes measurement in the Business of Nursing Program, and graduate research at Johns Hopkins University School of Nursing. I continued to develop expertise in organizational research and evidence-based practice. The importance of translating evidence to practice became more and more apparent.

As my research activities increased, I realized that I needed to develop additional competencies in health services research. I submitted an application for a K award, to the Agency for Healthcare Research and Quality, to study the effect of legislative, market and hospital forces on rural hospital nursing. Once again, exceptional mentors (Drs. Laura Morlock and Peter Pronovost) gave their time and expertise to help me develop - making an everlasting impact.

Upon reflection, I realized that I sought nurses whom I could mentor into leadership positions in each of my clinical positions. The realities and priorities of the clinical arena often took priority over my ability to mentor. It was during the K award that I began to understand the importance of working with developing nurse leader students. As I worked with graduate students, watching the development of their thoughts, engagement in evidence-based practice and development of well-synthesized literature became an amazing reward. Building professional practice though the use of evidence became a personal mission.

As Doctor of Nursing Practice (DNP) programs began to develop, I watched closely. The DNP made perfect sense, and the essential competencies well designed to meet current clinical and organizational challenges. I came to the conclusion that involvement in the DNP program was a means to merge my interest in developing nurse leaders, improving clinical quality, translating evidence into practice, and health services research. Teaching in the DNP program was perfectly aligned with my practice and research focus. I knew that I wanted to dedicate the rest of my career to mentoring and developing nurse leaders who would be able to affect quality of care - measuring outcomes, evaluating programs and translating evidence into practice.

At the same time, a position became available at University of Maryland School of Nursing for an Assistant Dean, Doctor of Nursing Practice Studies. In addition to the DNP, the University of Maryland has a strong focus on health systems leadership and management, as well as a number of students with interest in health services research. Realizing that I could have a role in helping nurse leaders develop, who would have a profound effect on the organizational environment, I assumed a full-time faculty appointment.

I thought the decision to move into a faculty position would be difficult. Instead, it was a natural transition from mentoring one or two potential leaders in a clinical setting to mentoring many potential leaders in an academic setting. The work became building a curriculum to meet the competencies needed in the clinical setting, instead of creating operational systems to meet the needs of our patient population. Moving to a faculty position was a personal decision, strongly influenced by the culmination of the benefit and guidance I received from my own mentors throughout my career.

When I interact with the students, I see a diamond field, with many diamonds in the rough. The talent, innovative thinking, expertise, drive and commitment of the students are breathtaking and encouraging. Moving to academia provided me the opportunity to dedicate time to mentoring future leaders in nursing. The complexity of our systems and the demand for quality care require strong leadership. What a privilege it is to be involved in developing what the world needs - exceptional nurse leaders.

Robin P. Newhouse, PhD, RN, CNAA, BC

Robin P. Newhouse is Assistant Dean, Doctor of Nursing Practice Studies and Associate Professor. As an expert in building evidence-based practice infrastructure, she consulted and presented internationally and nationally and has published books and peer-reviewed journals articles on the topic of evidence-based practice. She conducts health services research focused on nursing processes and related outcomes, with funding awarded by agencies such as Agency for Healthcare Research and Quality (K08) and the Robert Wood Johnson Foundation.

Dr. Newhouse has a PhD in nursing, an MS in Nursing, and a Masters of General Administration (MGA) with a focus on health care. She is Board Certified in Nursing Administration-Advanced and the operating room.

CHAPTER 17

Add a Pearl Necklace: Four Pearls on a String

by Carolyn Hope Smeltzer, RN, Ed. D, FAAN, FACHE

As I reflect on my nursing professional pearls, there are four that are non-traditional and stand out from the rest of the string. First the pearl of authorship, next the pearl of mentorship, third the pearl of partnership and last the pearl of trusteeship. I should mention, however, that these four pearls would have never been added to the string if it were not for all the skills, personal relationships and leadership knowledge I gained from the nursing profession, as well as from those who mentored me along the way. Although each pearl is distinct, it became the foundation for the next pearl to be added.

I have to thank the leaders in my original diploma school of nursing for beginning the sting of pearls, especially Marjorie Beyers for always believing that nurses need to be educated individuals who contribute to health care in a meaningful way throughout their lives and in many different roles. The philosophy that our learning was just beginning, not complete, at our nursing pinning was the pearl to be taken away from my graduation ceremony. Long after that pearl began the string, Marjorie was there to watch and encourage the rest to be strung. She became a lifelong thinker with me on "out of the box" professional and personal challenges and growth strategies.

I watched her through the years taking very non-traditional roles both on boards, as one of our first nurse trustees, and in healthcare systems. Her silent role modelling led me to believe that a nurse could achieve whatever she/he wanted. This pearl was the beginning of a long string that led to my becoming an author, mentor, partner, and board member. I actually learned how to be a mentor and author by watching and emulating how she strung her pearls.

Pearl of Authorship

It is easy to repeat the behaviors of those you admire and adopt as role models. Most of my professional life, I was surrounded by educational professionals who believed in sharing knowledge through publishing, which became a way of life. For example, during my nursing diploma program, I learned skills and authorship knowledge from instructors who were published or publishing. In fact, I took a course in leadership where the textbook was a written draft, which was being prepared for publication. In addition, the nursing class/school itself was an experimental learning program of self-paced, self-directed learning modules, all written by our faculty. As students, we actually contributed to the development of the program via the evaluation forms we completed. Thus, I was introduced to the merits of nurse writing, and writing myself, very early in my career.

My first writing reward came during nursing school. Based on an essay of leadership that I wrote, I was selected to represent our school at the student nurse association in Miami, Florida. What a reward - being recognized as a leader and getting to take my first plane ride! Writing had been proven to have merit and was now associated with having fun and being rewarded.

As a very young faculty member, I was asked to develop a program on nursing care planning. As I laid out the work and tried to make care planning part of the fabric of every course, I developed a paper. The paper was published and I was selected to present my thoughts on care planning to a national convention of educators. Again, I was rewarded for sharing knowledge and for writing.

Years later, after receiving a master's degree, a friend, Paula Dumas Vrba, and I opened up a cancer dictation clinic. It was recognized as one of the first in the country. We evaluated the merits of screening and cancer detection, and then we tracked results in terms of the percentage of patients who were diagnosed with cancer. We also educated the patients regarding their behaviors related to the risks of cancer and followed up to evaluate whether they changed these behaviors following education. Both these topics became articles, which enabled others to use some of our models and outreach programs for cancer detection and prevention in the early seventies. Through these experiences, I learned that writing had an impact and could be helpful to other nurse leaders ... and thus helpful to patients.

During the 1980s, I taught a course to graduate students on how to publish. Each student had to send off one article for potential publication within the timeframe of a single semester. Prior to an article being submitted to a journal, the entire student class became an editorial board, making suggestions/revisions to each other's written work. Thus I began sharing the "how of writing with other nurses.

My writing always reflected the practice area upon which I was focused at the time. The writing topics have included: teaching methods, cancer screening programs, program development and outcomes in patient education, nursing education, discharge planning, quality assurance and cost reduction programs. In addition, I have written about leadership development, restructuring organizations, merger integration, and storytelling as a leadership tool to shape culture. Eventually, I wrote interactive columns on coaching, where the readers would write in with a question on leadership and I would provide coaching by writing a response in a monthly column (in two journals).

In addition to writing articles, I was a member of two editorial boards, Journal of Nursing Administration and the Journal of Nursing Quality Care. Publication also became a way to develop relationships. As a consultant, I often wrote with other staff (teaching them both the importance and methods of publishing) and with clients. Publishing with a co-author is a powerful way to think together; it also provides a better thought process during the writing procedure and binds a relationship together.

With over 200 articles in print, today I am more interested in letting others do the writing while helping them through the process. I remain on an editorial board and support sharing knowledge through writing. I have expanded the pearl of writing articles to that of books. The first book was an idea of, "how to shape the image of nurses to the general public while using the silent stories of nurses as an energy force to increase self-esteem." At a health spa, Rio Caliente, I overheard two nurses talking about, "not having their ideas listened to." I realized the silent stories, skill sets and the way nurses lead their lives were not being heard. That night at the health spa, a Fulbright scholar was teaching creative writing skills. It was that night that I started writing a book, Ordinary People, Extraordinary Lives: the Stories of Nurses. After returning from the spa, I was discussing this concept of a "storytelling coffee table book" with a nursing assistant professor from Loyola University Chicago, Marcella Niehoff School of Nursing, Fran Vlasses. Without ever meeting, we agreed to write the book together and thus a new friendship was formed and a new soul mate was found.

We wrote the book by collecting stories and pictures of how nurses lead their lives to make a difference. The book signing alone was attended by over 700 individuals celebrating the lives of nurses. The book was the best seller of the publisher, Sigma Theta Tau International Society, for three years in a row; it also won -Honorable Mention Media Award from the American Academy of Nursing, and 'Best of Best Books' from Sigma Theta Tau. Our real rewards were: being able to highlight the work of nurses, release the silent stories of nurses, create a storytelling culture in healthcare, teach storytelling methods as a leadership tool, and learn about more stories.

One of those other stories we heard was about the history of a decade of nurse parades (from 1948 to 1959) that had been lost to nursing and to Chicago. This story/history became our second book, Chicago's Nurse Parade, published by Arcadia Publishing. The book recreated the forgotten history of a nurses' parade where merchants, churches, city government and healthcare came together to highlight the work of nurses during a time of a nurse shortage. This book won several awards also, two being the Media Award from the American Academy of Nursing and the St. Peregrine National Award, Our Lady of Sorrows Baasilica.

In addition, this book taught me the power of history, storytelling and photography as a way of learning and served as the impetus for my third book, Lake Geneva in Vintage Postcards. The knowledge of publishing that I gained from writing books about nursing was transferred to the place where I write most, Lake Geneva/Williams Bay Wisconsin..

I have used publishing to share my nursing knowledge in order to improve patient care, build relationships and/or improve leadership. Currently, I focus on teaching nurses how to write and share their nursing lives through storytelling. The sharing of nurse stories has created a media program that demonstrates the value of nurses to the public, while increasing the self-esteem of nurses in the healthcare setting. Ultimately, publishing helped me clarify thoughts/projects. Sharing authorship with others gave me new deep relationships. Writing also allowed me to explore other interests outside of nursing and to share history while transferring the writing skills I had learned from nursing to other fields.

Pearl of Mentorship

I learned the pearl of mentorship from those who mentored me. This is a pearl that can only be kept on the sting if it is reshaped and rearranged throughout the years. Since relationships are not stagnant, this pearl cannot remain the same. Many times, one who has been a mentor becomes the mentoree during the growth of a relationship. This pearl needs to be fostered and monitored, just like relationships, since it is always dependant upon the other individual as well as the wearer of the pearl. This pearl stands out for me with one illustration. The year was 1994; the month, January; the place Edmonton, Canada. My role: a healthcare project manager for a healthcare consulting engagement with an entrepreneur firm. The first morning of the project, I was introduced to Ruth Williams Brinkley. She came from the South. She had been a very successful Vice President of Nursing in a University Hospital. Her first morning of consulting was in the dead of a Canadian winter. Ruth was wearing tiny, ankle-high fashion boots, a lightweight suit, and a fall coat; she had slept the night before in a twin bed. She also had vouchers for cabs from T.J., so she would not take "joy rides" in the wilderness of Canada. My first impression was, "Why is Ruth working as a nurse consultant when she could be a model?"

Ruth's face showed her disappointment in the consulting world she had just elected to join, and I remember thinking that I could help her. She was amazed by this consulting world, without any of the comforts of home and without the leadership autonomy to which she had been accustomed. In short, Ruth was shocked at the "life of a consultant." As she talked about her family, home and her last very senior role, it seemed to me that she was questioning whether or not she had made a good choice in transitioning to consulting. Her eyes were even more telling. Her dark eyes did not smile behind her modest laugh. I would learn within a year that Ruth is a lady who loves life, smiles constantly, has sparkling eyes and an infectious laugh.

When I realized Ruth's self-doubt about her feelings on changing jobs, I started to build a relationship with her. I remembered my first days/years as a consultant and did not want her to "give up" a potentially great opportunity without giving consulting a fair chance. This pearl began with empathy, listening, trust and guidance. My goal was to make Ruth's consulting orientation and transition easier than mine had been, so that she could make an informed choice about being a consultant and not just react to the different lifestyle of a consultant. I decided to share with her the consulting skills that I had learned, offer encouragement/strategies on how to advance in the firm, and offer support/tips regarding how to make consulting fit in with a normal lifestyle.

I indicated to Ruth that this was the beginning of many opportunities for her to have leadership roles in the future. I listened to Ruth answer her portable phone and, many times, it appeared that there was a search firm on the other end discussing job opportunities. I continued to be a sounding board for her as she discussed other career opportunities, including returning to her previous role. I gave her feedback on her work accomplishments, taught her the skills of consulting/client relationships and provided her with sponsorship for promotion.

After our initial engagement in Edmonton, Ruth and I found ourselves in a classic consulting opportunity. The client was ready to buy the work and wanted to make the purchase from a woman partner. This time, I needed Ruth's support and presence. The mentorship not only paid off for her (she liked consulting) but helped me sell a large project. Ruth had an opportunity to lead a team to deliver excellent client work on operational effectiveness. She also learned how to leverage a team. Together, Ruth and I built lifelong relationships with the CEO, the project director and other client senior leadership.

I had promised Ruth the manager role on this engagement; however, the client had different ideas. Although they wanted a female partner, it was a surprise to find out they wanted a male manager, who happened to be Canadian. I eventually agreed; however, I remembered my promise to Ruth. I had to have an honest discussion with her, telling her that I felt she would eventually become the manager of this project. I asked her to trust me and to give me time. I asked her to demonstrate her skills and commitment to the client and to build a solid client relationship. The trust that had developed during our initial mentorship role became the foundation for working through this tough client issue.

The project was not leveraged by our consultants. We were using more of their staff to do the work, which made it a very time-intensive project, since both the client and our consultants were learning new skills. Within a month of the project, the client called me with an urgent request for Ruth to become the manager. She had developed a relationship with the client and was producing the work product for which they were looking.

The project went well, actually better than the firm and client expected. Ruth's relationship with the client was better than most. Eventually, we sold a large piece of add-on work to the client, contingent upon Ruth being the manager. After the project was sold, Ruth informed me she did not want to continue on with this client. I learned that Ruth wanted to reprioritize her life and focus on her teenage daughter, which required her to be on a consulting project closer to home. At first I was upset; I was actually devastated. I lost energy and thought that Ruth owed me more since I had given her opportunities in the firm that no one else would have afforded her.

I then realized that, in order to keep our relationship on my string of pearls, I had to restring the pearl. In restringing the pearl, I maintained my connection to Ruth, and our relationship evolved. Today, she is my mentor, friend and supporter. Ruth is a CEO of regional hospitals and I now reach out to her to verify my actions on boards. She coaches me on what a CEO needs from board members. She has coached me on my personal relationships in life ,on job transition and on retirement planning. In turn, Ruth often credits her interest in writing to me and continually uses the consulting skills she learned during our time together in all roles she holds.

This pearl is an example of all the pearls of mentorship: a mentor can remain friends with her mentee, be mentored or become a mentee, change roles in being coach/coached and always champion of the other's work and life. This pearl is a pearl of life, a pearl of support, a pearl of relationships that continue to have impact throughout one's life.

Pearl of Partnership

The pearl of consulting turned partnership took some polishing in order to be strung. The skills of consulting reminded me a lot of the skills I had gained and utilized in previous roles. Teaching, providing leadership/mentorship, research/analysis, writing and selling ideas were not new. I was actually surprised at how these skills transformed into the project management and business skills, staffing skills and budgeting skills that contributed to a successful consulting project. I wasn't surprised, though, by how naturally the relationship and respect skills I gained throughout my nursing career transferred over to partnership. I have often thought that walking into a stranger's room (a patient) and developing a helping relationship based on trust and competency during a difficult time (even a life and death situation), is a remarkable skill that most human beings never experience. So the relationship-building skills necessary to partnership were second nature to me, because of my work in nursing.

The polishing of this pearl was not focused on how to be a good consultant but rather on how to become a good partner. Figuring out how to use relationships to accomplish a recognized leadership role of partnership in a firm was a challenge. Frankly, I did not even recognize nor value the importance of this aspect of becoming partner at first. In addition, I had no one to describe how to travel the road to partnership. In a sense, I felt like I was going up a fence and did not know how high it was. In fact, it seemed to me that the fence was growing taller, or the bar was being raised higher as time went on. In all honesty, while I did not understand the road to partnership, the firm little understood the value of nurse leadership in becoming a partner.

Our Entrepreneur Health Care Consulting firm was started by partners who wanted to make a difference in healthcare while also making a profit. It was a very self-promoting culture. In the early 1990s, this firm did not have any infrastructure for hiring, orientation, mentoring, coaching, staffing or assignment allocation. In addition, there were no processes in place for promotion or evaluation. The majority of partners, if not all, had Harvard MBA degrees, were men and were Jewish. The firm was very successful and really had no reason to change their practices regarding partnership at that time. The firm had no diversity or any appreciation for it. There were definitely no nurse partners. In retrospect, I saw none of this; I saw only the work that needed to be done and rewarded on the road to partnership.

I knew the work and what I perceived as the accomplishments that were necessary to become partner. The revenue goals that had to be met in terms of selling and managing the work, as well as the new product development that had to be accomplished in order to be recognized and thought of in terms of potential leadership. Of course, a large aspect of the goals was how I could participate in growing the practice/firm. What I failed to recognize was the building up of support required in order to be marked for one of the available promotion slots, the posturing this required and how I needed a champion for all I had accomplished. I foolishly thought my work and sales revenue would stand on their own merits on the road to partnership. But when I did not get partnership during the first "go round," I became disorientated, yet even more determined to add this pearl to the string.

I had the list of accomplishments that were needed for partnership. It was transparent information, so I also had the histories of the managers who had made partner. I called the new partners and congratulated them on their promotions. I also called my partner sponsor and told him there must be some mistake and asked him to go back to the partnership to readdress their decision of not making me partner. It was clear that the work I had done met the targets in terms of client sales, deep client relationships that became firm references, marketing efforts, client work/satisfaction, developing staff and new products like implementation of cost reduction. Doing quality work and reaching the goals as I and others understood them for partnership gave me confidence to have the firm revisit and re-evaluate their position on me being admitted to the partnership.

Although the partner did not take my case back to the meeting, I was guaranteed a partnership within three months prior to the end of the year. In the meantime, they offered me all the partner perks, i.e. administrative assistant, phone, and office (to mention a few). While I waited for partnership, other firms began seeking me out with promises of partnership. It seems that the search firms knew who was in line for promotion to partner at various firms.

Just as my firm had made a commitment to me for becoming a partner in three months, I made a commitment to myself to explore other partnership options without leaving my current firm until the three months had played out. I decided to take control of my own career if need be and not rely on the promises of others. As it turned out, I added this pearl to my string at my original firm within the three-month timeframe; years later this pearl shifted, as I became partner in a big four accounting firm, PricewaterhouseCoopers.

I will always remember the very big celebration planned when I became a partner in my firm. The celebration was with all my nurse colleagues who were now hopeful that they, too, had the opportunity to become partners. Being the first nurse in my group to transition to partnership was not easy, but I was committed to having the process be more visible and less confusing to other nurses who wanted to make this milestone or add this pearl to their own strings. Very few nurses were partners in consulting firms in the early nineties, but now this option seemed very real from a career perspective.

I now look at becoming a partner as very similar as to achieving academic tenure, in terms of the actual work that needs to be accomplished, the processes used to evaluate the promotion and the politics that enter into both situations. In addition, I have found that being a partner in a consulting/accounting firm utilizes all the skills I learned in my doctorate programs: analysis of data is like research - developing the "so what" of the data is like developing the strategies to implement the solutions recommended to the client.

Selling/marketing is similar to teaching and negotiation. Writing a marketing proposal uses the same skills as writing a consulting proposal, in terms of understanding the needs, redefining the problems and stating the proposed solutions, budgeting both the time and dollar amount required to develop the solutions and creating an effective team that can be leveraged. Writing proposals can also be looked upon as using some of the same skills as writing an article for publication. Timelines and project management are also skills learned in a nursing administration or doctorate program.

The work of consulting or being a partner is not foreign to nurses; however, the process used to achieve the recognition and be promoted to partner might be foreign and, therefore, does require a champion and mentor. Even after one has become a partner, the pearl needs to be polished, as one's role intensifies and the bar is raised for marketing, selling and delivering on the client work. In addition product development, thought leadership and staff development are aspects of the partnership role.

The partnership pearl involves perpetual learning, and developing new skills based on the foundation of all the prior pearls. Partnership allows one to be an entrepreneur while participating in team structure and a learning culture. Due to various mergers, my own partnership pearl has been rearranged within two jobs at four different firms.

Pearl of Boardship

All of my previous pearls prepared me for the next phase of utilizing my skills in a strategic meaningful way ... becoming a trustee on healthcare boards. It was time to give back, on a volunteer basis, to healthcare for all that it had given me, in terms of leadership opportunities, career, relationships and friendships. This is another pearl that could not be strung alone. It required support and networking.

A nurse mentor came to the forefront and positioned me for a board seat and, at the same time, another nurse leader I had been mentoring recommended me for a different board seat. Both positions were on system boards, one local and one national. While serving as a vice-president, I had given many presentations and reports to various boards; this helped me understand the roles of boards. In my capacity as a partner, I had been allowed into boardrooms on a regular basis. These experiences, combined with my facilitation of board decision-making and my reading/teaching on how to be an effective board member, all prepared me for having a board presence.

I recognized that my pearl of nursing got me on the boards; however, once on the board, I was representing quality patient care rather than representing the nursing profession. I learned and came to respect the power, politics, and persuasion of nurse leaders as trustees. I share Don Berwick's belief that the performance of a healthcare organization is dependent upon the well being, engagement and capabilities of nurses as well as physicians (Boardroom Press, April, 2005). Nurses have powerful impact on and can make great contributions to the work of healthcare boards and thus to the work of patient care.

Landmark quality studies have summarized the need to have nurses on boards to ensure and improve the quality of and develop new models of care. Generative thinking of boards is a new framework utilized in the boardroom for strategic thinking. Nurses contribute greatly to the deep dives on strategies because they are knowledgeable about healthcare operations. Nurse leaders demonstrate strategies and thus gain board respect, which allows them (and me) to have persuasion and influence, thus helping to develop healthcare effectiveness. Board best practice knowledge, along with knowledge of the field and wisdom of leadership, all contribute to preparing oneself for the political and practical work on a board.

More healthcare institutions are focusing on quality/safety in their organizations and in their boardrooms. It has been cited that trustees should spend 25% of board time focused on the quality/safety of patients. A recent study (Health Research and Education Trust National Study, 2005) stated that 11 of the 14 hospitals studied had established board committees for monitoring patient care quality/safety. Those 11 quality committees all had physicians as voting members, but only 7 had nurses. The same study indicated that physicians comprise 25% of healthcare board seats while nurses comprise less than 2%. Since nurses can bring so much knowledge to the table regarding patient care, it stands to reason that boards lack power by not having nurses as voting members.

The exploration of consumer demands for healthcare reform, along with the need for different practices/models and hospitals wanting to have Magnet status, all support the visibility of nurse leaders in the boardroom. Larry Prybil's work, as reported in, "Nursing Involvement on Boards" (Journal of Nursing Quality Care, 2007), highlights the past barriers in positioning nurses to become voting board members. I have learned that a nurse trustee, like any board member, needs to be political and persuasive in order to influence the care of patients when shaping strategies of the board. Success in these roles requires the nurse to be packaged for a board "fit" and to function in an expanded executive role that is different from many of the operational roles s/he has demonstrated during the course of a successful career.

I am now in one of my most important roles – one that allows me to bring my values of advocating for patients strategically into the boardroom. I am currently on the system board of Advocate Healthcare in Illinois and the system healthcare board of Sisters of Charity of Leavenworth, Kansas. In addition, I serve on the audit committee of Loyola University Chicago (which has both a medical and nursing school housed in the medical center) and the finance committee of a Catholic Health Initiative Hospital, Memorial Health System.

Once on a board, the work or goal does not end, it just begins. Leadership in the boardroom has to be significant. Other board members have to see your contributions as useful to reaching/impacting the mission of the institution and the quality of care. Skills of negotiation, politics, networking and knowledge all need to be evident in order to be seen as a leader on a board. The board seat is just the start of being even more influential, in the way of becoming chair of committees, where much of the board work occurs. I have been chair of the Strategy and Quality Committee of Sisters of Charity Leavenworth, as well as on the executive committee. At Advocate Healthcare, I chair the Quality Committee and also am on the executive committee. To advance to this leadership role on the board of Advocate took approximately four years. So once on the board, the work just begins - leading to other leadership opportunities.

Re-framing the work of nonprofit healthcare boards is just the beginning task for this pearl. A larger role is to ensure a succession plan for other nurses to serve on boards, so they can also have a positive impact on the lives of patients. In my role as a financial steward, a strategist and a sense maker in generative thinking, I feel I am back to the very reason I entered nursing -- to help patients receive quality care. This pearl allows me to make a meaningful contribution to the organizational mission, to patients and to nurses and staff. My past roles created the skills needed to be effective in the boardroom: networking, relationship building, presentation style, and nursing and leadership core competencies, along with specific knowledge of how boards work. This pearl will be shared with others so they, too, can string this pearl on their necklaces.

Summary

My string of pearls is greater as a whole rather than any single pearl having the most significance. The pearl of authorship, the pearl of mentorship, the pearl of partnership and the pearl of trusteeship are all interdependent. These four non-traditional pearls make the complete strand of pearls very special. Each pearl has certainly lead to another pearl being added to the sting. It is very clear, however, that the most shining pearl is the original nursing pearl that became the foundation and strength of the rest of the pearls to be added to the string.

Carolyn Hope Smeltzer, RN, EdD, FACHE, FAAN

Carolyn Hope Smeltzer is a Partner in the Health Industry Advisory of PricewaterhouseCoopers. She has over 35 years of senior executive and nearly 20 years of consulting experience in the health care field. She has worked on a variety of engagements, including cost reduction, mergers, clinical integration, financial feasibility, recruitment and retention strategies, management training, patient satisfaction studies, quality assurance improvements and change implementation. The results of her consulting engagements range from 12 to 30 percent reductions in operating budgets ($10 to $40 million in savings) while improving quality and service standard as well as employee job enrichment. In addition, she has led post-merger engagements. Currently, she is the lead for the new "on boarding process for new hires" for the fastest growing sector of PwC.

Dr. Smeltzer is a national speaker and has published numerous articles on mergers, cost-effectiveness and the implementation of change. She currently is focused on leadership and customer service challenges and solutions. She has authored two published columns on executive coaching. Most recently, she co-authored the books, Ordinary People, Extraordinary Lives, The Stories of Nurses (nursing's only coffee table book, illustrating in words and pictures the lives of over 100 diverse nurses from around the world), Chicago's Nurse Parade and Lake Geneva in Vintage Postcards. Both nursing books received international awards from the American Academy of Nursing. Carolyn is an expert on the concept of story-telling as a tool for leadership to shape culture.

Prior to joining PricewaterhouseCoopers, Dr. Smeltzer was a Principal APM health care management consulting firm. Previously, she held executive vice president positions at the University of Chicago Hospitals, University Medical Center (University of Arizona), and Loyola University Medical Center (Chicago). She is on the following boards: Loyola University Chicago Board of Regents and Audit Committee, Poor Handmaids of Jesus Christ Linden

House for the Elderly, Chicago, Advocate Healthcare System, Oak Brook , Sister of Charity Leavenworth Health System, Kansas and CHI Memorial Hospital, Tennessee. She is focused on governance best practice and mentoring nurses to be on boards. Carolyn enjoys golfing, traveling on international immersions, swimming, teaching, reading and writing.

CHAPTER 18

Same Pearls, Different Look

by Patricia G. Turpin, PhD, RN, CNAA-BC

As the oldest of five children, I grew up in the role of a leader, as well as a mentor. My siblings ranged from 2 - 11 years younger than me, so I experienced "generational" issues before those particular problems had ever been identified as a concern for leaders. Nursing became a passion for me when I was very young, perhaps beginning with my first toy "nurse's bag" from which I dispensed sugar pills and Band-Aids, and offered care. I remember reading a Cherry Ames novel, either the one about the Visiting Nurse or the Private Duty Nurse, and thinking, someday, I want to be just like her and wear a wonderful nurse's cape!

I maintained the desire to become a nurse through junior and senior high school and was a member of the Future Nurses Club (I was the only member of that club who actually became a nurse). As I was graduating from high school, where college was the next expected step, my decision to go to a baccalaureate nursing program was simple: I wanted to be a nurse, and I wanted and was "expected" to go to college. The ANA White Paper on Entry into Practice (1964) was published about the time I entered college; it confirmed that I had made the right choice.

Early in my student career, there were many dialogues between the nearby diploma school nurses and those of us at the university. Many of those discussions were disheartening because we thought they were getting so much more clinical, hands-on experience than we were. When we brought our instructors into this dialogue, it was reinforced that we were being educated to become nursing leaders. So, nursing leadership was the foundation of my being a nurse.

Between my freshman and sophomore years, I got my first "real" job in a hospital as a nurse's aide. That experience opened my eyes to what would be expected of me after I finished school. It also re-confirmed that I had made an excellent choice to become a nurse: the work of a nurse's aide was repetitive, hard work. In fact, I probably learned many things that I had to 'unlearn' when I moved into my first clinical experience in school during the sophomore year.

When I finished my sophomore year, I went to stay with my grandmother in Louisiana for the summer and was able to get a job in a family-owned nursing home as a student nurse. In those days, a student nurse was allowed to pass medications to 80+ residents (many times I had to wait for the resident to spit out snuff in a coffee can before she could swallow medications), give enemas (oh joy), remove fecal impactions (oh joy, again), catheterize, and make assessments (skin assessments were made daily as we bathed residents unable to care for themselves). It was here that I managed my first patient having a cardiac arrest. I was expected to chart on more than one or two patients (which was the standard for us in school), and so much more! I acted as the "charge nurse" on the night shift: I had one or sometimes two aides taking my direction regarding the care to be given to the residents on my shift.

In my junior year at the university, we began our upper division, clinical rotations at the medical branch campus in south Texas. I had another opportunity to 'unlearn' some of the techniques I had "improvised" during my summer in the long-term care setting. After we completed our first clinical rotation in the program (mine was in the operating room), we were allowed to apply for a part-time position in the hospital. Although my parents sponsored me throughout my college program, "running around money" was my responsibility, so I jumped at the opportunity to have a job. As a student nurse, I was assigned responsibility as both scrub and circulating nurse for a variety of operating room suites; my favorite became plastic surgery. However, when I worked on the weekends, I was "in charge" and scheduled rooms for emergency procedures. We were staffed to open two rooms at a time on weekends and one during the night shift, so it was important for me to be able to prioritize cases, and sometimes negotiate with physicians, in order to have a smooth flow of patient care when I was in charge.

During the two years our class was at the medical branch, there was a movement to separate the nursing school from the medical school. There were many cancelled classes, due to faculty being in meetings during this climate of "uproar." There was also a movement among the RN to BSN students to eliminate some of the seemingly redundant parts of their baccalaureate education. For instance, even with 10+ years of clinical experience, the RN to BSN students were required to "learn" how to take a blood pressure along with us neophytes. I got involved in that political movement (my roommate at the time was an RN with many years of clinical experience; she was probably my first mentor). I spent the day before my final examination for Medical-Surgical Nursing meeting with a group of concerned students to write a petition to change the education process.

Since I was so busy being a political activist, I neglected to study for my final examination and failed it miserably. My burgeoning career almost came to a screeching halt at the end of my final semester as a senior! Thankfully, there was one other student in my class who failed the same examination and the faculty took pity on us (they knew we had been involved in the petition-writing episode) and allowed us to take a make-up exam, which we both passed. So I got to participate in graduation and I was on my way. I was not one of the school's "shining stars" during my undergraduate years, maintaining a strong "B" average; however, I was a "plodder."

Faculty strongly encouraged members of our class to sign up to enter graduate school immediately. Only one of my classmates elected to do that; the rest of us just wanted to get out of school and practice nursing. From my perspective, I decided that I had already obtained my "terminal degree" in nursing.

We were allowed to practice as student nurses while we waited for our Board of Nurse Examination scores, so I continued my career in the operating room, fully confident that I would remain an OR nurse for the rest of my career. What a shock it was when I received my Board scores and learned that I had failed the Medical portion of the exam! I was completely devastated! My score was so low that I was convinced that I must have mismarked the scantron; however, I had no opportunity to challenge those results. So, I retook the exam as soon as possible (without any preparatory classes) and waited for the results, which were to be reported in December.

In the meantime, I had fallen in love with the man who was to become my husband (we have now been married for 38 years) and had made the decision to move back to central Texas. I was still able to apply for a job as a student nurse, pending the Board results, so I applied for a job on the Medical unit of a community hospital. I will never forget going to that interview: the Director of Nurses was a formidable woman (ex-military, with "orthopedic shoes" and a crisp white cap and uniform). She sat with the Director of the ICU-CCU and told me that they had a position for me on the 3-11 shift in ICU-CCU. I told them that I was certain that I really wanted to work on the medical floor, since I had failed that portion of my examination and obviously needed that experience, but I was hired for ICU-CCU.

I believe it was God's will that I become a nurse. I passed the second Board examination (with room to spare) and was licensed as a full-fledged RN! And, my first real job as a professional nurse was in the critical care unit! The skills that I learned during those first months in ICU-CCU were phenomenal! During my education at the medical branch, there had been plenty of interns and residents to handle things, so there had been many tasks that student nurses (or RNs, for that matter) were not allowed to do. For example, we had been taught that there would "never be a reason" for an RN to start an intravenous line (IV) or monitor IV medications, such as Pitocin. My first day in the ICU-CCU, however, I was taught how to start an Inter-cath (a 3- to 4-inch catheter that was threaded through a large-bore needle) for a "routine" IV. I was expected to administer IV drugs, including antibiotics, hypotensive agents (Levophed was the drug of choice then), antiarrhythmics and more. One of my first patients was receiving peritoneal dialysis, which I was expected to administer and monitor. Talk about a culture shock!!

As I became proficient in clinical skills, my leadership skills were identified and I was named Charge Nurse within the first six months of beginning my new job. When the Head Nurse position became available, I had developed sufficient skills and rapport with staff, physicians, and families and was asked to accept that role. As Head Nurse, I managed assignments, identified staff opportunities for continuing education, and provided direct patient care. Within another year, which was my third year of experience as RN, I was promoted to Supervisor of ICU-CCU. My role expanded to be relief House Supervisor, rotating to all shifts. The ICU-CCU Supervisor position was also expanded to be responsible for a cardiac step-down unit and later a surgical step-down unit. As House Supervisor, I found myself supporting patient care in Labor and Delivery and the Nursery, an area about which I knew VERY little, since that was my rotation during the semester of cancelled classes – my mantra there was "I don't know nothing about birthing babies." In this position, I was viewed by the staff as someone who could manage a crisis and would be willing to help out in a crunch (I even bathed some of the infants in the Nursery on occasion).

During those years, the American Association of Critical Care Nurses was established and I was an early member of that organization, participating as a Board member for the local chapter. In addition, I was named to the local Board of the American Heart Association and began teaching CPR to community groups across central Texas. The program for Advanced Cardiac Life Support (ACLS) was introduced and I was one of the first in our community to become certified. I was a trainer in the 'train-the-trainer' process implemented to increase the number of critical care nurses certified in ACLS. I was also elected to the district board of the Texas Nurses' Association.

The regular evening supervisor at our hospital was a tremendous role model for me. I don't think there was anything that she couldn't do. In her 50s, she made the decision to return to school to attain her MSN. I was in awe of her courage and tenacity. I was certain that I didn't want to return to school; however, she encouraged me with the "carrot" of predicting that nursing management positions would very soon be offered only to nurses with master's degrees. Since I knew that I always wanted to stay in the manager role in ICU-CCU, I made the decision to apply to Graduate School.

I know that many people are reluctant to apply to graduate school because they are intimidated by the thought of taking the dreaded Graduate Record Examination (GRE). Because our faculty at the university had anticipated that fear, part of our undergraduate curriculum had been to take the GRE in our final semester as seniors. This was a requirement, despite our protesting that we "never" intended to go to graduate school! Oh, we were so sure of ourselves. We had no preparatory courses for the GRE like those that are offered today: we had some overview of the kinds of questions that would be on the exam, but no coaching. I had taken that examination and somehow attained the minimum scores necessary to be accepted into graduate school. That was quite interesting, since I just about failed out of the whole program that same semester by becoming a political activist, rather than a dedicated student. Luckily, I applied to the graduate program within the five-year window necessary to avoid re-taking the GRE and was accepted.

I attended classes for about three months in the fall semester. I was convinced that there was "absolutely nothing" that "they" could teach me that I didn't already know. After all, I was practicing in a life and death situation in critical care every day. The first course in the curriculum was a theory course, during which many abstract concepts were presented. I was totally frustrated: in ICU, you "plugged it in, turned it on, and it worked." Who cared about the theory as to why that happened? I dropped out at the earliest opportunity, salvaging the majority of my tuition fees. It took another three years before I realized that a master's degree was absolutely necessary for me. So, I re-enrolled, continued to work full time, and completed my master's within two years. Ten years after receiving my undergraduate degree, I had my Master's and a 4.0 grade point average – a far cry from my lackluster undergraduate academic career. I was inducted to the Sigma Theta Tau and Phi Kappa Phi Honor Societies. I was a successful scholar! Once again, we students were encouraged to continue our education and obtain our Ph.D. degrees. I reassured the faculty that I would "never" desire to have a Ph.D., and simply continued my practice in the critical care area.

One day, one of my former faculty members from the MSN program called me to let me know of an opportunity to apply for an Assistant Director of Nursing (ADN) for Critical Care position at the faith-based hospital across town, where an applicant with a Master's Degree was preferred. What a fantastic opportunity! Although I had spent nine years at the community hospital and had become something of a "fixture" there, I made the tearful decision to move

241

across town to work with the Daughters. Although I was seen as a superior clinician where I currently worked, no one knew me in my new setting and, initially, I had to prove myself all over again every day.

My unit responsibilities included the ICU-CCU, the Step-down Cardiac Care Unit, and the Outpatient Department (the Emergency Room). In the beginning, I had three head nurses who reported to me, and we worked together with the evening and night supervisors for coordination of care. The head nurses met with me, individually and as a group, to inform me that they did not believe that they needed any supervision. So I needed to build a foundation of trust, too. After a few experiences where I actively supported decisions that they had made, and intervened on their behalf with administration and physicians, we soon had a very strong, collegial relationship.

A short while later, the ADN position was upgraded to the Director level and my clinical areas of responsibility expanded to include three additional medical units. One of those subsequently became a specialty cancer therapy unit, the second became another step-down cardiac care unit, and the third remained a general medical unit. Under this new structure, the evening and night supervisors became ADNs and were assigned to specialty areas. My leadership role now included two ADNs, five head nurses and well over 200 staff.

I continued house supervisor responsibility on weekends and holidays, as well as full budgetary responsibilities (staffing, capital, operating, and construction) for six units. My critical care clinical skills continued to be enhanced as new surgeons and internal medicine physicians established practices in town and presented us with new technology and systems. I was challenged on a daily basis to assess, plan, implement and evaluate systems. Human resource (HR) issues were ever present. At one point, we successfully thwarted the Communication Workers of America from unionizing our registered nurse staff.

In those years, nursing staff all worked 8-hour shifts, and all staff rotated through all three shifts. A few articles were published that suggested the benefits of converting to 12-hour shifts and limiting rotating shifts, particularly in the ICU-CCU. A task force of our staff made a formal presentation, which I took to HR, and we successfully initiated the first 12-hour shifts at our hospital. We were thus able to reduce the number of staff who rotated shifts to those who remained on the regular 8-hour shifts. At that time, since our Wage and Salary designation was 8/80, those who chose to move to 12-hour shifts had to schedule one 8-hour shift during a two-week schedule in order to be considered full-time. We had no electronic scheduling system, so scheduling both 8-hour and 12-hour shifts to cover this 20-bed critical care unit was quite a challenge for the unit manager! It was also demanding for me, as the director, to support staffing that was so different from every other unit in the facility.

I worked in this exciting, challenging and stimulating position for five years. Once again, I was convinced that this would be "home" to me for the duration of my nursing career; I was age 35. Then, about two weeks after we had successfully received full accreditation from the Joint Commission and finished the annual budget process, our Vice President made an announcement one Tuesday at a regularly scheduled, early morning meeting. She informed us that three clinical Director positions and the Director of Education position had been eliminated from the budget and that those employees had one month to decide what they were going to do. We were strongly encouraged to leave the facility and take the paid month to find new positions. Suddenly, I was out of a job!!

Prior to that morning, the demands of my position were such that I believed the building would surely crumble and fall if I was not there at 6:00 a.m. every day. What a shock it was to drive by the hospital days and weeks after being told that I was no longer needed and see that the building was still standing!

This was what later became termed an "RIF" (reduction in force). It was the first one within our system, but certainly not the last. This first time, there were no such things as 'outplacement services' or counseling of any kind. During later "reductions," displaced employees were given career counseling and assistance with writing resumes, and coached in the interview process.

Without any of those support systems, I just cleaned out my office and went home, thoroughly wounded to the core.

My father had died five months earlier, so I decided to spend some quality time with my mother. My husband's business required him to travel away from home a great deal and I had no children at home, so this was an ideal time to explore life outside of nursing. I traveled with Mom to Florida and Colorado, visiting relatives and helping her to decide what she wanted to do with her life now that Dad was gone. I had decided that I was going to stay at home and take a "vacation" from nursing.

In mid-summer, I became aware of a position at a large long-term care facility very near my home. Hadn't I begun my early nursing career taking care of elderly patients in that family-owned nursing home in Louisiana? Maybe this was a calling that I should return to those roots. I made an appointment for an interview for the Director of Nursing position, confident that this was where I needed to be. When I entered the facility, I was almost knocked over by the stench! I was horrified!! I walked the length of the facility; the further down the hallway I walked, the less foul odor was present. When I arrived at the Administrator's office, I was almost ready to bolt and run. The Regional Nursing Supervisor for the company was present for my interview; she turned out to be the wife of one of the nurses who had worked with me in the ICU-CCU. She was very reassuring. She told me that her husband had told her about me, stressing what an asset I would be for the long-term care company. Networking was definitely a factor here. She convinced me that I could make a significant difference in the operation of this place. I decided to give it a try: after all, I loved working with older people and there were many advantages to my working so close to home.

I had another new look!

I did make a difference in that facility, by establishing a working relationship with the surveyors from the state health department, who were regular visitors. I also created a climate where good resident care was valued. Two of the three units within the facility had positive ratings from the Health Department; however, the third unit (the one through which I had walked on my first visit) remained a problem. There were structural problems (the roof leaked, commodes were stopped up, clothes washers were broken) and staffing problems (no one wanted to work there because the resident care was so demanding) that were not easily resolved. We implemented a "Check & Change" policy so that incontinent residents were diapered and changed regularly. This dramatically improved the odor within the facility and made it a much more pleasant place in which to work and live.

After one year, however, I realized that this was not the place where I was meant to be after all. My husband found a listing for a position as a consultant with the Texas Hospital Association (THA), working with management engineers who implemented patient classification and staffing monitoring systems in hospitals for a five-state region. I applied for the position, was hired, and entered into a new world.

I learned how to use a computerized spreadsheet to calculate staffing standards based upon time-motion study data – my first use of a personal computer. I was assigned to implement the patient classification system developed by THA in client hospitals in Texas and Louisiana, and developed a User Manual for that system. I was designated to market, sell, and implement an automated patient classification system, and later a combined scheduling/staffing system, throughout the Southwest. Once again, I was part of a new, expanded role as a nurse and I absolutely loved every day of my work.

After six years with THA, I was invited to see a demonstration of a bedside documentation system that was "designed by nurses for nurses." As I previewed this innovative technology, I thought, "This will never catch on. I will be in a wheelchair before hospitals buy into this technology, but it is certainly exciting!" Within a month, I was offered a position to be a regional sales executive for this company and began traveling across the country to develop a client base for this remarkable system. I set up training demonstrations at sites throughout the mid- and southwest, traveling by air, as well as by car. I was loved by skycaps all across the U.S., since I carried a minimum of 13 cases that weighed 10-15 pounds each everywhere I went!

Eventually, there were many companies developing stand-alone auto-mated documentation systems for nursing, but there was no connectivity to any other system or department within the hospital. The philosophy was that nurses needed a documentation system that worked for them and nurse administrators were eager to purchase systems that worked for their staff. Of course, once those systems were implemented, physicians, laboratory and radiology techni-cians, clinical dietitians, and every other healthcare worker who provided direct care to patients wanted to access the system to document their care, as well. So the usefulness of the standalone systems was limited.

During this period, I learned that, although systems were built to the design specifications of the client, very few clients used the full capability of a system once it was installed. I began to question, "Why don't nurses use the systems to full capacity?"

I was now traveling across the country every week, often leaving on a 6:00 a.m. flight on Monday morning to be in Baltimore, Maryland by 9:00 a.m. in order to work with clients. I worked all week, catching a 6:00 p.m. or later flight on Friday to get home by midnight for the weekend. Although the work was enjoyable and I liked the people with whom I came in contact, staying in a hotel night after night and navigating through airports soon lost its allure.

In the summer of 1994, I attended a conference on informatics in nurs-ing. There I was introduced to the Internet! It was amazing! I was using com-puters daily in my work, including remote email; however, I had no idea that the Internet existed. Imagine sitting in a classroom in Baltimore and connecting to a site in Iceland - I was astounded!

The conference I attended was held on a university campus; I realized that there was, indeed, a lot more to learn! I decided to apply for the nursing doctoral (Ph.D.) program at my alma mater to focus in informatics. By then, it had been 26 years since I had taken the GRE and obtained the "magical" entry-level score. Whether or not I would be required to re-take the GRE was at the discretion of the Graduate Advisor. I negotiated with my advisor: since I had proven 16 years before that I had the ability to be successful in graduate school, and since I had been working within the field of nursing ever since graduation, I should not be required to re-take the GRE. Fortunately, she agreed with me; however, she challenged me to spend my first semester developing and writing a National Institute for Nursing Research (NINR) pre-doctoral grant application.

At that time, the only two doctoral courses in the country with a focus in informatics were at the University of Maryland and the University of Utah. Since I was not interested in relocating to either of those states, I negotiated with my advisor to develop a degree plan that would allow me to attend my own university to get the foundation that I wanted for informatics. I was a maverick! I was accepted and entered the program with my research question in hand, planning to be finished in three years. My husband and I arranged our finances so that I could quit my traveling job (but I planned to return), not take out student loans, and just go to school. What a luxury!

Remember that I had just learned about the Internet a few months before? Now I was challenged to do a literature review related to my research question using that same Internet, as well as to develop a proposal that would provide me with federal funding for my research. I began this work in my opening full-term semester as an independent study. I successfully completed the application and submitted it by the deadline in December. My professor was totally amazed; she said that many students had accepted the challenge that she posed, but very few had completed it.

The following spring, I received word that the proposal had been accepted, but it was not to be funded. By that time, I was moving along through my coursework and thought, "Well, I don't need the money now, anyway." I had missed the concept that the game was to keep applying. Also, by that time, I had learned quite a bit in my coursework and discovered that the question that I had formulated when entering the program was not necessarily the right one.

The chairperson of my dissertation committee worked with me diligently. I framed a new research question and designed a study that included both quantitative and qualitative components. Within five years, I had graduated with a Ph.D. During those five years, I served as President of the Association of Nurses in Graduate School (ANGS) one year, worked as a Graduate Teaching Assistant for two years, and participated as a data analyst for a qualitative study for one of our faculty members. Wow! I really enjoyed the teaching assistant experience and began to think that teaching would be an exciting career, now that I had my terminal degree. The thought of getting on an airplane and staying in hotels all the time no longer interested me, but I needed a job!

Back when I was going through the process of applying to the doctoral program, I was cautioned that I wouldn't be invited to teach at my alma mater because both of my graduate degrees had been obtained there. Of course, at that time, I hadn't been interested in teaching. Well, now that I actually had my Ph.D., I really wanted to teach. But the school was true to its word, and I was not encouraged to apply for a teaching position there.

Fortunately, one of my colleagues in the doctoral program had a teaching position at another university in the state. She contacted me to see if I would be interested in making a move to join her on that faculty. Although this meant selling our retirement home and moving from a city where my husband had lived since age 3, we made the decision to try the move. We were fortunate enough to have a motor home for recreation. This gave us the opportunity to "camp" at the new location while maintaining our permanent home, to see whether or not I liked this new role and would choose to stay.

I came to the university in a part-time capacity and was assigned to teach courses in the three programs offered within the School of Nursing (RN to BSN matriculation program, generic BSN program, and Master's program). It was a very busy first semester. I was energized and thrilled to be working again! In the fall, I was invited to continue as full-time faculty. So, we sold our "retirement" home and relocated. Quite an expense for someone who hadn't had a paid job for five years!

I have now been teaching for seven years. I teach primarily in the graduate program in nursing administration, where I am lead teacher for the program's two finance courses. As an active full-time faculty member, I have been involved in the curriculum design for our Doctorate in Nursing Practice program. I also participate in multiple committees within the nursing school and the university.

Two years into this new job, my Director challenged me to take the ANCC certification examination for nursing administration. I already had a Ph.D., which I considered my "terminal" degree. Why would I need further certification? After some discussion, I accepted the challenge, took the examination for Certification Nurse Administrator, Advanced, and added six more letters after my name: CNAA-BC (the BC means Board Certified). This achievement is noteworthy, since I am one of 1% of the nurse executives in the U.S. to have achieved this distinction. Ever learning, ever growing.

Five years ago, I was invited to be liaison between the university and a local hospital as nurse researcher. I do this in conjunction with my teaching responsibilities. Initially, this position served the double purpose of helping me to focus on a research area and to help the hospital on its Magnet journey. The hospital did attain Magnet status; however, I am still interested in a myriad of research projects, not focused in one area.

My projects continue to be varied. I have worked with staff nurses and managers to develop protocols to successfully complete the requirement for research projects in a certification course in aromatherapy. I co-authored an article, published in WOCN, about whether pillows are necessary in the positioning of patients who are in continuous lateral rotation therapy. I helped in the development of a protocol to replicate a study that implemented a process of identifying Daily Goals in the surgical intensive care unit. The clinical educator for Women's Services and I co-investigated student outcomes in traditional classroom instruction vs. online instruction. We also co-investigated the outcomes of using Touchpoints™ in the training of healthcare employees in the area of women's health. These diverse topics of interest have helped me make the decision to remain on our faculty clinical track, rather than seeking tenure (which requires a much more focused area of research interest). I applied for a promotion to Associate Clinical Professor last year, and was successful.

Two years ago, I was invited to participate as a member of the Institutional Review Board for the University. After a number of administrative changes, I now chair that important committee and review research applications involving human subjects from all disciplines on campus. When I was invited to accept the position of Chairperson, I discussed my limitations in terms of rank and tenure with the Board. The Vice President of Research informed me that I was being asked to accept the position on the basis of my administrative skills and my abilities to interact with people. Within a few months, the Research Coordinator and I have successfully altered the culture within the Office of Research Compliance to be one of support for faculty research, while maintaining the integrity of the regulations that guide research involving human subjects.

At this point, I am approaching the fortieth anniversary of my graduation from undergraduate nursing school. My varied experiences during these years are unparalleled: clinical nursing, long-term care, consulting, sales and program implementation, academia, and guiding research for a top-tier university! The same pearls; a new look, and I am at the height of my career!

Patricia G. Turpin, PhD, RN, CNAA, BC

Patricia Turpin joined the faculty at UTA School of Nursing in January 2001, teaching in the undergraduate RN to BSN and BSN programs and the graduate Nursing Administration Program. She serves as the lead teacher for the two finance courses in the graduate program.

Since January 2003, she has served in an adjunct faculty role as Nurse Researcher at Harris Methodist Fort Worth Hospital (HMFW) (a designated Magnet Facility). In that capacity, she enhances the research skills of clinical nurses and facilitates/coordinates the approval process of research projects for nursing.

Dr. Turpin's previous clinical work experiences include critical care (in staff and manager roles) and long-term care (as nurse administrator). Outside of the clinical setting, she has had experience as a consultant for nurse staffing and scheduling programs (including computerized systems) and as director of sales and marketing for point-of-care computer systems designed to automate nursing documentation.

She is a member of TNA, ANA (District 3), N-TONE, TONE, AONE, and CGEAN, as well as Sigma Theta Tau International and Phi Kappa Phi Honor Societies. She serves as the Chairperson for the Institutional Review Board for UT Arlington.

CLOSING

CHAPTER 19

The Clasp - From Beginning to End

by Leslie Furlow, PhD, RN, MSN, FNP

I was the oldest child. That means I started being a boss early in my life. That's what the oldest child does, especially if she is a girl. You would think that all that early experience would translate into excellent people management skills. Well, guess again. To paraphrase Drucker, "telling people what to do isn't the same as being an effective executive."

Part of being a good leader is understanding priorities – we all have them. As a nurse executive and entrepreneur, I have said and heard, "I don't have time," more times than I care to remember. However, I have learned that it is a false statement. We all have the same amount of time; it is how we decide to spend it that differs.

One of the greatest lessons one can learn is how to identify and order one's priorities. I must admit that, for me, this has been a lesson that was difficult to master. I started out as compulsive people-pleaser.

One of my first jobs was as a lab tech. I worked in analytical support. I was the only person in the lab without a college degree. I was a "wanna be," so I volunteered for everything. I did any job, whatever my boss wanted done, and I was the eager beaver. So what is wrong with that? I learned a valuable lesson. First, your coworkers don't appreciate you when you are always trying to show them up, even if that isn't your motivation. Second, and most important, is that hard work doesn't always pay. After a year of putting the company's priorities at the forefront of my mind, review time came. I got a glowing evaluation. Then, this petrochemical company (where 'pay for performance' was in place long before healthcare decided to use it) gave me a 10% raise. Ten percent! The problem was that my coworkers, who hadn't worked as hard as I had, got 6% raises. And

6% of their salaries was a whole lot more than 10% of mine. Having a pretty good math aptitude, I figured it out quickly and questioned my boss. I prepared my statement and then asked why, when I had worked so diligently, did I get less of a raise than my coworkers? His reply still rings in my ears, and has helped me with developing my priorities. He said, "You did what you did because you chose to. No one required that you do extra work or volunteer for projects; you did it for your own reasons. So you should not be disappointed that the company doesn't feel obligated to pay you for your choices." Okay, lesson learned. People do what they do because they want to. If you are doing something with the expectation of more money, promotion or recognition, you need to clarify that in advance. There are not any guarantees that the boss is going to see your effort as beneficial for the organization, just because you think it is.

I then took another hiatus from nursing (I was an LVN before I went to RN school). This time, I went to work for an insurance company. I worked hard, and remembered the lessons I had learned in my last out-of-healthcare job. It wasn't long before I got my opportunity to move into management (a goal that I had made known to my boss during the interview process). Like most new managers, I wanted to be liked. I wanted my staff to be happy all the time. I wanted to meet everyone's needs. So, I let other people determine my priorities. I made schedules without filling the holes and ended up filling them myself by working way too many hours. I didn't want to hurt anyone's feelings, so I didn't hold people accountable. That meant that more infractions of the company's policies occurred. I thought I was being a good manager. After all, my job was my life. I was hurt and deflated when I realized that my "rescuer" style was not what my boss was looking for. I thought that my job was to advocate for the staff. I just didn't understand what that meant or what it looked like.

Once back in nursing, I got my RN. One of the reasons for this degree was that I wanted to be a manager. I had learned a lot and one of the things I knew was that I could manage better than I was managed. I wouldn't let anyone get away with anything. I would apply the rules equally to everyone. There would be no favorites. I would be a management machine. My priorities were based on: "doing it right," "making it fair," and "getting it done." Honestly, I was a drill sergeant. I did just what I said I would do, but I didn't listen and I didn't make friends. I met my productivity numbers. But I wasn't a great leader, a marvelous manager; I might have been a simple supervisor. But I didn't know that at the time. Ignorance is, indeed, bliss.

I began working on a master's degree. As far as I was concerned, this move was just a formality. I thought I already knew everything and just needed the degree to get my resume noticed. So I pursued a Master's of Public Health with a focus in Health Administration. Loma Linda University was internationally known, and their MPH-HA was the same curriculum as their MHA, except that they didn't require a residency. And I didn't need that anyway.

Have you ever been amazed to learn what you don't know? The old adage, "You don't know what you don't know," must have been written for me. I started out rather cocky. But, as we covered case studies, it seemed that all the things I had done as a manager were the examples of "what not to do." I thought to myself: I am a natural born boss, I am the oldest child; I have all the desire in the world. How could I be doing everything so wrong? One of the first things I learned is that a graduate education is to point out how little you actually know. The more you learn, the more you realize there is more to learn. The second thing I learned is that I didn't know how to listen. I could hear. Hearing is a physiologic process; listening is something else all together. They had taught me "therapeutic communication" in nursing school. I found it rather silly and not very useful. At Loma Linda, they got through to me that this technique is not just about repeating words; one should be trying to clarify ideas and thoughts. One should be communicating!!! Wow - what a concept. That one lesson has probably done more to change my life than any other. I started using it at work, at school, even at home. I began to clarify everything. I suddenly realized that shaking one's head did not mean agreement with a statement. People who don't speak your language will shake their heads as you ramble on, and not understand a thing you said.

I had been introduced to management theory in my BSN program. Now I was learning what it meant to apply it. I also begin to realize that, as Solomon said, "There is no new thing under the sun." Every new program was just a new light on an old idea. Furthermore, I learned that you can't adopt any program or process (no matter who developed it) wholesale and expect cultural change. 'Flavor of the month' had been the bane of my staff existence. Now I understood why. Executives wanted to enact change for everyone but themselves. The law of gravity is not just a law in the physical world. It is also a law in corporate culture. Whatever is at the top runs downhill. If there is no commitment to change at the top, change will only occur at the bottom when coerced and then those at the bottom will respond like a rubber band. When the pressure is off, the situation will return to its original shape, only less effective than before.

About half way through my program, I was blessed with another management opportunity. I was promoted to Assistant Director of Nurses (this is like today's assistant VP). I was put in charge of the medical section of the hospital, which included Medical Nursing, Telemetry, Pediatrics, ICU and ED. This time, armed with more knowledge and a lot more understanding, I set about to change the world. One of my favorite cartoons is of a dragon sitting against a tree picking his teeth with the knight's lance, with the knight's armor in pieces around him. The caption reads, "No matter how right you are, No matter how hard you try, Sometimes the Dragon WINS!" That cartoon pretty well describes my experience.

I applied all that I was learning. I listened to the staff. I held people accountable without stripping them of their dignity. I kept my boss informed. I worked with HR closely to insure that I enforced the spirit, as well as the letter, of the policies. I encouraged participation and growth. I really wanted to do the right thing, rather than just doing things right!

Again, life was about to teach me a very hard lesson. One of my staff was not happy with a decision I had made. It was the right decision, just not the one she wanted. She went around me to my boss. She didn't tell me that she was doing it. She didn't follow the chain of command. Didn't she know the management rules? The next thing I knew, my boss had me in her office reading me the riot act. "Who did I think I was? What right did I have to do what I did; why didn't I check with her first?" And, by the way, my boss had countermanded my edict with the nurse complainant.

Well, this was the lesson: ask before you act. I had talked with my boss; she had agreed with the action. When the nurse went to her, she told a totally different version of what had taken place. My boss had not only lost credibility in my eyes, she had effectively neutralized my effectiveness. She also was the type who could not admit a mistake, so the situation was entirely my fault. I should have left then, but I am, if nothing else, loyal. However, the next incident did lead to my departure.

The organizational structure that had been developed gave me one assistant and between us we had about 90 staff to supervise, schedule and evaluate. Now, I am no genius, but Christ was. If He chose 12 disciples and had one go bad, how could I manage 90? After all, I would at least sink to my waist when I tried walking on water. Span of control is a valid management principle. It's as old as the Exodus. Why do we in healthcare try to violate it so consistently? Back to the story: I went to my boss with my concern about not being able to adequately manage that many people. She informed me that, if I couldn't do it, she would find someone who could. The gauntlet had been dropped. So, not keeping in character, or regressing to my previous behavior, I told her that, if she was right, then she would do just that. And the next person she appointed would do a great job and everything would be wonderful. But, if I were right, she would end up with a series of managers who would burn out, much as I was doing after a few months. So there! I tendered my resignation the next day. Not to gloat, but the structure didn't work. Over the next two years, no less than five managers came and went.

But all's well that ends well. I sent out about 50 resumes - to every hospital looking for an assistant or director of nursing. I got several calls. I went on a couple of interviews, but only one organization really pursued me. I didn't really want to move to that part of the country, but the interview went very well. It was a job I could do (or so I thought) and when they asked me what it would take to get me there, I decided I would price myself out of consideration. I took my old salary, doubled it and added 10%. The CEO said he would get back to me. About two hours later, I had a job. Another lesson: don't say it if you won't do it!

Suddenly, my priorities had shifted. I had a lot of decisions to make. How would I deal with my family? How would I finish my degree? What if I wasn't as good as I thought? What if I wasn't as good as they thought? I had to change the world this time. They wanted a culture change; I embodied the change they wanted. I decided that I would live my values; it had to work! It was, indeed, a great experience. I made major changes, kept my integrity, and mentored the next layer of management. When I started, there were two masters-prepared directors; when I left, all but two had their degrees (and the final two were working on their degrees, as well). I got to know the staff nurses. I never undercut my directors; I always sent issues back to them before I got involved. The HR VP was wonderful and is still high on my list of mentors to this day. Overall, this was a very successful time; however, there were some lessons to be learned so that I could move into the future and on to my next phase of development.

Most of the time, consultants can be assets. They bring a fresh perspective to an organization; they challenge the status quo. They also are able to communicate the message of those who do the work to those who think they know what is going on. But, I had also seen my share of consultants who lacked both knowledge and integrity. Those who were out to make a name for themselves and line their pockets. I discovered that that type of consultant was willing to say what the client wanted to hear rather than what needed to be said. I knew both types of consultants existed. However, I had never been in a position to hire and work directly with consultants before. I had always been on the receiving end of their services. Now, I had an opportunity to select the right type. And I did. The consultant I hired ended up being a long-term friend. We shared and grew and made things better. What I didn't count on was my experience with the consultant my boss hired for me. I trusted her, too, and assumed (we all know what that means) that she had my best interest at heart. WRONG!

I was more than helpful. I gave her all the ammunition she needed to shoot me in the gut. And she did. When she gave her recommendations to the Board of Directors, nothing in the presentation seemed familiar. She essentially removed half of my departments. In a performance worthy of an Academy Award, my boss acted surprised! Then he had me meet with my staff to tell them that they were no longer reporting to me. To say I was devastated does not begin to express my emotional state. I should have gotten the "best supporting actress" award for my performance when I told the staff that this was the best decision for the organization. The lessons learned that time included: 1) Never trust a consultant you didn't hire, 2) Always ask to see a consultant's recommendations before they are presented to a group, 3) Always support your boss, even if you know you have been sabotaged, and 4) Never let them see you cry.

I didn't leave immediately, but I did start looking. I hated to leave; my heart was now tied to this place, where I hadn't even wanted to be only a few years earlier. And I know I left it in better shape than when I arrived. That job turned out well. The organization needed someone who could hold the course I had charted. But I was an explorer and it was time to explore new horizons.

My next adventure was as a consultant. The lessons previously learned were timely and I was able to use them almost immediately by moving into this new world. The fledging firm grew, and I will always believe that I was a very integral part of that growth. We found niches and ways to fill them. We were honest, and gave good value for our fees. I believed, and still do, that a consultant's role is to always improve a client's situation. I also felt that I could impact nursing more globally as a consultant than I could in the role of a nurse executive. As is so often the case, I was on a mission. I was going to change the world, yet again.

We did a lot of good work. I was able to help both clients and new consultants grow and reach new goals. I was maturing and, as a result, was able to "get over myself." The most valuable lesson I learned during my 8 years with that firm was, "it's not all about me!" Subsequently, as I have worked with consultants from many different firms (both small and large), I have found that the biggest obstacle they have to get over is their own egos. I learned that the answers to most problems that consultants are called upon to correct are locked within the people who do the work everyday. Sometimes, those people know they have the answer, but the administration will not ask for their input, or listen to suggestions. But sometimes people don't even realize they have the answer. This can be because they have not identified the problem and are fighting symptom fires, or because they can't articulate the issue. By "getting over myself" and recognizing that all of us are smarter as a whole than any of single one of us, I was able to facilitate many brilliant solutions.

The next lesson was that all good things come to an end. The owner of that company decided to sell the firm. I didn't want to work with the new owners, so I left. For a while, I tried one-on-one patient care again as a nurse practitioner. But, alas, I missed the challenges of groups and healthcare issues. So I did the only thing I knew how to do. I started my own company. This has been both a blessing and a curse. I work harder than when I had a boss. And having my office in my home means that I literally never leave the office. Three o'clock in the morning, I will find myself sitting at the computer in my jammies writing an article, adding to a report, or finishing a proposal. Even if I had gone to bed at 10:00 p.m., I would sometimes wake up at 2:00 a.m., walk to the back of the house and start working again.

I built a fairly nice company; at one point, I had 15 staff members working all over the US. I started a second company with a good friend and developed a speaking and writing career. Life was good. But even life has a way of putting you in your place. After 33 years, my husband, partner and best friend died suddenly. My staff kept my business alive while I languished in disbelief. Six weeks after burying my husband, my mom lost her battle with terminal cancer. I was suddenly both a widow and an orphan.

The end of this story is nowhere in sight. The business is alive and changing. My life is forever changed. And I now realize that the greatest lesson any of us can learn is, "identify your priorities and then live your life by them."

Leslie Furlow, PhD, RN, MSN, FNP

Leslie Furlow began her nursing career as a nursing assistant. She later finished an LVN program and then earned her AA degree as a Registered Nurse. To get into the ED, she became an EMT. At that point, she decided that nursing would be her life's purpose and finished a BSN two years later. After serving in different administrative positions, Dr. Furlow entered consulting. AchieveMentors, Inc., which she founded, provides a variety of operational, management and process consulting to hospitals nationally.

Dr. Furlow has a Doctorate in Management, as well as Master's degrees in Public Health and in Nursing. She has served, and continues to serve, as adjunct faculty for several colleges and universities teaching management, leadership and technical skills. She is certified as a Family Nurse Practitioner, Professional Behavioral Analyst, Facilitator, and in Total Quality Management.

Her interest in mentoring the next generation of nursing leaders lead her to receive Board Certification in Leadership from the Society for the Advancement of Consulting in 2006. Furthermore, that interest began her partnership with Dr. Sharon Judkins to create HardinessMentors, LLC, a research-based development process that increases personal hardiness in middle managers and shows proven decreases in stress response and unplanned absences. The results of their research received international attention, with presentation in Australia, Austria, England and Scotland and in numerous publications in such countries as Canada and Great Britain. Hardy leaders display increased job satisfaction, retention of quality staff and productivity, thus insuring their success and the future of nursing.